Bloom's Modern Critical Interpretations

Bloom's Modern Critical Interpretations

Gabriel García Márquez's

ONE HUNDRED YEARS OF SOLITUDE

Edited and with an introduction by
Harold Bloom
Sterling Professor of the Humanities
Yale University

CHELSEA HOUSE
PUBLISHERS
A Haights Cross Communications Company
Philadelphia

10 9 8 7 6 5 4 3 2 1

Library of Congress Cataloging-in-Publication Data
One Hundred Years of Solitude : [essays] / edited with an introduciton
by Harold Bloom.
        p. cm — (Bloom's modern critical interpretations)
Includes bibliographical references and index.
    ISBN 0-7910-7046-8
  1. García Márquez, Gabriel, 1928– Cien años de soledad. 2.
García
Márquez, Gabriel, 1928—Criticism and interpretation. I. Bloom,
Harold. II. Modern critical interpretations.
    PQ8180.17.A73 C535 2002
    863'.64—dc 21

                                                    2002009603

Contributing editor: Gabriel Welsch

Cover design by Terry Mallon

Layout by EJB Publishing Services

Chelsea House Publishers
1974 Sproul Road, Suite 400
Broomall, PA 19008-0914

http://www.chelseahouse.com

Contents

Editor's Note

My Introduction grants the marvelous richness of *One Hundred Years of Solitude*, while suggesting the parameters of the novel's achievement.

David T. Haberly discovers a highly plausible source for the novel in Chateaubriand's *Atala*, while Keith Harrison solves the mystery of the shooting-death of Jose Arcadio.

The major critic of Hispanic literature, Roberto González Echevarría, emphasizes the influence of Borges upon García Márquez.

Vexed relations between women and society in the novel are considered by John J. Deveny and Juan Manuel Marcos, after which Elizabeth A. Spiller traces the narrative search of Renaissance discovery in García Márquez.

A dialectic of "solitude" is argued by Paul M. Hedeen, while Jonathan Baldo regards that condition largely as an effect of language.

A Hegelian García Márquez is offered by Iddo Landau, after which Dean J. Irvine intimates Defoe's *Journal of the Plague Year* as crucial source.

Irvin D.S. Winsboro wryly contemplates differences between fiction and reality in the novel's women.

Virginia Woolf's *Orlando* is regarded by Alexander Coleman as another vital source, after which Mary E. Davis shows the deep influence of Faulkner upon not only García Márquez, but also upon Fuentes and Vargas Llosa.

Introduction

Macondo, according to Carlos Fuentes, "begins to proliferate with the richness of a Columbian Yoknapatawpha." Faulkner, crossed by Kafka, is the literary origins of Gabriel García Márquez. So pervasive is the Faulknerian influence that at times one hears Joyce and Conrad, Faulkner's masters, echoed in García Márquez, yet almost always as mediated by Faulkner. The *Autumn of the Patriarch* may be too pervaded by Faulkner, but *One Hundred Years of Solitude* absorbs Faulkner, as it does all other influences, into a phantasmagoria so powerful and self-consistent that the reader never questions the authority of García Márquez. Perhaps, as Reinard Argas suggested, Faulkner is replaced by Carpentier and Kafka by Borges in *One Hundred Years of Solitude*, so that the imagination of García Márquez domesticates itself within its own language. Macondo, visionary realm, is an Indian and Hispanic act of consciousness, very remote from Oxford, Mississippi, and from the Jewish cemetery in Prague. In his subsequent work, García Márquez went back to Faulkner and Kafka, but then *One Hundred Years of Solitude* is a miracle and could only happen once, if only because it is less a novel than it is a Scripture, the Bible of Macondo, Melquíades the Magus, who writes in Sanskrit, may be more a mask for Borges than for the author himself, and yet the Gypsy storyteller also connects García Márquez to the archaic Hebrew storyteller, the Yahwist, at once the greatest of realists and the greatest of fantasists but above all the only true rival of Homer and Tolstoy as a storyteller.

My primary impression, in the act of rereading *One Hundred Years of Solitude*, is a kind of aesthetic battle fatigue, since every page is rammed full of life beyond the capacity of any single reader to absorb. Whether the impacted quality of this novel's texture is finally a virtue I am not sure, since sometimes I feel like a man invited to dinner who has been served nothing but an enormous platter of Turkish Delight. Yet it is all story, where everything conceivable and inconceivable is happening at once, from creation to apocalypse, birth to death. Roberto González Echevarría has gone so far as to surmise that in some sense it is the reader who must die at the end of the story, and perhaps it is the sheer richness of the text that serves to destroy us. Joyce half-seriously envisioned an ideal reader cursed with insomnia who would spend her life in unpacking *Finnegans Wake*. The reader need not translate *One Hundred Years of Solitude*, a novel that deserves its popularity as it has no surface difficulties whatsoever. And yet, a new dimension is added to reading by this book. Its ideal reader has to be like its most memorable personage, the sublimely outrageous Colonel Aureliano Buendía, who "had wept in his mother's womb and been born with his eyes open." There are no wasted sentences, no mere transitions, in this novel, and you must notice everything at the moment you read it. It will all cohere, at least as myth and metaphor if not always as literary meaning.

In the presence of an extraordinary actuality, consciousness takes the place of imagination. That Emersonian maxim is Wallace Steven's and is worthy of the visionary of *Notes toward a Supreme Fiction* and *An Ordinary Evening in New Haven*. Macondo is a supreme fiction, and there are no ordinary evenings within its boundaries. Satire, even parody, and most fantasy—these are now scarely possible in the United States. How can you satirize Ronald Reagan or Jerry Falwell? Pynchon's *The Crying of Lot 49* ceases to seem fantasy whenever I visit Southern California, and a ride on the New York City subway tends to reduce all literary realism to an idealizing projection. Some aspects of Latin American existence transcend even the inventions of García Márquez. I am informed, on good authority, that the older of the Duvalier dictators of Haiti, the illustrious Papa Doc, commanded that all black dogs in his nation be destroyed when he came to believe that a principal enemy had transformed himself into a black dog. Much that is fantastic in *One Hundred Years of Solitude* would be fantastic anywhere, but much that seems unlikely to a North American critic may well be a representation of reality.

Emir Monegal emphasized that García Márquez's masterwork was unique among Latin American novels, being radically different from the diverse achievements of Julio Cortázar, Carlos Fuentes, Lezama Lima, Mario Vargas Llosa, Miguel Angel Asturias, Manuel Puig, Guillermo Cabrera Infante and so many more. The affinities to Borges and to Carpentier were noted by Monegal as by Arenas, but Monegal's dialectical point seemed to be that García Márquez was representative only by joining all his colleagues in not being representative. Yet it is now true that, for most North American readers, *One Hundred Years of Solitude* comes first to mind when they think of the Hispanic novel in America. Alejo Carpentier's *Explosion in a Cathedral* may be an even stronger book, but only Borges has dominated the North American literary imagination as García Márquez has with his grand fantasy. It is inevitable that we are fated to identify *One Hundred Years of Solitude* with an entire culture, almost as though it were a new *Don Quixote*, which it most definitely is not. Comparisons to Balzac and even to Faulkner are also not very fair to García Márquez. The titanic inventiveness of Balzac dwarfs the later visionary, and nothing even in Macondo is as much a negative Sublime as the fearsome quest of the Bundrens in *As I Lay Dying*. *One Hundred Years of Solitude* is more of the stature of Nabokov's *Pale Fire* and Pynchon's *Gravity's Rainbow*, latecomers' fantasies, strong inheritors of waning traditions.

Whatever its limitations may or may not be, García Márquez's major narrative now enjoys canonical status as well as a representative function. Its cultural status continues to be enhanced, and it would be foolish to quarrel with so large a phenomenon. I wish to address myself only to the question of how seriously, as readers, we need to receive the book's scriptural aspect. The novel's third sentence is: "The world was so recent that things lacked names, and in order to indicate them it was necessary to point," and the third sentence from the end is long and beautiful:

> Macondo was already a fearful whirlwind of dust and rubble being spun about by the wrath of the biblical hurricane when Aureliano skipped eleven pages so as not to lose time with facts he knew only too well, and he began to decipher the instant that he was living, deciphering it as he lived it, prophesying himself in the act of deciphering the last page of the parchment, as if he were looking into a speaking mirror.

The time span between this Genesis and this Apocalypse is six generations, so that José Arcadio Buendía, the line's founder, is the grandfather of the last Aureliano's grandfather. The grandfather of Dante's grandfather, the crusader Cassaguida, tells his decendant Dante that the poet perceives the truth because he gazes into that mirror in which the great and small of this life, before they think, behold their thought. Aureliano, at the end, reads the Sanskrit parchment of the gypsy, Borges-like Magus, and looks into a speaking mirror, beholding his thought before he thinks it. But does he, like Dante, behold the truth? Was Florence, like Macondo, a city of mirrors (or mirages) in contrast to the realities of the Inferno, the Purgatorio, the Paradiso? Is *One Hundred Years of Solitude* only a speaking mirror? Or does it contain, somehow within it, an Inferno, a Purgatorio, a Paradiso?

Only the experience and disciplined reflections of a great many more strong readers will serve to answer those questions with any conclusiveness. The final eminence of *One Hundred Years of Solitude* for now remains undecided. What is clear to the book's contemporaries is that García Márquez has given contemporary culture, in North America and Europe, as much as in Latin America, one of its double handful of necessary narratives, without which we will understand neither one another nor our own selves.

DAVID T. HABERLY

Bags of Bones: A Source for Cien años de soledad

Several scholars have discussed possible sources for Gabriel García Márquez's *Cien años de soledad*, focusing on European and North American writers he might have read; strong cases have been made for Faulkner, Virginia Woolf's *Orlando*, and Defoe's *Diary of the Plague Year*.[1] One source which has not been mentioned, however, is Chateaubriand's *Atala*. This brief novel, one of the most popular Romantic texts, has been available, in Spanish translation, in dozens of editions from 1801 to the present; the first translation was probably done by Fray Servando Teresa de Mier. Either printed by itself or together with two other brief works by Chateaubriand, *René* and *El último Abencerraje* (*Les aventures du dernier Abencérage*), both almost as popular in the Spanish-speaking world, *Atala* was certainly readily available in Colombia in the first decades of the twentieth century.[2]

Chateaubriand's short novel, moreover, has had a special importance in Colombia; in the greatest Colombian novel before *Cien años de soledad*, Jorge Isaacs' 1867 *María*, *Atala* is the favorite book of Efraín and María, and is prominently mentioned in the text.[3] One of the first critics to write about *María*, José María Vergara y Vergara, emphasized the influence of Chateaubriand's novel, an influence that is particularly evident in the Nay and Sinar episode, and many editions of *María* after 1878 included Vergara y Vergara's article as a preface.[4] It is impossible to believe that García Márquez

---

From *Modern Language Notes* 105 (1990) © 1990 by The Johns Hopkins University Press.

did not read *María*, and it seems very possible that the references in the text and in Vergara y Vergara's preface might have led him to read Chateaubriand's original.

In *Cien años de soledad*, Rebeca arrives in Macondo carrying "un talego de lona que hacía un permanente ruido de cloc cloc cloc, donde llevaba los huesos de sus padres."[5] The remains of her parents present a problem, since "en aquel tiempo no había cementerio en Macondo, pues hasta entonces no había muerto nadie,…" The Buendías therefore "conservaron el talego con los huesos en espera de que hubiera un lugar digno para sepultarlos, y durante mucho tiempo estorbaron por todas partes y se les encontraba donde menos se suponía, siempre con su cloqueante cacareo de gallina clueca." (p. 44) When Ursula decides to rebuild and expand the house, the workmen complain loudly, "exasperados por el talègo de huesos humanos que los perseguía por todas partes con su sordo cascabeleo." (p. 55) The bones are forgotten until several years later, when Pilar Ternera predicts that Rebeca will never be happy until her parents are buried. José Arcadio contacts the workmen, who reveal that the bones were immured to get them out of the way. The workmen search the house, at José Arcadio's request, and finally hear the "cloc cloc profundo" of the bones; they break through a wall and retrieve "los huesos en el talego intacto." Macondo now has a cemetery, as a result of the final death of Melquíades, and the bones of Rebeca's parents are quickly buried there. (pp. 72-73)

In the epilogue to Chateaubriand's novel, the narrator encounters an Indian woman and her family; they are among the last of the Natchez tribe, fleeing into exile in the interior of North America. The woman reveals to the narrator that she is the granddaughter of René, an exiled European who was adopted by the wise and brave Chactas and to whom Chactas told the story of his life; that story—Chactas's conversion to Christianity by Father Aubrey, his unconsumated love for Atala, the purest and most beautiful of Indian maidens, and Atala's final suicide—has been preserved and retold for generations. Chateaubriand, in fact, claimed to have heard and recorded this narrative during his wanderings "dans les déserts du Nouveau-Monde," and it is this narrative which comprises the text of *Atala*.[6] The epilogue reinforces that claim by placing the narrator in direct contact with René's Indian granddaughter.

But that is not the narrator's only contact with the origins of his text. When the narrator asks what happened to the main characters, the woman reveals that Father Aubrey was tortured to death by hostile Indians. When Chactas later returned to Atala's grave at the foot of the Natural Bridge in Virginia, he found that the bridge had collapsed and buried her tomb. A doe led him to a rock alter, and underneath it he found the bones of both Atala and Father Aubrey; "il les enveloppa dans des peaux d'ours, et reprit le chemin de son pays emportant les précieux restes, que résonnaient sur ses épaules comme le carquois de la mort." Both Chactas and René have since died in a massacre, but the bag of bones—which now includes those of Chactas as well—remains as concrete evidence of the narrator's story. "O étranger," the Indian woman tells him, "tu peux contempler ici cette poussière avec celle de Chactas luimême!" The narrator kneels before the bones and then watches the Indians move on, carrying both their children and the bear-skin of bones; Chateaubriand laments that "dans mon exil, je n'ai point emporté les os de mes pères." (p. 99)

The rattling bag of bones is not the only parallel between *Atala* and the world of Macondo. René, who links the narrator, the Indian woman, and the three characters whose bones lie in the bag, is in self-imposed exile in the New World; the reason for his exile (and, perhaps, for Chateaubriand's own voyage to America) is his need to escape from the incestuous desire he and his sister feel for each other.[7] That story of desire and evasion is recounted in *René*, *Atala*'s companion in Chateaubriand's *Génie du Christianisme* and in dozens of subsequent editions and translations; the Buendías' failure to escape incest and its ultimate consequences is, of course, the central argument of *Cien años de soledad*.

NOTES

1. See Jacques Gilard, "García Márquez, le groupe de Barranquilla et Faulkner," *Caravelle*, 27 (1976), 159-70, and Susan Jill Levine, *El espejo hablado* (Caracas: Monte Ávila, 1975), pp. 18, 46-56, and 82-7.

2. For a partial list of Hispanic translations and editions, see Antonio Palau y Dulcet, *Manual del librero hispanoamericano*, 2nd ed., vol. 4 (Barcelona: Palau, 1951), 262-3. *Atala* is one section of Chateaubriand's *Génie du Christianisme*, but was first published separately in 1801, a year before the rest of the *Génie*, including *René*, appeared.

3. In particular, chapters 12 and 13. Jorge Isaacs, *María*, ed. Donald McGrady (Barcelona: Labor, 1970), pp. 76-8.

4. See McGrady's introduction to *María*, p. 10. McGrady argues persuasively that despite its prominence in the text, *Atala* was not nearly as important an influence upon Isaacs as Bernardin de Saint-Pierre's *Paul et Virginie*.

5. *Cien años de soledad* (Buenos Aires: Ed. Sudamericana, 1976), p. 43. Subsequent page references in the text are to this edition.

6. François-René de Chateaubriand, *Atala*, in his *Oeuvres romanesques et voyages* (Paris: Gallimard, 1969), vol. I. The epilogue is on pages 93-9, and

subsequent references in the text are to this volume. Chateaubriand claimed, in its preface, that *Atala* was written "dans le désert, et sous les huttes des sauvages." (p. 18) Exactly where Chateaubriand went during his stay in America, from April to December of 1791, has been the subject of considerable discussion and controversy.

7. The nature of François-René's relationship with his older sister Lucile is even more polemical than the novelist's itinerary in the New World. For a brief recent discussion of the problem, see George D. Painter, *Chateaubriand: A Biography*, vol. 1 (New York: Knopf, 1978), 64-5.

KEITH HARRISON

"The Only Mystery" in
One Hundred Years of Solitude

In *One Hundred Years of Solitude* Gabriel Garcia Marquez describes the death of Jose Arcadio as "perhaps the only mystery that was never cleared up in Macondo." The qualifying word, "perhaps," hints that the novel does ultimately explain the following incident:

> One September afternoon, with the threat of a storm, he [Jose Arcadio] returned home earlier than usual. He greeted Rebeca in the dining room, tied the dogs up in the courtyard, hung the rabbits up in the kitchen to be salted later, and went to the bedroom to change his clothes. Rebeca later declared that when her husband went into the bedroom she was locked in the bathroom and did not hear anything. It was a difficult version to believe, but there was no more plausible, and no one could think of any motive for Rebeca to murder the man who had made her happy. That was perhaps the only mystery that was never cleared up in Macondo. As soon as Jose Arcadio closed the bedroom door the sound of a pistol shot echoed through the house. (p. 129)

Suicide is a possibility here, given details such as the strong smell of burned gunpowder on the corpse, "the thread of blood ... out of the right ear," and

---

From *Literature and Psychology* 32, no. 2 © 1986 by Keith Harrison.

"no wound on his body," but this explanation is improbable, not only because of Jose Arcadio's healthy animalism but also because no one could "locate the weapon" (p. 130). Murder is one aspect of this mysterious death.

Those with a motive to kill Jose Arcadio are numerous. The neighbouring peasants must have resented his seizure of their land:

> It was said that he had begun by plowing his own yard and had gone straight ahead into neighbouring lands, knocking down fences and buildings with his oxen until he took forcible possession of the best plots of land around. (p. 113)

It is thus conceivable that one of his cowed neighbours, emboldened suddenly by belated rage, murdered Jose Arcadio; however, his home would be an unlikely (albeit somewhat appropriate) place for such revenge, and there is also no evidence that Jose Arcadio ceased to be an intimidating physical force. An equally implausible explanation for his murder could be derived from obscure political motivations: unknown authorities wanted him dead as a result of his public intervention that recently saved a dangerous rebel, his brother Colonel Aureliano, from a firing squad. But there doesn't seem to be any intricate calculation in the circumstances of Jose Arcadio's death: "he returned home earlier than usual." Furthermore, both the setting of the bedroom and the fact Jose Arcadio "had just taken off" his leggings (p. 130) suggest intimacy, implicate Rebeca whose deafness is just not credible.

In another century, Rebeca aims an antiquated pistol at Aureliano Triste, nearly reenacting the murder of her husband:

> She remained motionless in the center of the room filled with knickknacks, examining inch by inch the giant with square shoulders and with a tatoo of ashes on his forehead, and through the haze of dust she saw him in the haze of other times with a double-barreled shotgun on his shoulder and a string of rabbits in his hand.
>
> "For the love of God," she said in a low voice, "it's not right for them to come to me with that memory now."
>
> "I want to rent the house," Aureliano Triste said.
>
> 'The woman then raised the pistol, aiming with a firm wrist at the cross of ashes, and she held the trigger with a determination against which there was no appeal. (p. 207)

This passage makes clear Rebeca's will and capacity to kill a vision of her husband, presumably with the very pistol that had murdered Jose Arcadio a century before. The mystery surrounding his death then ultimately concerns not the question of who but of why. As Philip Rahv comments on Dostoevsky's *Crime and Punishment*, detection is "not of the criminal ... but of his motive." To understand why Rebeca would "murder the man who had made her happy" it is first necessary to recognize the contradictions of her character, a duality that is partly reflective of an entire continent.

When Rebeca arrives at Macondo as a girl of eleven, carrying the bones of her parents in a bag, she exemplifies the condition of solitude that defines the novel. Orphaned, consigned to strangers in a remote village, she initially refuses to speak:

> From the moment she arrived she had been sitting in the rocker, sucking her finger and observing everyone with her large, startled eyes without giving any sign of understanding what they were asking her.... Her greenish skin, her stomach, round and tense as a drum, revealed poor health and hunger that was older than she was, but when they gave her something to eat she kept the plate on her knees without tasting anything. They even began to think that she was a deaf-mute until the Indians asked her in their language if she wanted some water and she moved her eyes as if she recognized them and said yes with her head. (pp. 49)

Her earliest communication, and affinity, in this context of hunger and displacement is with the Indians. Later, it will be revealed that she "spoke Spanish with as much fluency as the Indian language" (p. 49).

The two cultural modes that Rebeca expresses linguistically manifest themselves in her appearance:

> She wore a diagonally striped dress that had been dyed black, worn by use, and a pair of scaly patent leather boots. Her hair was held behind her ears with bows of black ribbon. She wore a scapular with the images worn away by sweat, and on her right wrist the fang of a carnivorous animal mounted on a backing of copper as an amulet against the evil eye. (p. 47)

In depicting Rebeca, Marquez discloses a state of contradiction. On the one hand he details elements of European traditions through her striped dress, patent leather shoes, and hair bows. On the other hand he denies the cultural premise for which those clothes are an emblem by the words, "scaly," "worn," and "black." The tensions inherent in Rebeca's appearance are most explicit in the juxtaposition of a fang with a scapular. This latter item is "an article of devotion composed of two small squares of woolen cloth, fastened together by strings passing over the shoulders, and worn as a badge of affiliation to the religious order which presents it" (S.O.E.D.). Rebeca's ostensible commitment to Christianity clashes with the indigenous magical beliefs symbolized by her amulet. The duality of her cultural inheritance, Indian and European, also signifies a correlative opposition that will define the contradictory impulses shaping her life: the physical ("sweat," "fang," and "animal") in conflict with the spiritual.

Rebeca's impulse to primitivism reveals itself at the outset by her pica, her craving for substances unfit for food:

> ...Rebeca only liked to eat the damp earth of the courtyard and the cake of whitewash that she picked off the walls with her nails. (p. 48)

In what is almost a parody of the "civilizing" forces that sought to transform a continent, Marquez describes how the Buendia family tied Rebeca up, made her swallow bitter medicine on an empty stomach, and, when she used "the vilest obscenities that one could ever imagine," they "added whipping to the treatment" in order to stop her "vice of eating earth" (p. 49). After this forced acculturation, Rebeca begins to express herself in Spanish and dreams of her dead parents who image her European inheritance:

> ...Rebeca dreamed that a man who looked very much like her, dressed in white linen and with his shirt collar closed by a gold button, was bringing her a bouquet of roses. He was accompanied by a woman with delicate hands who took out one rose and put it in the child's hair. (p. 51)

A vision of elegance transfigures Rebeca's primitivism, but only temporarily. Marquez, working in the language formed by Cervantes, is fully aware of the ironic distance between such dream elegance and a child's survival through the eating of damp earth.

One day, however, the idealized figure of Rebeca's vision actually seems to appear:

> Pietro Crespi was young and blond, the most handsome and well-mannered man who had ever been seen in Macondo, so scrupulous in his dress that in spite of the suffocating heat he would work in his brocade vest and heavy coat of dark cloth. (p. 64)

Crespi (Sp. *crespo*—curly; artificial) personifies cosmopolitan taste, arriving "with the Viennese furniture, the Bohemian crystal, the table service from the Indies Company, the tablecloths from Holland, and a rich variety of lamps and candlesticks, hangings and drapes." By a reference to Crespi as "the Italian" (p. 65), Marquez obliquely joins him to that other traveller alluded to frequently in the novel, Columbus: both bring European notions of civilization to a primitive continent. For Rebeca, Crespi's arrival is the actualization of a dream, both Freudian and Jungian. Rebeca falls in love with this image of her father, with this representative of a cultural elegance that is at once new and ancestral. When Crespi departs, Rebeca feels an archetypal vision has been betrayed. She goes back to eating earth.

The inner contradictions of her character, which Marquez correlates mythologically with the antithesis of civilized and primitive, show outwardly in the two contrastive men Rebeca loves. When Crespi returns to Macondo, she returns to her elegant self-image, and the two plan for a wedding that will take place upon completion of a new church, the paramount symbol of European culture in the New World. But events, particularly the death of Remedios, postpone indefinitely her marriage to this figure of refinement. "Inside the black dress with sleeves down to her wrists" (p. 91), Rebeca despairs of ever realizing her love for Pietro; it has become Quixotic in this "city of mirrors (or mirages)" (p. 383). A demoralized Rebeca begins eating earth once more. But physical life soon reasserts itself, personified by Jose Arcadio who has suddenly reappeared. "The day that she saw him pass by her bedroom she thought that Pietro Crespi was a sugary dandy next to that protomale whose volcanic breathing could be heard all over the house" (p. 94). The once desirable elegance of Crespi has now become inadequate, artificial. In an urge corresponding to her pica, "her ancestral appetite, the taste of primary minerals, the unbridled satisfaction of what was the original food" (p. 67), Rebeca seeks crude sexual experience "in the steaming marsh" (p. 95) of Jose Arcadio's hammock. Her gratification in each instance is primordial, a defiance of civilization: in Freudian terms, the return of the repressed.

The wild passion of their honeymoon scandalizes the neighbours; their cries of physical joy "woke up the whole district as many as eight times in a single night and three times during siesta" (p. 96). Marquez also writes that "her hunger for earth, the *cloc-cloc* of her parents' bones, the impatience of her blood as it faced Pietro Crespi's passivity were relegated to the attic of her memory" (p. 113). In short, her husband "made her happy." Why then did Rebeca kill Jose Arcadio?

The explanation of this mystery lies within her schismatic identity. Her physical needs satiated, Rebeca returns to her embroidery, a symbolic renewal of her need for images of refinement. In correlation with the feeling "of guilt" (p. 48) that accompanied her pica habit, Rebeca experiences a sense of guilt about her fleshly pleasures: later, "it was discovered that she was writing letters to the Bishop, whom she claimed as the first cousin... (p. 131). One passage indirectly shows the murderous hate that Rebeca ultimately felt towards Jose Arcadio's animalism:

> ...her only companion was a pitiless servant woman who killed dogs
> and cats and any tiny animal that got into the house.... (p. 206)

Out of causes that are at once spiritual and psychological, passion becomes loathing, Eros changes to Thanatos, and Rebeca kills Jose Arcadio in the bedroom with his leggings off.

In detailing the opposing elements that form Rebeca's character and that predetermine her frustrated life, Marquez illuminates the destructive contradictions that form South America. Her struggles of conscience against instinct, of spirit against flesh, and of dream against reality are familiar enough dichotomies, are nearly universal psychological, religious, and philosophical clashes. In *One Hundred Years of Solitude*, however, Marquez correlates these pan-human conflicts with historical and cultural dualities specific to South American experience. The antithesis of civilized and primitive, personified by Rebeca, mirrors the mythology of a Conquest in which Spaniards killed Indians. After Rebeca murders Jose Arcadio she lives on in embittered solitude, perhaps enduring the mysterious self-punishment of a continent.

ROBERTO GONZÁLEZ ECHEVARRÍA

Cien años de soledad:
The Novel as Myth and Archive

I

To most readers the Latin American novel must appear to be obsessed with Latin American history and myth.[1] Carlos Fuentes' *Terra Nostra* (1976), for instance, retells much of sixteenth-century Spanish history, including the conquest of Mexico, while also incorporating pre-Columbian myths prophesying that momentous event. Alejo Carpentier's *El siglo de las luces* (1962) narrates Latin America's transition from the eighteenth century to the nineteenth, focusing on the impact of the French Revolution in the Caribbean. Carpentier also delves into Afro-Antillean lore to show how Blacks interpreted the changes brought about by these political upheavals. Mario Vargas Llosa's recent *La guerra del fin del mundo* (1980) tells again the history of Canudos, the rebellion of religious fanatics in the backlands of Brazil, which had already been the object of Euclydes da Cunha's classic *Os Sertões* (1902). Vargas Llosa's ambitious work also examines in painstaking detail the recreation of a Christian mythology in the New World. The list of Latin American novels dealing with Latin American history and myth is very long indeed, and it includes the work of many lesser known, younger writers. Abel Posse's *Daimón* (1978) retells the story of Aguirre, the sixteenth-century rebel who declared himself free from the Spanish Crown and founded his own independent country in South America.[2] As the title of the book

From *Modern Language Notes* 99:2 (1984) © 1984 by The Johns Hopkins University Press.

15

suggests, Posse's fiction centers on the myth of the Devil and his reputed preference of the New World as residence and field of operations, a theme that had been important in two earlier Latin American masterpieces: Alejo Carpentier's *El reino de este mundo* (1949) and João Guimarães Rosa's *Grande sertão, veredas* (1956).[3]

Given that myths are stories whose main concern is with origins, the interest of Latin American fiction in Latin American history and myth is understandable. On the one hand, American history has always held the promise of being not only new but different, of being, as it were, the only *new* history, preserving the force of the oxymoron. On the other hand, the novel, which appears to have emerged in the sixteenth century at the same time as American history, is the only modern genre, the only literary form that is modern not only in the chronological sense, but also because it has persisted for centuries without a poetics, always in defiance of the very notion of genre.[4] Is it possible, then, to make of American history a story as enduring as the old myths? Can Latin American history be as resilient and as useful a hermeneutic tool for probing human nature as the classical myths, and can the novel be the vehicle for the transmission of these new myths? Is it at all conceivable, in the modern, post-oral period, to create myths? Latin American history is to the Latin American narrative what the epic themes are to Spanish literature: a constant whose mode of appearance may vary, but which rarely is omitted. A book like Ramón Menéndez Pidal's *La epopeya castellana a través de la literatura española* could be written about the presence of Latin American history in the Latin American narrative. The question is, of course, how can myth and history coexist in the novel? How can founding stories be told in this most ironic and self-reflexive of genres? It seems to me that the enormous and deserved success of Gabriel García Márquez's masterpiece *Cien años de soledad* is due to the unrelenting way in which these forms of storytelling are interwoven in the novel.

II

In order to explain why and how myth and history are present in *Cien años de soledad* I must first give a brief outline of the broad theory within which my arguments are couched, a theory that, I hope, will allow me to bring a new perspective to the study of the origins and evolution of the Latin American narrative. It is my hypothesis that the novel, having no fixed form of its own, assumes that of a given document endowed with truth-bearing power by society at specific moments in history. The novel, or what is called the novel at various points in history, mimics such documents to show their conventionality, their subjection to rules of textual engenderment similar to those governing literature, which in turn reflect those of language itself. The power to endow the text with the capacity to bear the truth is shown to lie outside the text; it is an exogenous agent that bestows authority upon a certain kind of document owing to the ideological structure of the period. In sixteenth-century Spain these documents were legal ones. The form assumed by the Picaresque was that of a *relación* (report, deposition, letter bearing witness to something), because this kind of written report belonged to the huge imperial bureaucracy through which power was administered in Spain and its possessions.[5] The early history of Latin America, as well as the first fictions of and about Latin America, are told in the rhetorical molds furnished by the notarial arts. These *cartas de relación* were not simply letters nor maps, but also *charters* of the newly discovered territories.[6] Both the writer and the territory were enfranchised through the power of this document which, like Lazarillo's text, is addressed to a higher authority. The pervasiveness of legal rhetoric in early American historiography could hardly be exaggerated. Officially appointed historians (*cronista mayor de Indias*) were assigned by the Crown and the Royal Council of the Indies a set of rules which included ways of subsuming these *relaciones* into their works. American history and fiction, the narrative of America, were first created within the language of the law, a secular totality that guaranteed truth and made its circulation possible. It is within this totality that Garcilaso de la Vega, el Inca, wrote his *Comentarios reales de los incas* (1609), for one must not forget that the *mestizo's* book is an appeal to restore his father's name to an honorable position.[7]

In the nineteenth century Latin America is narrated through the mediation of a new totality: science, and more specifically the scientific consciousness that expresses itself in the language of travelers who journeyed across the Continent, writing about its nature and about themselves. This was the second European discovery of America, and the scientists were the chroniclers of this second discovery. Except for a ground-breaking article by Jean Franco, little attention has been paid to this phenomenom, whose dimensions can be glimpsed by looking at the recent *Travel Accounts and Descriptions of Latin America and the Caribbean 1800–1920: A Selected Bibliography*, compiled by Thomas L. Welch and Myriam Figueras, and published by the Organization of American States (1982).[8] Though selective, this volume contains nearly three hundred pages of tightly packed entries. The names of these scientific travelers are quite impressive, ranging from Charles Darwin to Alexander von Humboldt, and including the likes of the Schomburgk brothers, Robertson, Koch-Grünbergh, and many others. Their fictional counterpart is Professor Challenger in Sir Arthur Conan Doyle's *The Lost World*, whose voyage to the origins of nature takes him to

South America. A scientific consciousness that expresses itself in the language of the travelogue mediates the writing of Latin American fiction in the nineteenth century. Domingo Faustino Sarmiento's *Facundo* (1845), Anselmo Suárez y Romero's *Francisco* (1880), and da Cunha's *Os Sertões* (1902) describe Latin American nature and society through the conceptual grid of nineteenth-century science. Like the chronicles, which were often legal documents, these are books that have a functional value and begin outside of literature. *Francisco* was originally part of a report sent to the British authorities documenting the horrors of slavery in Cuba.[9] Latin America's history and the stories of adventurers, who seek to discover the innermost secrets of the New World, that is to say its newness and difference, are narrated through the mind of a writer qualified by science to search for the truth. Both the self and science are, as Franco suggests, products of the power of the new European commercial empires. Their capacity to find the truth is due not to the cogency of the scientific method, but to the ideological construct that supports them, a construct whose source of strength lies outside the text. The "mind" that analyzes and classifies is made present through the rhetorical conventions of the travelogue. Sarmiento ranges over the Argentine landscape in a process of self-discovery and self-affirmation. In his book he dons the mask of the traveling savant, distanced from the reality that he interprets and classifies according to the intervening tenets of scientific inquiry. This particular mediation prevails until the crisis of the nineteen-twenties and the so-called *novela de la tierra*.[10]

The modern novel, of which *Cien años de soledad* is perhaps the best known example, avails itself of a different kind of mediation: anthropology. Now the promise of knowledge is to be found in a scientific discourse whose object is not nature, but language and myth. The truth-bearing document the novel imitates now is the anthropological treatise. The object of such studies is to discover the origin and source of a culture's own version of its values, beliefs, and history through a culling and re-telling of its myths. Readers of Mauss, Van Gennep, Lévi-Bruhl, Frazer, Lévi-Strauss and other anthropologists will no doubt recognize the inherent complexity of such works. In order to understand another culture, the anthropologist has to know his own to the point where he can distance himself from it. But this distancing involves a kind of self-effacement, too. This dramatic process has been beautifully expounded by Lévi-Strauss in *Tristes tropiques*, a book in which he devotes a good deal of time to his stay in Brazil. John Freccero and Eduardo González have studied how much this book has in common with Alejo Carpentier's *Los pasos perdidos*, a text to which we shall have to return shortly.[11]

Anthropology is the mediating element in the modern Latin American novel because of the place this discipline occupies in Western thought, and also because of the place Latin America occupies within that discipline. Anthropology is a way through which Western culture indirectly affixes its own cultural identity. This identity, which the anthropologist struggles to shed, is one that masters non-historical cultures through knowledge, by making them the object of its study. Anthropology translates into the language of the West the cultures of the others, and in the process establishes its own form of self-knowledge through a kind of annihilation of the self. Existential philosophy, as in Heidegger, Ortega and Sartre, is akin to this process, because it is only through an awareness of the other that Western thought can pretend to wind back to the origin of being. The native, that is to say Latin Americans or in general those who could be delicately called the inhabitants of the post-colonial world, provide the model for this reduction and beginning. The native has timeless stories to explain his changeless society. These stories, these myths, are like those of the West in the distant past, before they became a mythology. Freud, Frazer, Jung, and Heidegger sketch a return to or a retention of those origins. Anthropology finds their analogon in the contemporary world of the native. The modern Latin American novel is written through the model of such anthopological studies. In the same way that the nineteenth-century novel turned Latin America into the object of scientific study, the modern Latin American novel transforms Latin American history into originary myth in order to see itself as other. The theogonic Buendía family in *Cien años de soledad* owes its organization to this phenomenon.

The historical data behind my hypothesis concerning the modern novel and its relation to an anthropological model are vast. Miguel Angel Asturias, as is known, went to Paris to study ethnology under Georges Raynaud, an experience that produced in 1930 his influential *Leyendas de Guatemala*. One of Asturias' classmates at La Sorbonne was none other than Alejo Carpentier, who was then writing *¡Ecué-Yamba-O!* (1933), a novel that is, in many ways, an ethnological study of Cuban Blacks. Another Cuban writer was also preparing herself in Paris in those years: Lydia Cabrera, whose pioneering studies of Afro-Cuban lore would culminate in her classic *El monte* (1954). In more recent times Severo Sarduy has been a student of Roger Bastide, and his *De donde son los cantantes* is, among many other things, a sort of anthropological study of Cuban culture, seen as the synthesis of the three main groups inhabiting the island: the Spanish, the Africans, and the Chinese. Borges' 1933 essay "El arte narrativo y la magia," where the art of storytelling is compared to two kinds of primitive cures outlined in *The Golden Bough*, is but one indication of the wide-ranging impact of Frazer on Latin America. Traces of this influence are visible in Octavio Paz,

Carpentier, Carlos Fuentes, as well as in many others. Lydia Cabrera is perhaps the most significant author here, for she stands for a very important kind of Latin American writer who sits astride both literature and anthropology. Cabrera is a first-rate short-story writer, just as she is a first-rate anthropologist. Her teacher, Fernando Ortiz, was also claimed by literature and his influence upon modern Cuban letters is vast. Examples of writers straddling literature and anthropology are plentiful. The most notorious in recent years is Miguel Barnet, whose *Biografía de un cimarrón* not only contains all the perplexing dualities and contradictions of that relationship, but is also the perfect example of a book whose form is given by anthropology, but which winds up in the field of the novel. But the Peruvian José María Arguedas is without a doubt the most poignant figure among these anthropologist-writers: a novelist, anthropologist, and raised by Indians, Arguedas whose first language was Quechua, not Spanish, carried within him the contradictions and the tragedy inherent in the relationship between anthropology and literature with such intensity that he chose suicide in 1969.

Arguedas' radical gesture is a literal version of the reduction of the self inherent in the process of re-writing Latin American history in the context of the anthropological mediation. It is a gesture that has its literary counterpart, as we shall see, in *Cien años de soledad*. Arguedas' radical effacement of self, like the one practiced by Barnet as he turns or pretends to turn himself into Esteban Montejo, is part of the "unwriting" involved in the modern Latin American narrative. For the modern Latin American narrative is an "unwriting," as much as it is a rewriting, of Latin American history from the anthropological perspective mentioned. The previous writings of history are undone as the new one is attempted; this is why the chronicles and the nineteenth-century scientific travelogues are present in what I will call the Archive in modern fiction. The new narrative unwinds the history told in the old chronicles by showing that that history was made up of a series of conventional topics, whose coherence and authority depended on the codified beliefs of a period whose ideological structure is no longer current. Those codified beliefs were the law. Like the Spanish galleon crumbling in the jungle in *Cien años de soledad*, the history in the chronicles is a voided presence. Likewise, modern novels disassemble the powerful scientific construct through which nineteenth-century Latin America was narrated by demonstrating the relativity of its most cherished concepts, or by rendering literal the metaphors on which such knowledge is based. The power of genealogy is literalized in *Cien años de soledad* by, among other devices, the stream of blood that flows from José Arcadio's wound to Ursula. The presence of the European travelers Robertson and Bonplant in Roa Bastos' *Yo el Supremo* attests to this second voided presence. But the paradigmatic text among these unwritings is Alejo Carpentier's 1953 *Los pasos perdidos*. In this first-person narrative, a modern man travels up the Orinoco river in search of native musical instruments that will unveil the origins of music. As he travels upriver—clearly the river in which Melquíades dies many years later—the narrator-protagonist writes about his voyage as if it were a journey back not only through time, but through recorded history. Hence he passes through various epochs, the most significant of which are the nineteenth century of the traveling European scientists, who provide him with a way of interpreting nature and time, and the colonial period of Latin American history, characterized by activities such as the founding of cities, the indoctrination of Indians, the beginning, in short, of history in the New World as set down by the charters of those institutions—the *cartas de relación*. There are other epochs, reaching all the way back to pre-historic times, but the above are the most important ones, because they are present not only thematically, but through the mediating texts themselves: the era of the petroglyphs is narrated in the language of the scientific travelogue, and the founding of cities in that of the legalistic chronicles. The narrator-protagonist's text is organized according to a set of rhetorical conventions that reveal themselves as such in the process of reading. In the fiction of the novel, the narrator-protagonist cannot remain in what he has termed the Valley-of-Time-Detained, the origin of time and history, for he needs to secure enough paper to set down the music he has begun to compose. In the fiction the quest for that degree zero of time and history whence to inscribe a rewriting of Latin America history has not been found. But in the writing of the novel a clearing has been reached, a razing that becomes a starting-point for the new Latin American narrative. That razing involves the various mediations through which Latin America was narrated, the systems from which fiction borrowed truth-bearing forms, erased to assume the new mediation, which requires this level-ground of self and history. This is the point at which *Cien años de soledad* begins, and the reason why the world is so recent "that many things lacked names, and in order to indicate them it was necessary to point" (p. 1).[12] It is also the point that the last Aureliano seeks at the very end when he discovers how to translate Melquíades' manuscripts. He reads in a frenzy "discovering the first indications of his own being in a lascivious grandfather who let himself be frivolously dragged across a hallucinated plateau in search of a beautiful woman who would not make him happy" (p. 421). What is left for fiction after *Los pasos perdidos*? Clearly, only fiction; but novels are never content with fiction, they must pretend to deal with the truth. So, paradoxically enough, the truth with which they deal in the modern period is fiction itself. That is to say, the fictions Latin American culture has created to understand itself, the myths about the origin of its history.

III

The importance of myth in *Cien años de soledad* was noticed by the first commentators of the novel and later studies have again taken up the topic.[13] It seems clear that myth appears in the novel in the following guises: 1) there are stories that resemble classical or biblical myths, most notably the Flood, but also Paradise, the Seven Plagues, Apocalypse, and the proliferation of the family, with its complicated genealogy, has an Old Testament ring to it; 2) there are characters who are reminiscent of mythical heroes: José Arcadio Buendía, who is a sort of Moses, Rebeca, who is like a female Perseus, Remedios, who ascends in a flutter of white sheets in a scene that is suggestive not just of the Ascension of the Virgin, but more specifically of the popular renditions of the event in religious prints; 3) certain stories have a general mythic character in that they contain supernatural elements, as in the case just mentioned, and also when José Arcadio's blood returns to Ursula; 4) the beginning of the whole story, which is found, as in myth in a tale of violence and incest. All four, of course, commingle, and because *Cien años de soledad* tells a story of foundations or origins, the whole novel has a mythic air about it. No single myth or mythology prevails. Instead the various ways in which myth appears give the whole novel a mythical character without it being a distinct version of one given myth.

At the same time, there is lurking in the background of the story the overall pattern of Latin American history, both as a general design made up of various key events and eras, and in the presence of specific characters and incidents that seem to refer to real people and happenings. Thus we have a period of discovery and conquest, when José Arcadio Buendía and the original families settle Macondo. There is in this part of the book little sense that Macondo belongs to a larger political unit, but such isolation was in fact typical of Latin America's towns in the colonial period. Even the viceroyalties lived in virtual isolation from the metropolitan government.[14] The appearance of Apolinar Moscoso and his barefoot soldiers is the beginning of the republican era, which is immediately followed by the outbreak of the civil wars in which Colonel Aureliano Buendía distinguishes himself. Though Colombia is the most obvious model for this period, nearly the entire continent suffered from civil strife during the nineteenth century, a process that led to the emergence of dictators and *caudillos*. This period is followed by the era of neocolonial domination by the United States and the struggles against it in most Latin American countries. These culminate in the novel with the general strike and the massacre of the workers. There are, unfortunately, countless models for this last, clearly defined period in the novel. After the flood, there is a time of decay before the apocalyptic wind that razes the town at the end. The liberal priest and the various military types who surround Colonel Aureliano Buendía, are among the characters with counterparts in Latin American history. Lucila I. Mena has already demonstrated that some of the historical incidents in the novel can be documented, and a sedulous critic with time and the proper library can probably document many others.[15] But to carry this sort of research much further than Mena has would be a rather gratuitous critical exercise. Set against the global, totalizing thrust of the novel are these historical details which, without being specific, are nonetheless true in a general sense. Each of the above mentioned epochs is evoked not only through major historical events, but also through allusion to specific minor incidents and characters. For instance, early Macondo is inhabited by a *de jure* aristocracy made up of the founding families, which is analogous to that of colonial Latin America, where conquistadores and their descendants enjoyed certain privileges and exemptions.[16]

The blend of mythic elements and Latin American history in *Cien años de soledad* reveals a desire to found an American myth. Latin American history is set on the same level as mythic stories, therefore it too becomes a sort of myth. The lack of specificity of the various incidents, which appear to represent several related or similar events, points in this direction. The Latin American myth is this story of foundation, articulated through independence, civil war, struggle against U.S. colonialism, all cast within a genealogical line that weaves in and out, repeating names and characters. There is a Whitmanian thrust to the brash declaration of the existence of a literary language that underlies this mixture of historical fact with mythic story in *Cien años de soledad*. The novel is in fact intimately related to similar efforts in poetry, such as the ones by Neruda in his *Canto General* and Octavio Paz in his *Piedra de Sol*. *Canto General* in particular is one of the most important sources of García Márquez's novel. Framed by Genesis and Apocalypse, fraught with incest and violence, the story of the Buendía family thus stands as Latin American history cast in the language of myth, an unresolved mixture that both beckons and bewilders the reader.

This duality is present throughout *Cien años de soledad* separating the world of writing from the atemporal world of myth. But the play of contradictions issuing from this duality reaches a synthesis that is perhaps the most important feature of the novel. As we have seen, myth represents the origin. Latin America's history is narrated in the language of myth because it is the other, represented by incest, taboo, and the primitive act of naming. The novel's persistent preoccupation with genealogy and with supernatural acts performed by various characters belongs to this realm.[17] History, on the other hand, is critical, temporal, and dwells in a special place: Melquíades'

room in the Buendía house, which I have chosen to call the Archive. The
room is full of books and manuscripts, and has a time of its own. It is here
that a succession of characters attempt to decipher Melquíades' parchments,
and the last Aureliano, in an epiphanic inspiration, orally translates the whole
(or nearly the whole) manuscript and dies. What occurs here, the text of the
novel suggests, is unrepeatable. In the fiction of the novel, on the other hand,
there are many repetitions. Ursula, for instance, twice feels that time is going
around in circles and that members of the family follow one or two patterns
of behavior indicated by their names. Time is circular in the fiction, but not
in Melquíades' room. The Archive appears to be linear and teleological,
while the plot of the novel itself is repetitive and mythical. *Cien años de soledad*
is made up of two main stories: one has to do with the family and culminates
in the birth of the child with the pig's tail, while the other is concerned with
the interpretation of Melquíades' manuscript, a linear suspense story that
culminates in Aureliano's final discovery of the key to the translation of the
parchments.

That there should be a special abode for documents and books in *Cien
años de soledad* should come as no suprise to readers of modern Latin
American fiction. In spite of its apparent novelty, there are such enclosures
in *Aura, Yo el Supremo, El arpa y la sombra, Crónica de una muerte anunciada*
and *Oppiano Licario*, to mention a few of the novels where it plays a
prominent role. What is characteristic of the Archive is: 1) the presence not
only of history, but of previous mediating elements through which it was
narrated, be it the legal documents of colonial times or the scientific ones of
the nineteenth century; 2) the existence of an inner historian who reads the
texts, interprets and writes them; 3) and finally the presence of an unfinished
manuscript that the inner historian is trying to complete. In *Cien años de
soledad* the most tenuous presence is the legal texts, but one can infer it from
the allusions to the chronicles that were in fact *relaciones*, and particularly in
the founding of Macondo, for the founding of cities, primordial activity of
conquistadores, was closely connected to the writing of history. The
vagueness of this presence is only so in relation to the others, for at least two
critics have convincingly argued in favor of the overwhelming influence of
the chronicles in *Cien años de soledad*.[18] The nineteenth-century travel-books
are evident in the descriptions of the jungle and at a crucial moment when
José Arcadio Segundo hears Melquíades mumble something in his room.
José Arcadio leans over and hears the gypsy mention the name of none other
than Alexander von Humboldt and the word *equinoccio*, which comes from
the title of the latter's book, which in Spanish is *Viaje a las regiones
equinocciales del Nuevo Mundo*. In Macondo's Archive, there are in addition
two key words: the so-called English *Encyclopedia* and *The Thousand and One*

Nights. These two books play an important role in Melquíades' writing, and the *Encyclopedia* is instrumental in the decoding of his manuscripts. The existence in Melquíades' fiction of precisely these two books adds a peculiar twist to the Archive, one that points to its own literary filiation.

I do not think that it would be too farfetched to say that *The Thousand and One Nights* and the so-called English *Encyclopedia* together are allusions to that master of fictions called Borges. In fact, Melquíades is a figure of the Argentine writer. Old beyond age, enigmatic, blind, entirely devoted to fiction, Melquíades stands for Borges, the librarian and keeper of the Archive. There is something whimsical in García Márquez's inclusion of such a figure in the novel, but there is a good deal more. It is not too difficult to fathom what this Borgesian figure means. Planted in the middle of the special abode of books and manuscripts, a reader of one of the oldest and most influencial collections of stories in the history of literature, Melquíades and his Archive stand for literature; more specifically, for Borges' kind of literature: ironic, critical, a demolisher of all delusions, the sort of thing we encounter at the end of the novel, when Aureliano finishes translating Melquíades' manuscript. There are in that ending further allusions to several stories by Borges: to "Tlön, Ucqbar, Orbis Tertius," in that Macondo is a verbal construct; to "The Secret Miracle," in that Aureliano, like the condemned poet, perishes the moment he finishes his work; to "The Aleph," in that Aureliano Babilonia's glimpse of the history of Macondo is instantaneous and all-encompassing; and particularly to "Death and the Compass," for the moment of anagnorisis is linked to death. Like Lönnrot, Aureliano only understands the workings of his fate at the moment of his death.

The Archive, then, is Borges' study. It stands for writing, for literature, for an accumulation of texts that is no mere heap, but an *arché*, a relentless memory that disassembles the fictions of myth, literature and even history. The masterbooks in the Archive are, as we have seen, the *Encyclopedia* and *The Thousand and One Nights*. The *Encyclopedia*, which Aureliano has read according to the narrator from A to Z as if it were a novel, is in itself a figure of the totality of knowledge as conceived by the West. But how is it knowledge, and how has Aureliano read it? The moment we consider the order of knowledge in the *Encyclopedia* and the way in which Aureliano reads it, we realize the paradoxes inherent in the Archive as repository of history. The *Encyclopedia* is organized, of course, in alphabetical order, without the order of the entries being affected by any sort of chronological or evaluative consideration: Napoleon appears before Zeus and Charles V before God. The beginning is provided arbitrarily by the alphabet as well as by the sequence: apocalypse must appear in the first volume. *The Thousand and One*

Nights, on the other hand, stands for a beginning in fiction, or beginning as fiction, as well as for a series of individual, disconnected stories, linked only by the narrator's fear of death. Aureliano is like Scheherazade, who tells her stories on the verge of death. Neither book seems to have priority over the other. Both have a prominent place within the Archive, providing their own forms of pastness, of documentary, textual material. The order that prevails in the Archive, then, is not that of mere chronology, but that of writing; the rigorous process of inscribing and decoding to which Melquíades and the last Aureliano give themselves over, a linear process of cancellations and substitutions, of gaps.

Writing and reading have an order of their own which is preserved within the Archive. It might be remembered that in Melquíades' room, it is always Monday and March for some characters, while for others his study is the room of the chamberpots, where decay and temporality have their own end embodied in the very essence of eschatology. The combination of feces and writing in the Archive is significant enough. Writing appears as an eschatological activity in that it deals with the end. Yet writing is also the beginning, insofar as nothing is in the text until it is written. Hence the prevalence of Monday and March in the secret abode of Melquíades, the beginning of the week and of spring respectively (March, not April, is the "cruellest month" in García Márquez). Melquíades is both young and old, depending, of course, on whether or not he wears his dentures; he presides over the beginning and the end. The Archive, then, is not so much an accumulation of texts as the process whereby texts are written; a process of repeated combinations, of shufflings and re-shufflings ruled by heterogeneity and difference. It is not strictly linear as both continuity and discontinuity, held together in uneasy allegiance. This is the reason why the previous mediations through which Latin America was narrated are contained in the Archive as voided presences; they are both erased and a memory of their own demise, keys to filing systems now abandoned, but they retain their archival quality, their power to differentiate, to space. They are not archetypes, but an *arché* of types.

This process is evident in the way in which Melquíades' manuscript is written and translated. Throughout the novel we are told that Melquíades writes undecipherable manuscripts, that his handwriting produces something that looks more like musical notation than script, that his writing resembles clothes on a line. Eventually José Arcadio Segundo discovers, with the aid of the *Encyclopedia*, that the writing is in Sanskrit. When Aureliano begins to translate from the Sanskrit, he comes up with coded Spanish verses. These verses have different codes, depending on whether they are even or odd numbered. Aureliano is finally illuminated when he sees the dead newborn being carried away by the ants and remembers the epigraph of the manuscript, which is supposed to read: *"The first of the line is tied to a tree and the last is being eaten by the ants"* (p. 420, emphasis in the original). He realizes then that the manuscript contains the story of his family, and hurries on to translate it to discover his own fate and the date and circumstances of his death. We shall return to the significance of all this, but first let us complete our description of the manuscript and its translation, for it is very easy to leap to conclusions concerning Melquíades' writing. Aureliano begins to translate the text out loud, jumping ahead twice to get to the present faster. Once he reaches the present he has a second illumination: that he would die in the room where the manuscript is kept once he finished translating the last line of poetry ("el último verso"). Critics have been quick to say that what we have read is Melquíades's version of the history of Macondo, that is to say, *Cien años de soledad*. Even if in fact it is Aureliano's translation that we read, then some changes have been made. To begin with, the epigraph has been omitted, as we have seen. In addition, Aureliano's leaps to get to the present have either not been accounted for in this version, or the holes they left have been restored. But by whom? The only solution to this enigma is to say that our reading—that each reading—of the text is the text, that is to say, yet another version added or appended to the Archive. Each of these readings corrects the others and each is unrepeatable insofar as it is a distinct act caught in the reader's own temporality. In this sense, we, like Aureliano, read the instant we live, cognizant that it may very well be our last. This is the eschatological sense announced in various ways by the Archive.

The radical historicity to which the Archive condemns us belies its apparent atemporality and the bizarre order that the master-books within it have. It is a historicity that is very much like the one to which the narrator-protagonist of *Los pasos perdidos* is condemned at the end of that novel. In fact, Aureliano's reading of the manuscript in search of his origins and of an understanding of his being in the present is analogous to the reading performed by Carpentier's character in search of the origins of history and of his own beginnings. Such dearly achieved historicity in the face of the circularity and repetition of the family's history is somewhat ironic, given the sense of ahistoricalness with which many readers, intoxicated by the similarity of names and by Ursula's notion that time is going round and round, leave the novel. Such historicity, however, is needed to represent, within the anthropological mediation posited, the lucid consciousness of the West, able to understand itself by posturing as the other, but unable to abandon the sense of history to which writing sentences it. This is a sentence from which we can gain acquittal by means of a wilfull act of delusion, but one that *Cien años de soledad*, for all its fictive force does not allow the reader.

There is a curious fact that few readers of *Cien años de soledad* remark upon: even though the novel begins with Colonel Aureliano Buendía facing the firing squad, the one who dies at the end is not Aureliano the soldier, but Aureliano the reader. It seems to me that this displacement, plus the fact that Aureliano's moments of vision are flashes of insight parallel to those of the rebel, seems to suggest a most significant connection between the realms of history and myth, one that constitutes a common denominator between the repetitions of the family history and the disassembling mechanisms of the Archive. In the Archive, the presence of Melquíades and Aureliano (and in *Aura*, Felipe Montero, in *Yo el Supremo*, Patiño, etc.) is an insurance that the individual consciousness of a historian/writer will filter the ahistorical pretense of myth by subjecting events to the temporality of writing. But in *Cien años de soledad* the death of these figures is indicative of a mythic power that lurks within the realm of writing, a story that makes possible the Archive. In *Yo el Supremo* this is clearly indicated by Patiño's being a "swollen foot," that is, an Oedipus who pays a high price for his knowledge. In *Cien años de soledad* Aureliano suffers a similar fate. He commits incest with his aunt, engenders a monster with her and dies the moment he has a glimpse of his fate. Aureliano is the necessary victim for us to be able to read the text, for us to acquire the knowledge we need to decode it. He (we) is no Oedipus, but more likely a Minotaur, which would bring us back to Borges (and also Cortázar). The ritualistic death—which prefigures that of *Crónica de una muerte anunciada*—is necessary because of the incest committed both at the genealogical and the textual level. In both cases, what has been gained is a forbidden knowledge of the other as oneself, or vice-versa.

As we have seen, the most salient characteristic of the text we read is its heterogeneity. However, this heterogeneity is made up of differences within similarity. The various versions of the story are all related, yet differ in each instance. Their difference as well as their relation is akin—*valga la palabra*—to the relationship between the incestuous characters and to the broader confrontation between writer and a primitive other who produces myth. Put differently, the self-reflexiveness of the novel is implicitly compared to incest, a self-knowledge that somehow lies beyond knowledge. A plausible argument can be made that the end results of both are similar, in the most tangible sense, or at least related. When the ants carry away the carcass of the monstrous child engendered by Amaranta Ursula and Aureliano, its skin is described in terms that are very reminiscent of Melquíades' parchments. The English translation blurs that similarity. It reads: "And then he saw the child. It was a dry and bloated bag of skin that all the ants in the world were dragging..." (p. 420). The Spanish reads: "Era un pellejo [it was a skin] hinchado y reseco, que todas las hormigas del mundo iban arrastrando..." (p.

349). I need not go into the etymological and historical kinship uniting skin and parchment because the novel itself provides that link. The parchments are once described as "parecían fabricados en una materia árida que se resquebrajaba como hojaldres" (p. 68), and the books in the Archive are bound "en una materia acartonada y pálida como la piel humana curtida" (p. 160). The English reads, "the parchments that he had brought with him and that seemed to have been made out of some dry material that crumpled like puff paste" (p. 73), and "the books were bound in a cardboard-like material, pale, like tanned human skin" (p. 188).

The monster and the manuscript, the monster and the text, are the product of the turning onto onself implicit in incest and self-reflexivity. Both are heterogeneous within a given set of characteristics, the most conspicuous of which is their supplementarity: the pig's tail, which exceeds the normal contours of the human body, and the text, whose mode of being is each added reading. The novel is a monster, engendered by a self-knowledge of which we too are guilty, to which we add our own pig's tail of reading and interpretation. The plot line that narrates the decipherment of the manuscripts underscores our own falling into this trap. Like Aureliano, we follow along in search of the meaning of the manuscripts, constantly teased by scenes where Melquíades appears scratching his incomprehensible handwriting onto rough parchment, by scenes where José Arcadio Segundo or Aureliano make preliminary discoveries that eventually lead them to unravel the mystery. But like Lönnrot in "Death and the Compass," and like Aureliano himself, we do not discover, until the very end, what the manuscripts contain. Our own anagnorisis as readers is saved for the last page, when the novel concludes and we close the book to cease being as readers, to be, as it were, slain in that role. We are placed back at the beginning, a beginning that is also already the end, a discontinuous, independent instant where everything commingles without any possibility for extending the insight, an intimation of death. This independent instant is not the novel; it is the point to which the novel has led us. By means of an unreading, the text has reduced us, like Aureliano, to a ground zero, where death and birth are joined together as correlative moments of incommunicable plenitude. The text is that which is added to this moment. Archive and myth are conjoined as instances of discontinuity rather than continuity; knowledge and death are given equivalent value.

It is a commonplace, almost an uncritical fetish, to say that the novel always includes the story of how it is written, that it is a self-reflexive genre. The question is why and how it is so at specific moments. Clearly, *Cien años de soledad* is self-reflexive not merely to provoke laughter, or to declare itself literary and thus disconnected from reality or from history. In García

Márquez, and I daresay in all major Latin American novelists, self-reflexivity is a way of disassembling the mediation through which Latin America is narrated, a mediation that constitutes the pre-text of the novel itself. It is also a way of showing that the act of writing is caught up in a deeply rooted, mythic struggle that constantly denies it the authority to generate and contain knowledge about the other without at the same time generating a perilous sort of knowledge about one's mortality and capacity to know oneself.

What do we learn about Latin American history in *Cien años de soledad*? We learn that while its writing may be mired in myth, it cannot be turned to myth, that its newness makes it impervious to timelessness, circularity, or any such delusion. New and therefore historical, what occurs in America is marked by change, it is change. García Márquez has expressed this by tantalizing the reader with various forms of myth, while at the same time subjecting him to the rigors of history as writing, of history as Archive. He has also achieved it by making Borges the keeper of the Archive, for the figure of the Argentine ensures that no delusions about literature be entertained. In a sense, what García Márquez has done is to punch through the anthropological mediation and substitute the anthropologist for an historian, and to turn the object of attention away from myth as an expression of so-called primitive societies to the myths of modern society: the book, writing, reading, instruments of a quest for self-knowledge that lie beyond the solace mythic interpretations of the world usually afford. We can always use *Cien años de soledad* to escape temporality, but only if we wilfully misread it to blind ourselves of its warnings against it. American history can only become myth enmeshed in this very modern problematic that so enriches its most enduring fictions.

For it is not toward a high-pitched rationality that *Cien años de soledad* moves, but toward a vision of its own creation dominated by the forces that generate myth. This is perhaps most evident if we consider that the Archive may very well be the most powerful of cultural retentions. The Archive is, first of all, a repository for the legal documents wherein the origins of Latin American history are contained, as well as a specifically Hispanic institution created at the same time as the New World was being settled. As is known, the great Archive at Simancas, begun by Charles V, but finished by the King Bureaucrat Philip II, is the first and possibly most voluminous such storehouse in Europe. The same Herrera who designed the Escorial had a hand in planning the Archive, that is to say, in turning a castle that was originally a prison into the Archive. America was discovered by Columbus, but really became a historical entity as a result of the development of the printing press. Latin America was created in the Archive. It may very well have been Carlos Fuentes in his *Terra Nostra* who most clearly saw the connection, making Cervantes the inner historian in that novel. In terms of the novel's ability to retain and pass on cultural values, the message contained in books such as Fuentes' and *Cien años de soledad* is indeed disturbing, for they tell us that it is impossible to create new myths, yet bring us back once and again to that moment where our desire for meaning can only be satisfied by myth.

NOTES

1. This paper was originally the keynote address in a Symposium on the Works of Gabriel García Márquez held at Wesleyan University, on April 9, 1983. I wish to thank Professors Diana S. Goodrich and Carlos J. Alonso for their invitation and hospitality. I also wish to thank the Guggenheim Foundation for a fellowship that allowed me to do some of the research that led to many of the ideas put forth here.

2. Abel Posse (Argentina, 1934), is the author of *Los Bogavantes* (1967), *La boca del tigre* (1971—Premio Nacional de Literatura), *Daimón* (1978) and *Los perros del paraíso* (1983).

3. The topic of the presence of the Devil in Latin American culture has been the object of many studies. A useful introduction to the topic in relation to literature may be found in Sabino Sola, *El diablo y lo diabólico en las letras americanas* (Madrid: Castalia, 1973).

4. Ralph Freedman made a useful suggestion about the study of the origins of the novel that is my point of departure here: "Instead of separating genres or subgenres artificially and then accounting for exceptions by stipulating mixtures and compounds, it is simpler to view all of prose fiction as a unity and to trace particular strands to different origins, strands which would include not only the English novel of manners, or the post-medieval romance, or the Gothic novel, but also the medieval allegory, the German *Bildungsroman*, or the picaresque. Some of these strands may be close to folk material or to classical epics, others may have modeled themselves on travelogues and journalistic descriptions of events, and others again suggest drawing-room comedies and even lyrical prose poetry, yet all, to varying degrees, seem to mirror life in aesthetically defined worlds (life as myth, as structure of ideas, as worlds of feeling or quotidian reality)..." "The Possibility of a Theory of the Novel," in *The Disciplines of Criticism. Essays in Literary Theory, Interpretation, and History*, ed. Peter Demetz, Thomas Greene and Lowry Nelson Jr. (New Haven: Yale University Press, 1968), p. 65.

5. For further details on this, see my "The Life and Adventures of Cipión: Cervantes and the Picaresque," *Diacritics*, 10, no. 3 (1980), pp. 15-26.

6. On the *relaciones* there are the following studies: Vittorio Salvadorini, "Las 'relaciones' de Hernán Cortés," *Thesaurus* (Boletín del Instituto Caro y Cuervo), 18, no. 1 (1963), pp. 77-97; Roberto González Echevarría, "José Arrom, autor de la *Relación acerca de las antigüedades de las indios:* picaresca e historia," *Relecturas: estudìos de literatura cubana* (Caracas: Monte Avila, 1976), pp. 17-35; Walter Mignolo, "Cartas, crónicas y relaciones del descubrimiento y la conquista," in Luis Iñigo Madrigal, coordinador, *Historia de la literatura hispanoamericana*, Tomo I "Epoca Colonial" (Madrid: Cátedra, 1982), pp. 57-110; Tzvetan Todorov, *La conquête de l'Amérique. La question de l'autre* (Paris: Editions du Seuil, 1982); Roberto González Echevarria, "Humanismo, retórica y las crónicas de la conquista," *Isla a su vuelo fugitiva: ensayos críticos sobre literatura hispanoamericana* (Madrid: Porrúa, 1983), pp. 9-25. Mignolo's work is particularly useful, for he carefully distinguishes between the various kinds of discourse available to chroniclers in the colonial period, without falling into the trap of considering their work literary or imaginative before taking into account first what each text was (letter, chronicle, history, etc.) Todorov's book rediscovers a good deal of material available in the extant bibliography in Spanish, which he apparently did not consult, and reaches conclusions that are fairly predictable. Todorov was unable to keep clear of the dramatic moral issues raised by the conquest of the New World, which have continued to determine much of the scholarship on the colonial period. His confession of being chiefly a moralist does not absolve him for being banale: "Pour Cortés, la conquête du savoir conduit à celle du pouvoir. Le retiens de lui la conquête du savoir, même si c'est pour résister au pouvoir. Il y a quelque légèreté à se contenter de condamner les méchants conquistadores et à regretter les bons Indiens, comme s'il suffisaint d'identifier le mal pour le combattre. Ce n'est pas faire l'éloge des conquistadores que de reconnaître, ici ou là, leur supériorité; il est nécessaire d'analyser les armes de la conquête si l'on veut pouvoir l'arrêter un jour. Car les conquêtes n' appattiennent pas qu'au passé" (p. 258). In my own work, as sketched briefly in the text of this paper, I intend to study how through notarial rhetoric the newly deployed Spanish State controlled historical discourse. To do so one has to follow the development of legal rhetoric from Bologna to the Renaissance, and then its application in America through the various institutions created or developed in the late XV and early XVI century. For the history of legal rhetoric see Rafael Núñez Lagos, *El documento medieval y Rolandino (notas de historia)* (Madrid: Editorial Góngora, 1951). I draw from Núñez Lagos' extensive discussion of the *carta* my assertion concerning the *cartas de relación*.

7. For details of Garcilaso's legal maneuvers, see John Grier Varner, *El Inca. The Life and Times of Garcilaso de la Vega* (Austin and London: The

University of Texas Press, 1968), pp. 213-26. The first century of colonization was characterized by spectacular legal cases that matched the fabulous adventures of the conquistadores: first Columbus and his successors, later Cortés and Pizarro. Even an adventurer and marvellous storyteller like Alvar Núñez Cabeza de Vaca ended his life embroiled in costly legal proceedings that left him as devoid of wordly goods at the end of his life as he had been among the Indians of North America.

8. Jean Franco, "Un viaje poco romántico: viajeros británicos hacia Sudamérica: 1818-28," *Escritura* (Caracas), Año 4, no. 7 (1979), pp. 129-41. On scientific travelers there is also: Christian C. Chester, Jr., "Hispanic Literature of Exploration," *Exploration* (Journal of the MLA Special Session on the Literature of Exploration and Travel), 1 (1973), pp. 42-46; Evelio A. Echevarría, "La conquista del Chimborazo," *Américas* (Washington), 35, no. 5 (1983), pp. 22-31; Hans Galinsky, "Exploring the 'Exploration Report' and Its Image of the Overseas World: Spanish, French, and English Variants of a Common Form Type in Early American Literature," *Early American Literature*, 12 (1977), pp. 5-24; C. Harvey Gardiner, "Foreign Travelers' Accounts of Mexico, 1810-1910," *The Americas*, 8 (1952), pp. 321-51; C. Harvey Gardiner, ed. *Journeys Accross the Pampas and Among the Andes* (Carbondale: Southern Illinois University Press, 1967); Mary Sayre Haverstock, "La fascinación de los Andes," *Américas*, 35, no. 1 (1983), pp. 37-41; Ronald Hilton, "The Significance of Travel Literature With Special Reference to the Spanish-and Portuguese-Speaking World," *Hispania*, 49 (1966), 836-45; S. Samuel Trifilo, "Nineteenth Century English Travel Books on Argentina: A Revival in Spanish Translation," *Hispania*, 41 (1958), 491-96; Victor Wolfgang Von Hagen, *South America Called Them: Explorations of the Great Naturalists La Condamine, Humboldt, Darwin, Spruce* (New York: Alfred A. Knopf, 1945).

9. The book was not included in the report, which did contain the autobiography of the Cuban slave poet Juan Francisco Manzano: *Poems by a Slave in the Island of Cuba, Recently Liberated; translated from the Spanish by R. R. Madden, M.D., with the History of the Early Life of the Negro Poet, Written by Himself; To Which are prefixed Two Pieces Descriptive of Cuban Slavery and the Slave-Traffic* (London: Thomas Ward and Co., 1840). There is a modern edition by Edward J. Mullen (Hamden: Archon Books, 1981).

10. On the *novela de la tierra* the most advanced work is by Carlos J. Alonso in his, "The *novela de la tierra*: The Discourse of the Autochthonous," Doctoral Dissertation, Yale University, 1983.

11. John Freccero, "Reader's Report," Cornell University. John M. Olin Library Bookmark Series, no. 36 (April 1968); Eduardo González, *Alejo Carpentier: el tiempo del hombre* (Caracas: Monte Avila, 1978).

12. All references are to Gabriel García Márquez, *One Hundred Years of Solitude*, tr. Gregory Rabassa (New York: Harper & Row, 1967), and *Cien años de soledad* (Buenos Aires: Editorial Sudamericana, 1967).

13. See, for example, Ricardo Gullón, *García Márquez o el olvidado arte de contar* (Madrid: Taurus, 1970) and Carmen Arnau, *El mundo mítico de Gabriel García Márquez* (Barcelona: Ediciones Península, 1971). There have been many studies since along these lines. The most convincing is by Michael Palencia-Roth, "Los pergaminos de Aureliano Babilonia," *Revista Iberoamericana*, nos. 123-124 (1983), pp. 403-17. Palencia-Roth's splendid piece argues in favor of the Biblical myth of Apocalypse as the principal one in the organization of the novel and insists on the influence of Borges on García Márquez. There is much to be learned from his interpretation. However, it seems to me that Palencia-Roth allows himself to be intoxicated by the mythic quality of the novel when he writes that the meeting of times at the end elevates time to eternity, and jumps to the conclusion that Melquíades' manuscripts are the novel. As I will argue further below, no myth controls the novel, and no transcendence is allowed by the constantly undermined and undermining world of writing. To believe in the possibility of eternal time, or to think that there is a text to which the title of the novel gives a name, requires that we accept that visions such as Colonel Aureliano Buendía and Aureliano Babilonia have in the fiction of the novel exist outside of the verbal realm. If we could escape the verbal, then the sort of simultaneity and atemporality of which Palencia-Roth speaks so persuasively, and which are characteristic of myth, would be possible. On the influence of Borges on García Márquez, see: Roberto González Echevarria, "With Borges in Macondo," *Diacritics*, 2, No. 1 (1972), pp. 57-60 and Emir Rodríguez Monegal, "*One Hundred Years of Solitude*: The Last Three Pages," *Books Abroad*, 47 (1973), 485-89. I have learned a good deal from this article, in which the author singles out Melquiades' room as an important feature of the novel, and insists on the notion of the Book as a key to an understanding of the text.

14. C. H. Haring, *The Spanish Empire in America* (New York: Harcourt, Brace and World, Inc., 1963 [1947]). Such isolation did not mean that the colonial towns were independent, nor that they could develop according to the whims of their inhabitants.

15. Lucila I. Mena, "La huelga bananera como expressión de lo 'real maravilloso' americano en *Cien años de soledad*," *Bulletin Hispanique*, 74 (1972), 379-405.

16. For details on this see Haring and Varner, op. cit. Much of the legal jousting mentioned before had to do with the claims of this spurious aristocracy.

17. Patricia Tobin has written an illuminating chapter on genealogy in *Cien años de soledad* in her *Time and the Novel. The Genealogical Imperative* (Princeton: Princeton University Press, 1978). Another excellent study, carried out incidentally by someone trained in anthropology, is Mercedes López-Baralt's "*Cien años de soledad:* cultura e historia latinoamericanas replanteadas en el idioma del parentesco," *Revista de Estudios Hispánicos* (San Juan de Puerto Rico), año 6 (1979), pp. 153-75.

18. Iris M. Zavala, "*Cien años de soledad, crónica de Indias,*" *Insula*, no. 286 (1970), pp. 3, 11; Selma Calasans Rodrigues, "*Cien años de soledad* y las crónicas de la conquista," *Revista de la Universidad de Mexico*, 38, no. 23 (1983), pp. 13-16. García Márquez's interest in the *crónicas de Indias*, established beyond doubt in Zavala's article, was made evident again in his speech accepting the Nobel Prize: "Los cronistas de Indias nos legaron otros incontables [testimonies of astonishing events and things in the New World]. El Dorado, nuestro país ilusorio tan codiciado, figuró en mapas numerosos durante largos años, cambiando de lugar y de forma según la fantasía de los cartógrafos. En busca de la fuente de la eterna juventud, el mítico Alvar Núñez Cabeza de Vaca exploró durante ocho años el norte de Mexico [sic], en una expedición venática cuyos miembros se comieron unos a otros, y sólo llegaron cinco de los 600 que la emprendieron. Uno de los tantos misterios que nunca fueron descifrados, es el de las once mil mulas cargadas con cien libras de oro cada una, que un día salieron del Cuzco para pagar el rescate de Atahualpa y nunca llegaron a su destino. Más tarde, durante la colonia, se vendían en Cartagena de Indias unas gallinas criadas en tierras de Aluvión, en cuyas mollejas se encontraban piedrecitas de oro." *El Mundo* (San Juan de Puerto Rico), Sunday, December 12, 1982, p. 21-C. In a long interview published as a book in that same year, he said: "Yo había leído con mucho interés a Cristóbal Colón, a Pigafetta y a los cronistas de Indias, que tenían una visión original [del Caribe], y había leído a Salgari y a Conrad..." *El olor de la guayaba. Conversaciones con Plinio Apuleyo Mendoza* (Bogota: Editorial La Oveja Negra, 1982), p. 32. The early history of Macondo furnished in "Los funerales de la Mama Grande" links the origins of the town to colonial Latin America through legal documents setting down the proprietary rights of the Matriarch: "Reducido a sus proporciones reales, el patrimonio fisico [de la Mamá Grande] se reducía a tres encomiendas adjudicadas por Cédula Real durante la Colonia, y que con el transcurso del tiempo, en virtud de intrincados matrimonios de conveniencia, se habían acumulado bajo el dominio de la Mamá Grande. En ese territorio ocioso, sin límites definidos, que abarcaba cinco municipios y en el cual no se sembró nunca un solo grano por cuenta de los propietarios, vivían a título de arrendatarias 352 familias." *Los funerales de la Mamá Grande* (Buenos Aires: Editorial Sudamericana,

1967), pp. 134-35. In *Crónica de una muerte anunciada*, the Archive is full of colonial documents: "Todo lo que sabemos de su carácter [the lawyer whose version of the crime would have been the first of the story being told] es aprendido en el sumario, que numerosas personas me ayudaron a buscar veinte años después del crimen en el Palacio de Justicia de Riohacha. No existía clasificación alguna en los archivos, y más de un siglo de expedientes estaban amontonados en el suelo del decrépito edificio colonial que fuera por dos dias el cuartel general de Francis Drake. La planta baja se inundaba con el mar de leva, y los volúmenes descosidos flotaban en las oficinas desiertas. Yo mismo exploré muchas veces con las aguas hasta los tobillos aquel estanque de causas perdidas, y sólo una casualidad me permitió recatar al cabo de cinco años de búsqueda unos 322 pliegos salteados de los más de 500 que debió tener el sumario." *Crónica de una muerte anunciada* (Bogotá: Editorial La Oveja Negra, 1981), pp. 128-29. The interplay of this floating history in legal cases, the absent first author (a lawyer) and the "pliegos salteados" as a version of the origin of the fiction being narrated deserves a commentary for which I have no space here.

JOHN J. DEVENY, JR. AND JUAN MANUEL MARCOS

Women and Society in
One Hundred Years of Solitude

Gabriel García Márquez' 1967 novel, *One Hundred Years of Solitude*, has been considered by many critics as a mosaic of historical and mythical elements which profoundly reflects the social and cultural reality of Latin America and, in particular, of Colombia, the author's native land. This combination of poetic-folkloric resources and testimony of a sociological nature seems, of course, quite natural in a writer with an intense Caribbean imagination, who brings together in his work the professional training acquired during long years as a journalist and the sensitivity of a poet of great aesthetic perception. In this study, nevertheless, we propose to analyze an aspect which heretofore has been scarcely dealt with by specialists, from a point of view which is also different. We are not going to attempt a critical reading of *One Hundred Years of Solitude* as a *reflection* of Latin American society, but rather as an ideological interpretation of it. We believe that, in spite of García Márquez' well-known political position, this investigation will yield rather surprising results. In effect, the view which takes shape from such a reading is quite conservative and pessimistic and seems to be in accord with the last sentence of the novel, to the effect that the inhabitants of that Latin American metaphor, Macondo, have no hope of "a second opportunity on earth."[1]

This study consists mainly of a critical inventory of the treatment of

From *Journal of Popular Culture* 22 (Summer 1988). © 1988 by Popular Press.

37

female characters in the Colombian author's novel, with the purpose of establishing the ideological coordinates which move them.

The main female character of *One Hundred Years of Solitude* is Ursula Iguarán, the co-founder of Macondo, with her husband, José Arcadio Buendía. Moreover, she has in the novel a role equalled only by that of her son, Col. Aureliano Buendia. She is the only one whose presence cuts across seventeen of the twenty chapters of the book: she dies one Holy Week, between one hundred fifteen and one hundred twenty years of age (316). García Márquez has often stated his belief that women symbolize stability and judiciousness, while men tend to be more given to adventure and extravagance. The following quotation from García Márquez shows, in his own words, what he calls "the historical view which I have of the two sexes": "Women uphold the order of the species with an iron fist, while men go through life dedicated to all of the infinite folly which drives history."[2]

It cannot be denied that García Márquez' characters fall completely within these parameters. What seems surprising is to assign the role of keeping "order" to women, both Latin American and others, who historically have been the victim of all sorts of social discrimination and who have begun to see their rights reaffirmed only in our century; in the lineage of Romulo Gallegos' character, doña Bárbara, novelistic matrons such as Mamá Grande and the many such characters to be found in *One Hundred Years of Solitude* are not even close to representing the supposed despotism or matriarchal nature of the Latin American woman, whose society has suffered and continues to suffer dictatorships operated exclusively by men and whose only two female presidents, in Bolivia and Argentina, never managed to exercise properly, the power which was rightfully theirs.

Furthermore, a Manichean division such as the one established by García Márquez is sexist in and of itself, without regard for which role is attributed to one sex or the other. The real question is that of seeking both men and women who are interested in creating more just social conditions rather than merely following platonic stereotypes. Halfway between the bourgeois tradition of the Enlightenment and blind Bakuninian anarchism, García Márquez forgets the essentially dialectic nature of the concept of authority, brilliantly studied by Herbert Marcuse,[3] and thus his view of society becomes as dismal as Col. Buendía's old age, with its repeated failures.

What sort of values does Ursula symbolize? They are these: the middle class stinginess with which she mourns the loss of a mule, a few goats, and three pieces of colonial money (11-12); the stupidity by which she refuses to admit that the earth is round (14); the superstition through which she scorns Melquiades' scientific experiments, confusing them with black magic (16);

the xenophobia with which she rallies Macondo against the gypsies (17); the insanity with which she submerges herself in housework (18); the reactionary activism with which she opposes the search for a more adequate site for Macondo (22); the mercantile enthusiasm with which she introduces into Macondo the peddlers from the other side of the swamp (42-43); the prejudicial scorn with which she orders that Arcadio's true identity be hidden from him, the illegitimate son of the second José Arcadio Buendía and Pilar Ternera (44); the repressive brutality with which she lashes Rebeca for eating whitewash from the walls and for speaking an Indian language (49); the petit bourgeois instinct with which she broadens her industrial activities in the bakery, going—we are told in a rather admiring language—from the candy business to an oven "that went all night" (59); nevertheless, a short time later we find out who is really the one who works all night: "the Indian woman took care of the bakery" (77), "she turned the responsibility of the bakery over to the Indian women" (88). The slave seems not to have the right, let's not even say for the narrator to take pity on her social situation or to describe her in more objective terms, but rather even for him to tell us her name. In reality, the narrator's denial of the name is in accord with Ursula's attitude in scorning the *guajiros'* language: the Indians do not have the right to their own identity, which is expressed in a language, in a name.[4] Ursula's prejudice is clearly reinforced later by the fact that her daughter-in-law, Santa Sofía de la Piedad, the daughter of two shopkeepers who were so poor that they sold her virginity for fifty pesos (112), winds up in the most abject servitude of the house, while Fernando del Carpio, Ursula's granddaughter-in-law, although she is almost as poor as Sofía because her father has to mortgage the house in order to give her a dowry (195-196), but who believes herself to be a blue-blood, flaunts her arrogance in the Buendía's territory without every worrying about manual tasks.

The problem is not that Ursula's behavior is worthy of repudiation, since villains have always existed in literature and in reality, but rather that the narrator presents her as a pillar of virtue. Is it a virtue for Ursula to violate the private correspondence between Rebeca and Pietro Crespi? (70) Is it a virtue for her to undermine the idealistic effort of her own son Aureliano, who symbolizes the quixotic Latin American desire to create a more modern and more human society? In effect, Ursula ridicules the authority of Arcadio, Macondo's liberal commandant during the revolution. She revokes his orders and re-establishes Sunday mass (106);[5] she organizes a demonstration of women in defense of the conservative general José Raquel Moncada (153); and she boards in her own house the six lawyers who come to Macondo seeking to reclaim the property titles of the landowners affected by Colonel Buendía's revolution, as well as to ask the colonel to renounce his intent of granting equal rights to both illegitimate and legitimate children (161). It is true that, at the beginning, the narrator tells us that Ursula contributed from her savings to her son's military campaign (133-134), but soon we know that by means of exploiting Santa Sofía de la Piedad's work force in her confectionery shop, Ursula "not only recovered the fortune that her son had spent in the war, but she once more stuffed with pure gold the gourds buried in the bedroom" (143). What is Sofía's share in this fabulous wealth? To sleep always "on a mat she laid out on the pantry floor in the midst of the nocturnal noise of the rats" (33).

The ideological values that issue from the character of Ursula, presented as a paradigm of the loftiest feminine virtues, are flagrantly patriarchical. Ursula believes that arranging children's marriage is "men's affairs" (74); that the duty of every good wife consists essentially of cooking, sweeping and stoically putting up with suffering (221); and that a good mother should give the example of "a century of conformity" without even permitting herself to say a bad word (236).

There are numerous episodes and statements in the book, although not all of them have female protagonists, which reinforce the patriarchical values of the story. The assassination of Prudencio Aguilar by the first José Arcadio Buendía is conducted by a strictly *machista* code of honor, in the strictest tradition of Lope de Vega (29). The exaltation of the second José Arcadio's sex organ in Catarino's store suggests that women have no other "covetousness" than the promiscuous satisfaction of their sexual appetite, to the point of raffling it off for ten pesos (93). During the civil war, mothers send their daughters to the bedrooms of the best-known warriors "to improve the breed" (123). According to an anonymous soldier, the object of the liberal insurrection is none other than that of abolishing the incest taboo, thus to satisfy any pathological oedipal tendencies: "we're fighting this war against the priests," he tells Aureliano José, who feels attracted by his aunt Armaranta, "so that a person can marry his own mother"(145). Colonel Buendía's illegitimate children must carry the last name of the mother because—the narrator says in neutral language—the law does not permit them to use the father's last name unless they are recognized, something which Aureliano never does (146). The *machista* tendency reappears in the stereotype of the North American women from the plantation, who are described as "languid," an adjective of doubtful objectivity with respect to its reference, and which, in spite of the social difference in relation to the Macondo women, unites both groups in one passive view of women (214). The narrator, finally, insults homosexuals in passing. This group is represented first by Catarino and, on a more prominent plane, by the last José Arcadio and his assassins, the "four oldest children" who take pleasure in practicing their "equivocal pleasures" (343). These contradictions underscore the debility of the internal harmony of the novel, which permits the reader to be assured that *all* of the colonel's seventeen children "were exterminated one after the other on a single night" (104), only to find out later that in reality one of the seventeen, Aureliano Amado, had survived for many years (345).

The rest of the female characters follow three models: the patriarchal model of Ursula, the servile model of Visitación, and a new one, the rebellious model of the sisters Meme and Amaranta Ursula, who, as we shall see, pay dearly for their boldness.

The Patriarchical Model

The characters who come under the first model include, in the first place, Pilar Ternera, a sort of grotesque replica of Ursula, whom she manages to surpass in longevity, since when she becomes one hundred forty five years old, she stops keeping track of her age (363); she is, further, the only character who is included in nineteen chapters of the novel, since the first appears in the second chapter (32–35), and she dies in the last chapter (367).[6] Pilar, unlike her noble namesake in Hemingway's *For Whom the Bell Tolls*, lacks ideals. She begins as a servant in the Buendía household (32), where she seduces young José Arcadio by showing her admiration of the unusual size of his penis (33–34). This devotion to male physical characteristics pushes her to quarrel with another woman, who had commented that her son Arcadio had a woman's buttocks (67). Later, Pilar gets involved in the business of procuring. She promises the first Aureliano "to serve him on a tray" the impuberate Remedios Moscote (72). After producing Arcadio with José Arcadio, she produces Aureliano José with the former's brother, which she communicates to Aureliano in this way: "Where you put your eye, you put your bullet" (79). Finally, she manages a brothel in which she spends her hyperbolic old age, until she dies and is buried "among the psalms and cheap whore jewelry" (367).

Pilar is not the only madam who parades through the pages of *One Hundred Years of Solitude*. In the third chapter, the heartless grandmother of another of García Márquez's stories is mentioned in passing (56–58). Nor is Pilar the only novelesque character who permits García Márquez to make use of his Rabelaisian imagination: Camila Sagastume, a singing teacher who enters into a rivalry with the second Aureliano in a repugnant eating contest, is described as a "totemic female" (239), while Nigomanta, "a large black woman with solid bones, the hips of a mare, [and] teats like live melons," who seduces Aureliano Babilonian in her room, is described as a "wild dog" (354–

355). It is clear that García Márquez' hyperboles are far from praising the female condition of these characters. All the characters of this type seem to reinforce the notion of woman as the natural servant of male appetites.

Rebeca Ulloa (47), Amaranta Buendía, and Fernanda del Carpio also belong to this group, although in a peculiar way. The three have in common an invincible pride, not of being women but rather of occupying a pre-eminent position in Macondo's high society, following Ursula's example. Life, nevertheless, is less generous with them and they respond to this circumstance by withdrawing from the world into cynical mysanthropy. After spending their lives dedicated to tasks which are no more intellectual than embroidery (129), Rebeca shuts herself in her house until her death after the suicide of her husband, the second José Arcadio (131). From the time she closed herself in the bathroom to vent her feelings (72) until she dies a virgin (262), Amaranta symbolizes a world of reclusion and supposed self-sufficiency, with her back to worldly reality. Fernanda also shows pathologically self-repressive traits, like the calendar "with the small golden keys" on which her confessor had marked days of sexual abstinence (198). Fernanda's cynicism becomes evident in her tolerance of the extra-marital affair which her husband, Aureliano Segundo, establishes with Petra Cotes (199); as well as the spiteful avarice with which she laments the sheets that Remedios the Beauty has carried off to heaven (235). Driven by atavistic social prejudice, Fernanda throws Mauricio Babilonia, a modest mechanic's apprentice, out of the house because she will not let him see Meme nor mingle with "decent" people (265); actually, she considers herself the "godchild of the Duke of Alba" and "a noble dame of fine blood" who is entitled to sign "eleven peninsular names" (299).

In spite of so much pride, Fernanda ends up supported in reality by Petra Cotes (320), a widowed mulatto woman who sold raffle tickets and who years ago had shared her bed with the brothers José Arcadio Segundo and Aureliano Segundo (180), and later had become a parallel wife of the latter, instilling in him "a pleasure in spending and celebrating" (193). Petra is a character who combines elements of Ursula, because of her economic providentalism, and of Pilar, because of her protean eroticism.

The last group within this series is made up of Remedios the Beauty, Fernando's sister-in-law, and Mercedes the pharmacist, whom some critics have interpreted as a novelesque interpretation of García Márquez's real wife.[7] Neither is given to the wildness of Pilar and Petra; neither assumes the authoritarianism of Ursula or Fernanda. Each in her own way, however, reflects patriarchal values. Remedios continues the example of misanthropy which she inherited from her great aunt, Amaranta and although not as ugly as she, Remedios withdraws into herself and abstains from even the most basic means of communication, such as at least learning to read (188); curiously, the narrator presents her as a model of lucidity, paralyzed "in a magnificent adolescence" (217). Like her great aunt, she dies a virgin, but furthermore, reinforcing her supposed Marian image, she ascends into heaven in body and soul (222-223). Her symbolism, nevertheless, is far from reflecting sentiments which are Christian or from any other religious tradition based on solidarity with and love for one's neighbor, since she never stops exercising an immense disdain for the human beings that surround her. With regard to Mercedes, to whom of the four times she is mentioned, García Márquez twice dedicates the adjective "stealthy" (343), the same adjective he applies to the self-sacrificing Sofía (330), she is the last pharmacist remaining in Macondo, "Gabriel's stealthy girlfriend" (371).[8] In the last chapter's atmosphere of devastation, the young pharmacist is the sole owner of the medicines (*remedios*) of Macondo, from whose scene the other Remedios have disappeared: Remedios Moscote, Remedios (the Beauty) Buendía, and Renata Remedios (Meme) Buendía. She seems to symbolize the innocence of the first Remedios, the beauty of the second, and the romanticism of the third. Predicting the end of Macondo, Aureliano Babilonia goes to the pharmacy for the last time but finds it transformed into a carpenter shop (379): the tragedy of Macondo has no remedy. In García Márquez' rhetorical system, these coincidences are more than a mere play on words. They announce, from the author's vantage point, Melquíades' mythic omens. This same Melquíades is, in turn, the author of the parchments. Both prophecies converge to identify García Márquez and his deepest ideological laws with those of the text's narrator. Although the brief character of Mercedes is doubtless lovely and positive, because of the character's symbolism within the novel, it contributes to reinforcing the patriarchial sense of the real-life Gabriel's values by identifying him with the fictionalized narrator.

The Servile Model

The *guajira*, Visitación, is not the only person who fills the role of a household servant for the Buendía family. We have already seen that Santa Sofía de la Piedad, "the condescending one, the one who never contradicted anyone, not even her own children" (168), also fills the role for many long years. Ursula establishes with her the same Hegelian relationship as with Visitacíon. Only upon Ursula's death does Sofía make a bundle of clothing and leave the household forever (332). Argénida, Rebeca's maid (131), also maintains such a relationship of servitude with the lady of the house.

Besides these examples, and the implicit subservience of several of the characters studied in the previous section, there are two more who astound the reader with special intensity because they are little girls who are completely at the mercy of brutal circumstances: Remedios Moscote, nine years old (63), whom the future Col. Buendía courts with unusual lasciviousness and whose marriage is arranged by her parents before she even reaches puberty. Remedios dies later because she is pregnant with twins (89). The other is the Eréndira of another story, an adolescent mulatto girl whom her grandmother drags from town to town, bedding her for twenty cents apiece with an average of seventy men a night (56-58). This economic information, in addition, gives us a guideline for the number of clients that the other prostitutes of Catarino's store must have endured, about whom we know that they earned about eight pesos a night (93): to earn them, they would have to be with at least forty clients, although since the mulatto girl was younger, the others probably charged less and thus would have to be with more clients.

This state of abjection does not draw from the narrator the slightest compassion. And although it is not a question of seeking morals to the story, it is worth noting his fatalistic dauntlessness in the face of circumstances which doubtless arise from social structures of backwardness and injustice with very clear historical roots. Is this kind of "order" the one which García Márquez recommends to Latin American women?

The Rebel Model

Meme and Amaranta Ursula Buendía, daughters of Fernanda and Aureliano Segundo, are the noblest female characters in *One Hundred Years of Solitude*. They can be reproached for nothing in the stoicism with which Meme suffers "Fernanda's rigidity and Amaranta's bitterness" (230) and offers her pure love to the modest worker Mauricio Babilonia (270). Nothing, in the stoicism with which her sister suffers at her "small private school" (314), without doubt as conservative as the nuns' school where her parents had sent Meme to learn to play the clavichord and to avoid her being a witness to the *ménage à trois* which they maintained with Petra Cotes (242).

Amaranta Ursula seems, in effect, "a happy, modern woman without prejudicies" (319), as if in the last of the Buendias there flourished the positive attitudes that were absent in her elders. In spite of the fact that the parish priest puts her under the vigilance of some Franciscan nuns on her trip to Europe (325), the young girl breaks free from the repression in Brussels (Cortazar's native city[9]), and returns to Macondo married to a Fleming who supports her in disposition (347). She thus becomes the only Buendía woman who marries. Some time later she exchanges her husband for the young

Aureliano Babilonia, ignoring the fact that he is her nephew, the son of Meme and Mauricio. In describing their erotic encounters, García Márquez' prose relapses into terms which are degrading to the female condition, upon calling the girl's modesty "the astuteness of a wise woman" (365). He also relapses into his machista anatomical hyperboles in describing "Aureliano's portentous creature" (373).

Nevertheless, with these two characters García Márquez had a magnificent opportunity to become partially reconciled to a more objective and optimistic view of women. Both, nevertheless, receive a severe and unjust sanction. Meme's is of a social nature, since Fernanda, scandalized by her affair with Mauricio Babilonia, interns her in a convent, and Meme dies many years later in "a gloomy hospital in Cracow" (275). Meme, like the Indians in the novel, is condemned to losing her identity and is forced to change her name, which is just another form of anonymity. Regarding her younger sister, her sanction seems to be of a mythic type because she dies during the birth of the last Aureliano, a child with the tail of a pig, according to Melquíades' prophecies (378-379). The child also dies immediately (381), in the presence of the desperation of his father, Aureliano Babilonia. Many critics have interpreted this as the consummation of the mythic curse for the transgression against the incest taboo.

Even within the novel's symbolic system, nevertheless, Amaranta Ursula's death does not fail to constitute a social sanction because Fernanda's prejudices are the cause of the concealing of Aureliano's filiation. It can then be asserted that the only two heroines of the novel succumb to the implacable force of intolerance and degradation of human values.

One Hundred Years of Solitude has doubtlessly achieved the status of a classic of contemporary fiction. Its poetic plasticity, the symbolic energy of its imaginative universe, and its brilliant combination of fantastic and realistic elements earn it a very prominent place in this century's Latin American culture. It is not, nevertheless, an insuperable work nor should it be seen as the culmination of the continent's narrative potentiality. Other writers, before and after García Márquez, have contributed to enrich the Latin America narrative tradition with words where society (and within it, the female condition) follow more noble and hopeful paths than the ones that are described in the darkly fatalistic book by the great Colombian author.

NOTES

1. Gabriel García Márquez, *One Hundred Years of Solitude* (New York: Avon, 1971), trans. Gregory Rabassa, p. 383. Other references to this translation will be noted in parentheses in the text.

2. Gabriel García Márquez and Plinio Apuleyo Mendoza, *El olor de la guayaba* (The Smell of Guava) (Barcelona: Bruyera, 1982), p. 156. Three pages later, García Márquez involves himself in a strange contradiction by defining Latin American society as a "matriarchical society" of *machista* essence."

3. See Herbert Marcuse, *From Luther to Popper* (London: Verso, 1983; first edition, 1972), pp. 128-143.

4. There are, nevertheless, two Indians who appear with their names, Visitación and Cataure, two *guajiros* who, according to García Márquez, flee "a plague of insomnia that had been scourging their tribe" and who were "so docile and willing to help that Ursula took them on to help her with her household chores" (44). To speak of "insomnia" in the case of South American Indians, who have suffered for centuries extermination and eradication of their cultural traditions by a white and mestizo society, does not turn out less offensive than to claim they are virtual beasts of burden or natural servants. Cataure soon escapes the Buendía household but his sister remains because she is convinced that the plague of insomnia is a destiny from which one cannot save himself, until he loses "the awareness of his own being" and until "he sank into a kind of idiocy that had no past" (50). Besides the Indian women, the gypsy women also remain anonymous, the only one of whom is included is the one who seduces the second José Arcadio (39-40). This destiny is not necessarily thus, however, and the Indians and other Latin American "insomniacs" can in effect be saved, as has indicated José Carlos Mariategui, in a society where democratic forces manage to abolish reified conditions of existence.

5. This religions fundamentalism is reinforced by its manifest aversion to protestantism.

6. In fact, it can be said that Pilar is present in every chapter, since even in the first one she anonymously forms part "of the exodus that ended with the founding of Macondo" (35).

7. See the introductory study by Joaquín Marco, "García Márquez y sus *Cien años de soledad* ("García Márquez and his *One Hundred Years of Solitude*"), in Gabriel García Márquez, *Cien años de soledad* (Madrid: Espasa-Calpe, 1983), p. 13.

8. The word "sigilo" (stealthy), from the Latin *sigillum* (stamp, seal, mark, brand), means etymologically a means to record on paper and it also means a secret. Perhaps García Márquez' use of this word alludes to the abnegation (comparable to that of Sofia) with which his wife Mercedes accompanied him through difficult times to the extent of becoming a necessary resource for his work as a writer and also to the sense of privacy

with which he has clearly protected his long and stable married life (cf. the Mendoza text, p. 163). On page 373, nevertheless, García Márquez uses the adjective "silenciosa," (silent) which could refer to the silent messages of his letters, not to his indifference. Viewed etymologically and not in its usual sense of silence or concealment, the use of the adjective takes on without doubt the character of a tender and well-deserved tribute.

9. Characters from the works of Carpentier, Cortázar, and Fuentes are mentioned on pages 144, 374, and 278, respectively, likely as a tribute of friendship. The choice of Brussels as the place of Amaranta Ursula's freedom can also be interpreted in this sense.

ELIZABETH A. SPILLER

"Searching for the route of inventions": Retracing the Renaissance Discovery Narrative in Gabriel García Márquez

If, as Harold Bloom suggests, *One Hundred Years of Solitude* (1967) is a "supreme fiction," it achieves that status as it reformulates early modern narratives of self-discovery and dominion.[1] García Márquez signals his intention of rewriting the great Renaissance narratives of discovery when he begins his 1982 Nobel Prize acceptance speech with an account of Antonio Pigafetta's *Viaggio attorno al mondo* (1522). As a navigator aboard Magellan's 1519-21 voyage around the world, Pigafetta kept a log that García Márquez categorizes as an ancestor "of our contemporary novels."[2] Where many Latin American writers might describe their work as postcolonial, García Márquez here suggests that his writing is post-Columbian. In *One Hundred Years of Solitude*, García Márquez defines for his reader what it means to experience the world from the perspective of post-Columbian Europe as much as he does from post-Columbian America. Thus, the voyage of discovery into Latin America that is *One Hundred Years* cannot but begin with the Renaissance narratives that created a real story that is not yet finished. Over and over, García Márquez dramatizes how Latin America is known—created—through these ways of seeing that have been inherited from the European Renaissance. Where revisionist histories focus primarily on what stories have been told, García Márquez invokes these narratives of discovery to force us to rethink what kinds of stories can get told. Thus, this

From *Clio* v. 28 (Summer 1999). © 1999 by *Clio*.

"epic" of the New World, as it is sometimes called, can be told only through the forms which it has inherited. As we shall see, these forms have invented not only García Márquez but a culture, America, that, in the end, has become not what the Europeans imagined but what their imagining has wrought.

Critical responses to García Márquez's work have, in part, been determined by the demands that magical realism makes on its readers to accommodate both fantasy and reality within a single narrative structure. As Mario Vargas Llosa remarks, García Márquez's novel is plural in "being at one time things which we thought to be opposites: traditional and modern; regional and universal; imaginary and realistic."[3] This essay will expand on this observation by considering why García Márquez insists on this plurality, that is, why the book complicates the binary oppositions that Vargas Llosa correctly sees as hopelessly entangled. García Márquez's *One Hundred Years of Solitude* is not just the product—the culmination—of three centuries of post-Conquest history. Rather, taking the intermixture of cultures in the Conquest as a point of origin, *One Hundred Years of Solitude* responds to and critiques the European narratives of discovery that as much created the Conquest as they retell it. Writing on Renaissance discovery narratives, Humberto Robles has shown us how accounts such as Pigafetta's need to be re-interpreted in a Latin American context.[4] Not a conventional revisionist history attempting to correct facts, offer new perspectives, or give voice to previously unheard testimony, García Márquez's great work rewrites the narratives that were most important during the "Age of Discovery" as western Europeans defined themselves in relation to the rest of the world. *One Hundred Years of Solitude* is at once both mythic and historical because it emerges out of a Renaissance genre which used myth to create what then became history while it also transformed existing history into a form of myth.

García Márquez invokes Pigafetta in his Nobel speech to extend and redefine Alejo Carpentier's classic definition of "lo real maravilloso." Carpentier first introduced the term "marvelous real" to distinguish what he saw as the artificiality of European surrealism from the essential truth of his own writing about Latin America.

> I found myself in daily contact with something which might be called *marvelous reality*. I was treading on land where thousands of men anxious for freedom had believed in the lycanthropic powers of Macandal, to the point where this collective faith produced a miracle on the day of his execution.... I had breathed the atmosphere created by Henri Christophe, a monarch of incredible exploits, far more astonishing than all the cruel kings invented by the surrealists.... At every step I encountered this *marvelous reality*.[5]

For Carpentier, what separates the kinds of stories he wants to tell from those written by Europeans are differences in political experience. European writers were forced to rely on "conjuring tricks" to "invoke the marvelous." Latin America, by contrast, had experienced the unimaginable as a reality, which meant that Carpentier could tell unimaginable stories as a realist.

Carpentier's definition of the marvelous real has been integral to critical identifications of this genre as inherently postcolonial. Wendy Faris, while herself arguing for a broader category of the "marvelous real," delineates the way that, for Carpentier, this kind of writing was a specifically American and specifically postcolonial form:

> this magical supplement to realism may have flourished in Latin America not only because it suits the climate there, as Alejo Carpentier has argued ... but because in dismantling the imported code of realism "proper" it enabled a broader transculturation process to take place, a process within which postcolonial Latin America established its identity.[6]

The model formulated by Carpentier, though, relies on metaphors of growth to naturalize Latin American literature: as an indigenous product, Latin American literature: as an indigenous product, Latin American literature springs up from the land itself. Because the literature is produced by the land of Latin America, it is uniquely Latin American and inherently postcolonial: a break in every way with Europe. García Márquez, however, encourages us to take a longer historical perspective. Where Carpentier refers to Bernal Díaz's *Chronicle* as the one real book of chivalry in which "the evil doers are lords one could see and touch, where unknown animals are real, unknown cities are discovered," García Márquez redefines the basis for that opposition between real and imaginary by reminding us that what Europeans such as Bernal Díaz did was re-enact originally aesthetic experiences as political ones. As a result, the "reality" that is America is for García Márquez never separable from its inherently fictive moment of European origin.[7]

In Carpentier's account, the history of Latin American fiction is a reaction against a repressive aesthetics imposed during the Colonial period. As Irving Leonard has demonstrated, Latin American literary critics and historians through the nineteenth century argued that Spanish authorities prohibited the reading and circulation of imaginative literature. Carpentier's claims about the impact of authoritarian politics in Latin American thus accord with arguments about equally authoritarian aesthetic policing. As one prominent literary scholar argued, "No books except of a certain kind ever came to the colonies which were so jealously guarded; they wanted to make us a race of hermits and they made us a race of revolutionists."[8] Leonard's analysis of the colonial book trade in Latin America makes clear, though, that these accounts do not adequately represent the historical reality: despite being officially prohibited, romances of chivalry and other "marvelous histories" nonetheless remained widely available.[9] While Carpentier's arguments about the "marvelous real" as a reaction against an externally imposed "realism" reflect the literary history of the colonial and postcolonial period, García Márquez's work implicitly recognizes what Leonard's larger historical analysis confirms. That is, the Conquistadors who carried *Amadís de Gaula*, *Don Quixote*, and other fabulous tales in cargo holds filled with books just off the presses in Seville almost certainly imposed not the rigors of realism but rather the marvels of fictive romance onto the New World.

By suggesting that marvelous realism begins in the Renaissance with Antonio Pigafetta, García Márquez thus transforms what is for Carpentier a thirty-year literary history into a four-hundred-year one:

> [Pigafetta] kept a meticulous log on his journey through our Southern American continent, which, nevertheless, also seems to be an adventure into the imagination. He related that he had seen pigs with umbilicus on their backs and birds without feet, the females of the species of which would brood their eggs on the backs of the males, as well as others like gannets without tongues whose beaks looked like a spoon. He wrote that he had seen a monstrosity of an animal with the head and ears of a mule, the body of a camel, the hooves of a deer and the neigh of a horse.... [in this] short and fascinating book ... we can perceive the germs of our contemporary novels.

García Márquez insists that the marvelous real way of writing originated with Pigafetta and other early European "Chroniclers of the Indies."[10] The "marvelous real" that Carpentier experiences as a distinctly Latin American response to the world is for García Márquez more specifically a consequence of the first European responses to America. What is "imported" from Europe is thus not its comparatively recent realism but its sense of what constitutes the marvelous.

As Stephen Greenblatt points out, the marvel is a prominent component of the European discovery narrative: "the production of a sense of the marvelous in the New World is at the very center of virtually all of Columbus's writings about his discoveries."[11] Writers such as Columbus, Vespucci, and Pigafetta use the term "marvel" to describe phenomena which they cannot explain: the abundance of gold, the size of the trees, and the nakedness of the people all fill observers with wonder. Where ordinarily passions stand in opposition to reason, marveling is an epistemological passion that exists in the interval between ignorance and knowing. For Albertus Magnus, men wonder in "the desire to know the cause of that which appears portentous and unusual.... wonder is the movement of the man who does not know on his way to finding out."[12] While an integral part of the discovery narrative, the marvel is often at odds with its claims to knowledge. Thus, when Amerigo Vespucci finds that he cannot be the "author" of the southern pole star as he had hoped, he instead offers Lorenzo de' Medici a narrative of the "marvels" he has discovered.[13] Yet, at the same time, the marvel can also serve paradoxically to validate the truth of the rest of the narrative precisely because of its own unverifiability. As Theodore Cachey notes, the marvel of the birds with no feet that García Márquez mentions are, in fact, the most conventional part of the *Viaggio* and "serve as an authorizing frame for what's new and most true in Pigafetta's narrative."[14] Although the unknowable marvelous may seem to threaten the epistemological plot of the discovery narrative, it finally becomes an essential part of what makes narrative like Pigafetta's successful.

When Europeans like Columbus went to the New World, they were searching for Arcadia. Whether in Virgil, Sannazarro, Lope de Vega, or Sidney, arcadias exist as ideal and imaginary places from which characters in exile or retreat comment on the national and imperial politics of the central court. As a genre, the arcadia is probably the most prominent European literary form that at least seems to write from the periphery of the dispossessed "other" in response to the dominant center of the culture being critiqued. If narratives of discovery in some sense involve the self-idealizing "invention" of an "other," García Márquez constructs Macondo as a form of arcadia in order to demonstrate how the "other" imagined by arriving Europeans was from its origin a way of telling a story of the European "self."[15] Thus, Macondo initially exemplifies not so much a New World as it does the return to the lost Golden Age that Renaissance explorers thought they had found in America. A model of the Golden Age "commonwealth," Macondo is a place, as Shakespeare expresses it, with "no kind of traffic / ... no name of magistrate / ... but nature should bring forth,/Of it own kind, all foison, all abundance."[16] Macondo was "a village that was more orderly and hard-working than any known until then by its three hundred inhabitants. It was a truly happy village where no one was over thirty years of age and where no one had died."[17] The town exemplifies the "social initiative" promoted by José Arcadio: every house receives equal access to the water from the river and equal protection from the sun in the streets (9-10). When the outsider Don Apolinar Moscote testifies to his belief in the name of magistrate by hanging a sign that reads "Magistrate" on his door, José Arcadio explains that laws are not needed in Macondo: "In this town we do not give orders with pieces of paper … we don't need any judges here because there's nothing that needs judging" (57).

Founded through José Arcadio's self-imposed exile, Macondo takes shape as a geographical expression of his separation from the world. Like Thomas More's Utopia, Macondo is situated in a mysterious no-place, somewhere in South America, that defies rational explanation. Bounded by an "enchanted region," Macondo is an uncharted site that does not even appear on the maps of the dead (336, 80). As a utopia, Macondo is a place that is in some sense created rather than founded because it is a physical realization of the idea of isolation. In a project of incredible labor, the founders of Utopia dig their island out of what was originally a peninsula in order to distance themselves from the problems of the mainland.[18] José Arcadio, in the same way if less consciously, reshapes the land of Macondo in the image of his ideals. In his case, however, although José Arcadio becomes convinced that Macondo is a utopian isle, "surrounded by water on all sides" (13), he never reaches the sea that was his initial goal. He thus constructs Macondo as a peninsula, not through physical labor as the Utopians do, but through an act of imagination and self-representation: "The idea of a peninsular Macondo prevailed for a long time, inspired by the arbitrary map that José Arcadio Buendía sketched on his return from the expedition" (13).

García Márquez imagines Macondo as a kind of arcadia to comment on Latin America's relationship to European narratives of self-knowledge and empire. If the marvelous real is a product of America's difference from Europe, it is so in the sense that it contains that cultural difference within itself. García Márquez's arcadia emerges from Pigafetta's *Viaggio* in that it is both a "meticulous log" and "an adventure into the imagination": a world that already contains within it the divergent qualities that Carpentier used to distinguish European and American writing. I am not suggesting here that García Márquez be seen as a kind of colonial apologist who regards Latin American writing as a derivative, a hybrid of European writing. Rather, García Márquez, invokes these prior European literary forms to make an argument more politically radical than Carpentier's. For Carpentier, experience is responsible for the kind of art a culture produces; for García Márquez, art—how Europeans imagined America—becomes responsible for political reality. Pigafetta's images of birds without feet and pigs with umbilical cords on their backs lead to a world in which twenty million children die before their second birthday and the population of whole villages disappears. García Márquez demands that, if we ask if Latin American writing is the ultimate product of a European response to America, are those representations not also responsible for the unimaginable reality of contemporary Latin America?

Reinventing the early modern narrative of discovery as the point of origin for *One Hundred Years*, García Márquez portrays how these narratives of discovery continue to shape representations of America. Úrsula and José Arcadio decide to leave their native village to found Macondo because their families fear that they will breed a race of pig-tailed descendants (20). The race of pig-tailed humans, born with a "cartilaginous tail in the shape of a corkscrew and with a small tuft of hair on the tip" (20) that Úrsula and José Arcadio's family fear is a marvel first told of in Columbus's 1493 Letter to Luis de Santangel.[19] As one of the few "marvels" that Columbus never himself sees, the "pig-tailed" men become a future that García Márquez imagines as a consequence of those first encounters between Columbus and the Indians. Even earlier, the meeting of Úrsula and José Arcadio can be traced back, however indirectly and comically, to what might be called a misadventure of discovery: Úrsula's great-great-grandmother first moves to the Indian village in the mountains after she sits on a lighted stove in panic during Sir Francis Drake's attack on Rio Hacha (19). Just as Amerigo Vespucci's ship follows the singing of "countless birds of various sorts" as they search for land in the New World, Melquíades's gypsies subsequently find Macondo by following the singing of José Arcadio's parrots.[20]

Once "discovered," Macondo is bounded by the early voyages of discovery and conquest. José Arcadio thus attempts to reverse the trajectory of the narratives of discovery when he sets out on an exploration of the outside world in order to find out not what is out "there," but to discover the "here" where he is. After weeks of expedition whose ardors match the deadly travels reported by Pigafetta or Ralegh, all José Arcadio and his men find is "an enormous Spanish galleon":

> Tilted slightly to the starboard, it had hanging from its intact masts the dirty rags of its sails in the mist of its rigging, which was adorned with an armor of petrified barnacles and soft moss, was firmly fastened into a surface of stones. The whole structure seemed to occupy its own space, one of solitude and oblivion, protected from the vices of time and the habits of the birds. Inside, where the expeditionaries explored with careful intent, there was nothing but a thick forest of flowers. (12)

This Spanish galleon becomes the outer boundary of Macondo: at the edge of the "enchanted region," it is what finally causes José Arcadio to admit defeat and return to Macondo. José Arcadio cannot get beyond the galleon, which "lay across his path like an insurmountable object," because in some sense there is nothing before or beyond the originary voyages of discovery that it represents. In this moment, we must recognize how the original sea-going voyages of discovery have, like the galleon, literally become grounded in Macondo. The people of Macondo have become the new "expeditionaries," continuing those original sea-going voyages in the land of Macondo.

The "truth" of *One Hundred Years of Solitude* consists equally in magnets and magic carpets, butterflies and cameras. While critics are correct to attribute this combination of science and magic to García Márquez's "magical realism," I would extend that argument by suggesting that what García Márquez has done is transform the organizing epistemological structure of the discovery narrative.[21] As a genre, the discovery narrative tells a story of intellectual dominion: where Caesar's imperial epigram was "I came, I saw, I conquered," early modern discovery narratives write a new nationalist identity in the terms "I came, I knew, I conquered." Yet discovery narratives are also moments of epistemological challenge in that they achieve intellectual dominion through stories they tell of confrontation with the unknown. In this context, marvels are isolated interludes which appear within and contribute to a larger narrative of progress and truth. By virtue of its familiar inexplicability, the marvel functions to confirm the truths of the narrative as a whole. García Márquez, by contrast, asks us to imagine a world in which the balance between knowing and marveling has been reversed: the marvel is no longer a brief interlude but rather a three-hundred-year experience that overtakes the novel as a whole. In doing so, *One Hundred Years of Solitude* explores the tension between the teleological plot of knowing and the interludes of marvelous unknowing that characterize early discovery narratives.

The history of José Arcadio's interaction with the gypsy Melquíades illustrates the historical and narrative consequences of rewriting the epistemology that characterizes European narratives of discovery. Just as Pigafetta uses marvels to establish the "truth" of his narrative, García Márquez begins with the marvels of Melquíades as a way of establishing his novel's concern with "truth." The treasures that Melquíades first brings to Macondo—the magnet, the telescope, magnifying glass, maps and charts, astrolabes, and sextants—are icons of discovery. On the one hand, such objects are wonders to be shown to natives as evidence of the divinity of the Europeans. Thomas Hariot, for example, records that the natives responded to compasses, magnifying glasses, and other European inventions with wonder, "so strange … that they thought they were rather the workes of gods then of men."[22] At the same time, such instruments also represent the progress of knowledge that characterizes the age. One of the most popular and widely reproduced representations of the "progress of knowledge" in the Renaissance was thus Johannes Stradanus's *Nova Reperta*, a series of engravings featuring the age's new inventions—magnet, telescope, printing press.[23] Constantly reappearing in the discovery narrative, these inventions are figures of the production of wonder in the Indian and of knowledge for the European. Simultaneously illustrating both the marvel and the knowledge, these inventions typify the epistemological doubleness of the act of "discovery."

Conscious of this duality, García Márquez uses Melquíades's marvels to imagine a rediscovery narrative in which the discoverers and the discovered have become one and the same just as the Europeans and the Americans now coexist in the inhabitants of Macondo. When Melquíades and the gypsies first arrive in Macondo they bring magnets, invented by the "learned alchemists of Macedonia" (2). The magnet is the first invention that Melquíades brings to Macondo because, as an instrument of navigation in the compass, it was what enabled sailors like Columbus to discover places like Macondo. Yet, it is not the gypsies who are directed by the magnet for they have been led to Macondo by the singing of José Arcadio's parrots. Rather, it is José Arcadio Buendía himself who seeks to follow the science of the magnet. In proposing to use the magnet to discover gold—in what is the first of his expeditions of and from Macondo—he acts like the Conquistadors who followed their compasses across the Atlantic with the hope of finding gold. What José Arcadio finds, however, is not gold but the Conquistadors themselves: "The only thing he succeeded in doing was to unearth a suit of fifteenth-century armor which had all of its pieces soldered together with rust and inside of which there was the hollow resonance of an enormous stone-filled gourd.... [which contained] a calcified skeleton with a copper locket containing a woman's hair around its neck" (2). In this initial "discovery," José Arcadio finds not new land, people, or knowledge; instead, he finds the past as he himself reenacts it.

While the past that consists of the lived experience shared by the characters within the novel is highly complex, the historical past that predates that experience is reductively simple: it is the Conquest. In juxtaposing these two different expressions of the past, I do not mean to suggest that the "Conquest," as a historic phenomenon, occurred as a single event: obviously, Columbus departs on his voyage to the New World in 1492, Drake attacks Rio Hacha in 1565-66, while Sir Walter Ralegh published his account of his explorations in 1596. Yet, that historic complexity disappears in the novel as such events are largely reduced to material artifacts which seem to exist in a single, undifferentiated past. The land becomes a kind of repository of the colonial past: whenever characters dig up the land, they unearth the past as artifacts of that past. Thus, José Arcadio first uses the magnet to "unearth a suit of fifteenth-century armor ... soldered together with rust"; his subsequent "expedition" finds the half-buried Spanish galleon, "covered with an armor of petrified barnacles and soft moss" (12); the coins that Úrsula digs up from under the house to give to her husband for his alchemy experiments are "colonial" doubloons, a legacy from her father's family (8, 3). Even when José Arcadio's son seems to escape from Macondo and its history, he does not really get beyond this history but instead only discovers alternative versions of it. Thus, for example, José Arcadio returns from his voyages and tells of killing a sea dragon, "in the stomach of which they found the helmet, the buckles, and the weapons of a Crusader" (94). The Crusader does not so much represent a different history—or a different future for José Arcadio—but rather a transposed version of the same history of discovery and conquest that is encrusted in the Spanish galleon and Úrsula's gold coins. It is not the land, but the acts of discovery and conquest, which produce the marvelousness of Latin America.

In this context, it is appropriate that the inhabitants of Macondo receive news of the outside world through the medium of the past. Francisco the Man sings his news using his "old out-of-tune voice" and plays on "the same archaic accordion that Sir Walter Ralegh had given him in the Guianas" (52). Macondo learns what is new in this way because whatever future they have comes from and is determined by that point of origin represented by Ralegh's songs and stories. In some sense, before Macondo, there is only a myth of discovery.

As the narrative progresses, however, the arcadian nature of Macondo alters as a result of the town's changing relationship with the outside world. The event that precipitates this fundamental change in Macondo is the death of Melquíades. Before Melquíades's death, Macondo is a naive utopia—the utopia that we approach nostalgically as a lost, idealized place; afterwards, it remains utopian as an expression of the death and destruction that is always present in Arcady. As a death that has already occurred once and that Melquíades will overcome through an act of resurrection that allows him to continue visiting Macondo as he has always done, this event is less about the mortality of Melquíades than it is about the mortality of Macondo. In making Melquíades's death the event that transforms Macondo, García Márquez critiques the dangerous nostalgia of Renaissance representations of the New World as a utopian paradise. At the same time, he also suggests that modern recollections of the Conquest participate in an equally nostalgic and thus equally inadequate relationship to the past. By placing death at the center of Macondo's transformation, García Márquez allows us to realize, in the Virgilian phrase, "Et in Arcadia Ego" (Even in Arcadia, there I am [Death]). When Renaissance writers such as Columbus transported Arcady from northern Greece to South America, they did so in a gesture of nostalgia: Columbus, for example, thought he had rediscovered a "lost Paradise" and perhaps even Eden itself. Yet, as Erwin Panofsky suggests, the sort of Renaissance arcadia that Macondo looks back to is not just a "retrospective vision of an unsurpassable happiness.... a happiness ended by death"; it cannot simply be a nostalgic "meditation" on "the idea of mortality." Rather, death is always present within Arcady in a way that transforms nostalgia for the past into an ominous morality lesson which "warn[s] of an implacable future."[24]

A figure of the arcadian quality of Macondo, Melquíades himself warns against nostalgia and prophesies an equally "implacable future" for Macondo. As readers, our initial response to Macondo mirrors Columbus's first response to the New World—it is an ideal, if inaccessible, place to which we stand in a relation of nostalgia and desire. While the first section of the book, dealing with the generation that founded Macondo, reads quickly, the remainder of the book becomes entropic: repetition replaces progress and personal nostalgia competes with collective forgetfulness. We read and reread different versions of the same events: when the gypsies ultimately return to Macondo with the magnet, people are just as surprised as ever (351). History is not just cyclical but regressive. The death of Melquíades thus asks us to recognize the limitations and self-indulgence of our attraction to and for this type of naive arcadia. García Márquez offers us an allegory of the self-delusion involved in some of the histories we tell ourselves: we are living out an arcadian narrative without recognizing that living in Arcady means death.

After Melquíades's death, his study becomes the new arcadian space in Macondo. The study is both the representation of the histories we tell and the place where we see what happens to history. In some respects, Melquíades's study exists outside of time and death: books that were from the beginning "almost destroyed by dust and moths" and manuscripts made of a material that "crumpled like puff paste" nonetheless remain intact a century later (73), the room never needs cleaning (188), and it is "always March there and always Monday" (355). Yet, at the same time, the study is also the site of the decay and death that destroy Macondo. Many of the characters who enter Melquíades's study can see it only as a place of death, full of "rubble, trash, piles of waste": the army officer searching for José Arcadio Segundo after the massacre simply does not see José Arcadio sitting on the bed because he cannot see any life in the room. At the end, the nostalgia for a timeless arcadian past finally coincides with the death it seeks to avoid. For Aureliano Babilonia, nostalgia becomes a form of death at the moment when understanding his past entails recognizing that he will die and "never leave that room" (422).

Where the swamps around Macondo were for José Arcadio once an "enchanted region," the gypsy's study now becomes a magical center of the Buendía world. Carefully built "far from the noise and bustle of the house," this study becomes an architectural realization of the same combination of isolation and knowledge that originally defined the arcadian character of Macondo (73). By that I mean that the male descendants of José Arcadio— Aureliano Segundo, José Arcadio Segundo, and Aureliano—retreat from the outside world into the study where they undertake utopian quests for knowledge. José Arcadio had, in his way, followed the paths of Columbus and Vespucci when he set out on "expeditions" in "searching for the route of inventions" (335). The last of his descendants, Aureliano, has never gone anywhere but has nonetheless acquired a more than encyclopedia knowledge of the world in the space of Melquíades's study (379, 388). The originary act of discovery in which knowledge was "found" by a search of and through the world has turned inward, has retreated, in textual exploration. Discovery is no longer a voyage in the land but in books. By supplanting physical acts of discovery with textual ones, however, Melquíades's study makes it possible to understand what happens to the discovery narrative as it is subsequently transformed into a model for writing history. That is, José Arcadio's descendants try to read Melquíades's manuscripts by adhering to different understandings of what history is and where it comes from. Where José Arcadio writes and lives a version of the originary discovery narrative, his descendants are essentially post-Columbian historians: their historiography is a post-Columbian adaptation and transformation of the discovery narrative.

José Arcadio's affiliation with Columbian understandings of historical knowledge can be seen in the way he educates his children. Having been chastised by Úrsula for letting the children run wild, José Arcadio transforms his laboratory into a schoolroom. Like José Arcadio's search for alchemical knowledge, these educational enterprises are pursued with the pre-lapsarian innocence that pervades Macondo before Melquíades's death:

> In the small separate room, where the walls were gradually being covered by strange maps and fabulous drawings, he taught them to read and write and do sums, and he spoke to them about the wonders of the world [*maravillas del mundo*] … the boys ended up learning that in the southern extremes of Africa there were men so intelligent and peaceful that their only pastime was to sit and

> think, and that it was possible to cross the Aegean Sea on foot
> from island to island all the way to the port of Salonika. (16)

Covering the walls with "strange maps and fabulous drawings," José Arcadio transforms the room into a graphic rendering of the marvel-filled Renaissance discovery narrative. If José Arcadio's drawings look back to the engravings of Theodore de Bry and Johannes Strandanus, his fabulous histories recreate Prester John and Mandeville. For Columbus, the marvelous literature of such writers provided an imaginative, if not necessarily a navigational, guide to the New World. What begins as the marvelous thus becomes a form of truth insofar as it takes a man beyond "where his learning had extended, but forc[ed] the limits of his imagination to extremes" (16).

Once Macondo no longer exists in the arcadian world of the initial discovery, however, this kind of history becomes impossible. When Aureliano Segundo first explores Melquíades's study, he reads stories of fish with diamonds in their stomachs, magic lamps, and flying carpets (189). This *Arabian Nights* compendium becomes, for Aureliano, the true history of Macondo. Just as Melquíades's manuscripts write the future of Macondo, his books narrate its past. The way that life in Macondo is created in and through texts is thus appropriately suggested in the format of Melquíades's books: as artifacts of the cultural cannibalism implicit in the history that they tell, they are bound in a material as pale as "tanned human skin" (188). García Márquez here represents the long-term consequences of that textualization of life and history. That is, the correspondence between the magic carpets brought by the gypsies and the magic carpets of Melquíades's storybooks should not simply suggest to us that Macondo is a fictional construct that exists only as a result of the imposition of another culture's fears and fantasies. Writing from a European perspective, Tzvetan Todorov thus argues that "the Conquest of America heralds and establishes our present identity.... we are all direct descendants of Columbus, it is with him that our genealogy begins." While it is true that the Conquest was for the Europeans largely a discovery that "the self makes of the other," García Márquez suggests that we also need to recognize how Aureliano Segundo participates in that act of cultural imposition.[25] What Aureliano has done here is to take a myth, a literary fiction, and use it to create a historical narrative. Aureliano Segundo differs from both Columbus and his great-grandfather, however, in that he does this to himself: he allows someone else's fable to become his history. The discovery narrative may be an act of cultural exogamy; Aureliano Segundo's history is an act of cultural cannibalism.

José Arcadio inverts the Columbian discovery narrative by making physical retreat—to Macondo and then to his laboratory—a means of intellectual exploration. For José Arcadio Segundo, by contrast, physical isolation leads not to eccentric escapism but rather to a truly dangerous intellectual retreat into madness and self-imposed ignorance. José Arcadio Segundo initially hides himself in Melquíades's study to escape from the military police after the banana strike massacre (316-19). As time goes on, however, he remains in the study in order to flee from his own knowledge of the massacre. José Arcadio Segundo's problem is not simply that he saw the massacre, but that no one will believe what he saw. Ironically echoing the utopian description that José Arcadio gives when the first government representatives arrive in Macondo, government military forces now respond to questions about the massacre victims by insisting "You must have been dreaming ... Nothing has happened in Macondo, nothing has ever happened, and nothing will ever happen. This is a happy town" (57-58, 316). For José Arcadio Segundo, the denial of a truth he experienced only too fully forces him to retreat into madness. Having found that a history which is only too real has been made into a myth, José Arcadio Segundo seeks refuge in Melquíades's manuscripts precisely because he cannot understand them: "José Arcadio Segundo dedicated himself then to peruse the manuscripts of Melquíades many times, and with so much more pleasure when he could not understand them" (318). Because the massacre that he understood is no longer true, the manuscripts that he does not comprehend provide an alternative "truth" for his madness. With Aureliano Segundo, Melquíades's texts innocently allow historical fact to be replaced with myth. Yet, while it may not seem to matter whether or not there were magic carpets, that precedent leads to a more dangerous situation in which the inhabitants of Macondo become complicit in the revisionist history practiced by their own totalitarian government. In some sense, having once believed in the arcadian myth that nothing ever happens in Macondo, the inhabitants must now accept that same argument when it is used as a repressive history. As the culmination to this sequence, Melquíades's prophetic manuscripts represent not just, as critics have demonstrated, an alternative novel to the one we are reading, but also an alternative history to the one we are experiencing, to the one we have been telling.[26]

García Márquez dramatizes how intimately connected the New World's birth is with the Old World's imagining of it through interbreeding that takes place between the Europeans and the Native Americans. If European representations of the "discovery" are structured on an initial perception of "otherness" that becomes an image of the "self," García Márquez recognizes that this narrative contains within it a genealogy of Latin America in which fear of radical exogamy alternates with and gives way to fear of incest. The family narrative that García Márquez tells, not just of

José Arcadio and Úrsula, but of all Latin America, thus takes Columbus's account of a race of pig-tailed men as its moment of origin. Columbus first mentions the pig-tailed men in his 1493 Letter to Luis de Santangel when he discusses some of the further provinces he has not yet reached, including one "they call 'Avan,' and there the people are born with tails."[27] In this first letter, the pig-tailed man appears as a figure of radical and monstrous otherness. Despite what Greenblatt has identified as the pervasive rhetoric of the marvelous in this letter, the pig-tailed men are the only truly supernatural phenomenon mentioned by Columbus.[28] Indeed, Columbus admits that he is surprised at the absence of human marvels: "In these islands I have so far found no human monstrosities, as many expected, but on the contrary the whole population is very well-formed" (1.14). As a point of departure for Columbus's definition of the New World "marvel," this monstrosity thus appears as a paradoxically familiar image of otherness.

The pig-tailed men are again mentioned in Columbus's second voyage. In his account of this voyage, Andres Bernaldez recounts how Columbus received reports of people inhabiting the region of Magón: "all the people had tails, like beasts or small animals, and that for this reason they would find them clothed." Bernaldez doubts the veracity of this story and concludes that "This was not so, but it seems that among them it is believed from hearsay and the foolish among them think that it is so in their simplicity ... it seems that it was first told as a jest, in mockery of those who went clothed" (1.138). This second, more elaborate, version of the tailed men has an obviously different conclusion. Whatever this story may say about native attitudes toward clothing, Bernaldez's interpretation reveals much about changes in the Europeans' attitudes toward the peoples they have met. Where the humans with tails are in some sense expected, what comes as more of a surprise ultimately are the tribes that wear clothing. Clothing becomes a cultural mark of the apparently natural differences that seem to separate the Europeans from the natives. In its subsequent reinterpretation, then, this story is no longer about otherness; rather, it suggests the more threatening possibility of a tribe which, in wearing clothing, may violate what the Europeans had come to see as a fundamental difference that separated them from these peoples. That is, the people of Magón represent the possibility of a kind of "mixed breed." They are not the familiar myth of otherness, but a tale of something too close to the Europeans themselves.

In Columbus, a monster of racial otherness (unnatural tails) becomes a monster of self-reflection (unnatural clothing); here, interbreeding produces inbreeding. As Claude Levi-Strauss argues in his classic analysis of the Oedipus story, myths work through conflicting and unresolvable cultural beliefs. For Levi-Strauss, the Oedipus myth is characterized by both an overrating of family relationships (incest) and an underrating of them (patricide, fratricide, genocide) because it attempts to reconcile the theological belief in the autochthonous origin of man with the conflicting experiential knowledge "that human beings are actually born from the union of man and woman."[29] Columbus's myth of a race of pig-tailed men becomes, in García Márquez, a similar story of origin for Latin America. García Márquez's *One Hundred Years* thus tells a myth about the birth, not of man as a biological being, but of Latin America as a culture. In this cultural birth narrative, we see Carpentier's belief that Latin America is born, Spartoi-like, out of the land competing with a recognition that it is instead created out of the union of two peoples and their cultures.

As Roberto González Echevarría has demonstrated, the work of Levi-Strauss has been a key influence on contemporary Latin American novelists. Adopting the language of anthropology that has been a "mediating element" between European science and Latin American experience, writers tell the story of Latin America in "the language of myth because it is always conceived of as the history of the other."[30] García Márquez follows this tradition, but also demands that we recognize how, in Latin America objectivity, the separation of the observing (European) "self" from the observed (native) "other" that anthropology aspires to is perhaps even more unattainable than is ordinarily the case. For García Márquez, the history of Latin America begins through a confounding of the categories of self and other.

If the people of Columbus's Magón are thus the symbolic ancestors of the inhabitants of García Márquez's Macondo, they are so in the sense that García Márquez uses the pig-tailed men to show his readers this link between the threat of otherness and the threat of the self.[31] Identifying incest as the "motivating theme" of the novel, Edwin Williamson argues that incest becomes a "symbolic equivalent" to the way that the Buendías read and understand history.[32] Just as Aureliano Babilonia succumbs to incest, he also gives in to a solipsistic and self-annihilating reading of history. Williamson suggests that the reader is able to move outside the self-enclosed fantasy of Macondo and is thus ultimately capable of an objective, distanced view of the history that is *One Hundred Years*. While our position as readers is partly modelled by the character named Gabriel García Márquez, I would suggest that because the kind of incestuous history that Williamson identifies is at the same time a consequence of racial and cultural exogamy, García Márquez gives us a perspective from which there is no truly objective stance. While the character Gabriel does manage to leave Macondo for Paris, as the history of Latin America attests, there has been no leaving this story, perhaps because the only forms in which the story can be told are ones that are themselves the products of cultural intermixture.

While critics have noted that this marriage violates incest taboos, what needs to be recognized is that it also breaks taboos against intermarriage. The marriage of José Arcadio to Úrsula Iguarán is initially described as the culmination of a partnership that unites these two families and the "two healthy races" they represent: "the great-great grandson of the native-born planter married the great-great-grand-daughter of the Aragonese" (20). Yet, at the same time, in a way that the narrative does not detail, the two families have already been united in the intervening three generations: while from different ethnic backgrounds, Úrsula and José Arcadio are nonetheless also "cousins." Incest is presented as the ultimate consequence not so much of inbreeding within the family as it is of interbreeding between races: The people "were afraid that those two healthy products of two races [salubales cabos de dos razas] that had interbred [entrecruzadas] over the centuries would suffer the shame of breeding iguanas" (20). In stressing that Úrsula and José Arcadio are, at once, of different racial descent and yet also cousins, García Márquez suggests that interbreeding between races leads to and culminates in inbreeding within a family; incest appears as a threat, a desire, and an ultimately unavoidable fate.

In the Buendía family and the cultural history it represents, the threat of incest appears as a consequence of overrating of family relations: incest seems to occur through failure either to recognize or make distinctions that need to be made to preserve the family. At the same time, the history of the Buendías is also characterized by an underrating of family relations in acts, real and imagined, of genocide, fratricide, infanticide, and suicide. In this lineage, Aureliano Babilonia becomes the conclusion to the inability to recognize family and community: in his case, failure to recognize how he is related to the rest of the world becomes figured as a form of "cannibalism." When Aureliano Segundo discovers the existence of his grandson Aureliano Babilonia, he sees in the last generation of his family what Columbus saw when he first arrived in Caribe islands: his grandson stands "naked, with matted hair, and with an impressive sex organ that was like a turkey's wattles, as if he were not a human child but the encyclopedia definition of a cannibal" (299). Amaranta Úrsula likewise recognizes Aureliano as a cannibal when she greets him, "Hello, cannibal" (397). Later, after she falls in love with Aureliano, she jokes that they have "end[ed] up living like cannibals" and predicts that their son will be "a real cannibal" (416-17). Although incest and cannibalism may both end in forms of self-annihilation, *One Hundred Years* demands that we recognize how they conflict with one another. Cannibalism is a cultural taboo—at least from the perspective of the Europeans—because it involves not a failure to make a distinction between self and other as incest does (shared family), but rather a failure to see a fundamental identity between self and other (shared humanness).[33] In this combination we see the culmination of the history of self and other that has created Latin America when incest and exogamy come together, however apocalyptically, in Aureliano Babilonia.

Considered from this perspective, it becomes clear why the pig-tailed progeny frame the narrative of Macondo, why the threat that initiates the founding of Macondo becomes its symbolic end when the "cousins" Amaranta Úrsula and Aureliano give birth to a pig-tailed child (417, 420). In the six intervening generations, the thematic tensions between incest and exogamy—the simultaneous threats of breeding too closely together and breeding too far apart—reappear in narrative form in a corresponding tension between a forward-moving epic teleology and a regressive romance cycle of repetition. The occurrence of incest, between Aureliano and Amaranta Úrsula, involves then an act of repetition by which the narrative closes down on itself and time essentially stops. Just as Pigafetta's *Viaggio* used familiar marvels in some sense to discover an unknown self, so does García Márquez end this family narrative at the point where the self and other, cultural discovery and incestuous cannibalism, finally converge. García Márquez's *One Hundred Years of Solitude* enacts both the Conquest and our endless repetitions of it, histories we cannot help retelling as if we had found at last the birth that initiates not our own history but the new one that invents the we who never arrive.

NOTES

1. Harold Bloom, Introduction to Harold Bloom, ed., *Modern Critical Views: Gabriel García Márquez* (New York: Chelsea House, 1989), 2. On writing as an act of conquest, see Tzvetan Todorov, *The Conquest of America: The Question of the Other*, trans. Richard Howard (1982; New York: Harper and Row, 1984), 54, 77-81, and Irving Albert Leonard, *Books of the Brave, being an account of books and men in the Spanish conquest and settlement of the sixteenth-century New World* (1949; New York: Gordian P, 1964).

2. Gabriel García Márquez, "The Solitude of Latin America, Nobel Address 1982," in Bernard McGuirk and Richard Cardwell, eds., *Gabriel García Márquez: New Readings* (Cambridge: Cambridge UP, 1987), 207. For earlier comments that anticipate the Nobel Prize address, see Gabriel García Márquez, "Fantasía y creación artística en América Latina y el Caribe," *Texto Crítico* 5 (1979): 4.

3. Mario Vargas Llosa, "García Márquez: From Aracataca to Macondo," in Bloom, ed., *Modern Critical Views*, 5.

4. Humberto E. Robles, "The First Voyage Around the World: From Pigafetta to García Márquez," *History of European Ideas* 6.4 (1985): 388.

5. Alejo Carpentier, "Prologue," *The Kingdom of this World* (1949); cited in Franco Moretti, *Modern Epic: The World System from Goethe to García Márquez*, trans. Quintin Hoare (London: Verso, 1996), 234. For the full text of the expanded version of this essay which was published in the same year as *Cien años*, see Lois Parkinson Zamora and Wendy B. Faris, eds., *Magical Realism: Theory, History, Community* (Durham: Duke UP, 1995), 75-88.

6. Wendy B. Faris, "Scheherazade's Children: Magical Realism and Postmodern Fiction," in Zamora and Faris, eds., *Magical Realism*, 165.

7. Carpentier, "Marvelous Real in America," in Zamora and Faris, eds., *Magical Realism*, 83. In the 1967 version of his essay, from which this passage is taken, Carpentier does discuss the Conquest but nonetheless continues to emphasize what are, for him, the fundamental differences between European and Latin American experiences. In doing so, Carpentier repeats arguments that he used in distinguishing European surrealists from the new Latin American "realists," so that what is merely aesthetic for Europeans is real with him. This argument thus supports Carpentier's larger claim that a Latin American culture and aesthetic predates Europe's: with a "legacy of thirty centuries ... *our style* is reaffirmed throughout *our history*" ("Marvelous Real in America," 83).

8. José María Vergara y Vergara, *Historia de la literatura en Nueva Granada*; cited in Leonard, *Books of the Brave*, 79.

9. Leonard, *Books of the Brave*, 75-90.

10. García Márquez, "The Solitude of Latin America," in Bernard McGuirk and Richard Cardwell, eds., *Gabriel García Márquez: New Readings* (Cambridge: Cambridge UP, 1987), 207. García Márquez elsewhere identifies Christopher Columbus's *Diary* as "the first masterwork of the literature of magical realism" and, as Michael Palencia-Roth demonstrates, García Márquez's knowledge of Columbus is "extensive and largely accurate" ("The New Worlds' of Columbus and García Márquez" in Bloom, ed., *Modern Critical Views*, 251).

11. Stephen Greenblatt, *Marvelous Possessions: The Wonder of the New World* (Chicago: U of Chicago P, 1991), 73; see also, 52-53, 72-85.

12. Albertus Magnus, *Opera Omnia* (1890), 6:30; cited in J. V. Cunningham, *Woe or Wonder: the Emotional Effect of Shakespearian Tragedy* (Denver: U of Denver P, 1951), 79-80. See further Peter Platt, "'Not Before Either Known Dreamt of': Francesco Patrizi and the Power of Wonder in Renaissance Poetics," *RES*, New Series, 43:171 (1992): 387-94.

13. Amerigo Vespucci, *Letters from a New World*, ed. Luciano Formisano, trans. David Jacobson (New York: Marsilio, 1992), 3-8.

14. Theodore J. Cachey, Jr., ed. and trans., *The First Voyage Around the World, 1512-1522* (New York: Marsilio, 1995), xxviii.

15. Although critics have commented on the idyllic and paradisal qualities of José Arcadio's Macondo, what has not been recognized is how García Márquez uses the conventions of early modern utopia so that his readers reenact the same moment of aesthetic nostalgia experienced by explorers such as Columbus. See, for example, Stephen Minta, *Gabriel García Márquez: Writer of Columbia* (London: Jonathan Cape, 1987), 149-50.

16. William Shakespeare, *The Tempest*, in G. Blakemore Evans, ed., *The Riverside Shakespeare* (Boston: Houghton Mifflin, 1974), 2.1.149-65.

17. Gabriel García Márquez, *One Hundred Years of Solitude*, trans. Gregory Rabassa (1967; New York: Harper, 1970), 9. All further references are given parenthetically in the text.

18. Thomas More, *Utopia*, ed. Edward Surtz, S.J. (New Haven: Yale UP, 1964), 60.

19. Cecil Jane, trans. and ed., *The Four Voyages of Columbus*, 2 vols. (1930, 1933; New York: Dover, 1988), 1.12, 138.

20. Vespucci, *Letters from a New World*, 37.

21. On the role of science and pseudo-science in Macondo, see Brian Conniff, "The Dark Side of Magical Realism: Science, Oppression, and Apocalypse in *One Hundred Years of Solitude*," *Modern Fiction Studies* 36.2 (1990): 167-79, and Floyd Merrell, "José Arcadio Buendía's Scientific Paradigms: Man in Search of Himself," *Latin American Literary Review* 2.4 (1974): 59-70.

22. Thomas Hariot, *A Briefe and True Report of the New Found Land of Virginia* (London, 1588), cited in William M. Hamlin, "Attributions of Divinity in Renaissance Ethnography and Romance; or, Making Religion of Wonder," *Journal of Medieval and Renaissance Studies* 24.3 (1994): 429.

23. For a modern edition, see Jan van der Straet, *New Discoveries*, ed. Martha Teach Gnudi et al. (Norwalk, Conn.: The Burndy Library, 1953), np.

24. Erwin Panofsky, *Meaning in the Visual Arts* (1955; Chicago: U of Chicago P, 1982), 296, 313.

25. Todorov, *Conquest of America*, 5, 3.

26. Scott Simpkins, "Magical Strategies: The Supplement of Realism," *Twentieth Century Literature* 34.2 (1988): 152.

27. Columbus, *Four Voyages*, 1.12.

28. Greenblatt, *Marvelous Possessions*, 72-85.

29. Claude Levi-Strauss, *Structural Anthropology*, trans. Claire Jacobson and Brooke Grundfest Schoepf (New York: Basic Books, 1963), 216.

30. Roberto González Echevarría, *Myth and Archive: A Theory of Latin American Fiction* (1990; Durham, NC: Duke UP, 1998), 13, 21.

31. Magón is "in reality" the name of a banana plantation near García Márquez's birthplace in Aracataca; see Minta, *Gabriel García Márquez*, 144-45.

32. Edwin Williamson, "Magical Realism and Incest: *One Hundred Years*," in McGuirk and Cardwell, eds., *Gabriel García Márquez*, 47.

33. For compelling accounts of how Renaissance Europe's understanding—or misunderstanding—of cannibalism arose out of both the fear and the rejection of identity with native Americans, see Peter Hulme, *Colonial Encounters: Europe and the Native Caribbean, 1492-1797* (New York: Routledge, 1992), 14-17, 33-41, and Stephen Greenblatt, "Eating of the Soul," *Representations* 48 (1994): 97-116.

PAUL M. HEDEEN

Gabriel García Márquez's Dialectic of Solitude

In her essay "Labyrinthine Solitude: The Impact of García Márquez" (*Southwest Review*, Summer 1973), Linda B. Hall states that *One Hundred Years of Solitude* is "a deep exploration of the aspects of solitude." She writes that the characters have "a profound sense of their solitude and vacillate between an attempt at communion and a return to total absorption in themselves." She correctly links García Márquez's philosophical base for solitude to those writings of Octavio Paz which define solitude as that state of being, that "nostalgic longing for the body from which we were cast out, ... a longing for place."[1] For Paz and García Márquez this solitude is a state of fundamental psychological disharmony; all effort then becomes a reaction to this state, a quest to establish or reestablish a sense of harmony. This effort is labyrinthine by nature, but at the center of the labyrinth is the hoped-for place of harmony, a place of reunification. Hall writes that in the novel this labyrinth is symbolized by the set of parchments left behind by the gypsy Melquiades, the parchments that off and on passionately interest various male members of the Buendia family. She maintains, however, that the center of the parchments—that hoped-for reunification—becomes the mythological beast, the child with the tail of a pig, and because the parchments are a history of the family, this deformed child "symbolizes the complete destruction of the family, rather than the hoped-for release from

From *Southwest Review* 68 (Autumn 1983). © 1983 by Paul Hedeen.

solitude." For Hall, the various Buendias are "the mutations and interactions of only a few personalities" that "show us dozens of variations of solitude" and "reveal to us what Borges and Paz had suggested: that man is always alone." But García Márquez's novel has meaning beyond that seemingly conclusive statement.

One Hundred Years of Solitude portrays many characters whose isolation ranges from the sheer loneliness and physical longings of actually being alone in time and place, to the solitude of being alone in power, to the paradoxical solitude of a personal and intimate love. While García Márquez's philosophy of solitude is heavily indebted to Paz, perhaps even more heavily than Hall cites in her essay, and while García Márquez does see solitude as a fundamental psychological state, he does not intend it as a conclusive, unredeeming, and irreconcilable condition. The novel's ultimate message is not that man is always alone. Paz states that "this primitive sense of loss becomes a feeling of solitude, and still later it becomes awareness." This awareness is reaction, not simple acceptance, a reaction to solitude which García Márquez applies to culture, society, and politics in a revolutionary way. As a culture consists of individuals connected with each other through a psychic relatedness, the solitude of the individual becomes the solitude of a culture, of a striving humanity. Solitude, then, is not merely a personal state of being, but the individual's reaction to it is projected into attitudes toward place and modes of action which create a climate of social awareness in which creative change becomes possible. Ultimately *One Hundred Years of Solitude* is a revolutionary novel.

The Buendias personify solitude. Indeed, García Márquez describes the household as "the desert of solitude." Regardless of the natural machinations of birth, life, and death, the characters at various times in their lives and in various situations experience the grip of solitude. Paz writes that "when we are born we break the ties that joined us to the blind life we lived in the maternal womb, where there is no gap between desire and satisfaction. We sense the change as separation and loss, as abandonment, as a fall into a strange or hostile atmosphere." This is the primal loss, common to all. It becomes the primal solitude, a state of being, the state of being human. He goes on to say that "death and birth are solitary experiences. We are born alone and we die alone." Life becomes, then, a process of separation, the realization of this separation which is solitude, the reaction to this separation—the labyrinthine search for the physical, primal antidote—and the final subsumption by solitude again. The experience of this primal solitude and the process described above are repeated again and again in the lives of the Buendias.

The adolescent José Arcadio, the oldest son of José Arcadio Buendia, becomes interested in a neighbor woman, Pilar Ternera, who works in the household. This experience first awakens in him a sudden loss and then a sudden longing: "José Arcadio felt his bones filling up with foam, a languid fear, and a terrible desire to weep. The woman made no insinuations. But José Arcadio kept looking for her all night long, for the smell of smoke that she had under her armpits and that had got caught under his skin." Later, after an initial confusing physical encounter with the woman, he knows he must have her, although he does not know why. During the night, in "a world he had not noticed until then," he enters her dark house, which is described by García Márquez as "that abyss of abandonment." There they find each other and he gives himself to her:

> Then he gave himself over to that hand, and in a terrible state of exhaustion he let himself be led to a shapeless place where his clothes were taken off and he was heaved about like a sack of potatoes and thrown from one side to the other in a bottomless darkness in which his arms were useless, where it no longer smelled of woman but of ammonia, and where he tried to remember her face and found before him the face of Ursula, confusedly aware that he was doing something that for a very long time he had wanted to do but that he had imagined could never be done … and feeling that he could no longer resist … [the] fear, and the bewildered anxiety to flee and at the same time stay forever in that exasperated silence and that fearful solitude.

José Arcadio is suddenly in an oddly violent, womblike world, which though physically sexual is not really experienced as such. He confuses his lover with his mother, Ursula. He has journeyed to, and is experiencing, both a new and an ancient state of being. He is performing a primal act, something that for a very long time he had wanted to do, that is accompanied by fear and a bewildered anxiety, and has awakened for him that fearful solitude. García Márquez describes Arcadio's ensuing nightly pilgrimages and sexual union as following "her path every night through the labyrinth of the room." Infected with a "virulent rancor against the world," which is a hatred of disharmony, he continues to long for the comfort of the woman who has defined, by opposition to her womblike control, that sense of primal separation. After the woman becomes pregnant, he seeks solace at the fair of the gypsies, where he finds another sexual partner and disappears with her. But this feeling of separation he seeks to escape is not simply a tumultuous, adolescent phenomenon.

When the aging Ursula, in "the impenetrable solitude of decrepitude," looks out to her invisible husband tied to the chestnut tree in the yard, she is "obeying a habit of her solitude." As Amaranta weaves her shroud, it is "not with any hope of defeating solitude … but, quite the contrary, in order to nurture it." After being spurned by Amaranta, Colonel Gerineldo Márquez becomes lost in thought as he "looked at the desolate streets, the crystal water on the almond trees, and he found himself lost in solitude." When Colonel Aureliano Buendia opens the door to seventeen men, he knows they are his sons for they are stamped "with a solitary air." When old age comes to the Colonel, he knows grace is simply "an honorable pact with solitude." These characters can be read as Hall chooses to read them: as symbolic of Paz's philosophy and as examples of the condition of man, separated eternally from his mother, his fellow man, his society, and his God. Various characters seek and find, however, a grudgingly temporary but sweet solace from this primal solitude.

For Paz, the pact with solitude is a dialectic. The awareness of solitude is actually an awareness of self which brings about an intense desire to negate the self and end the solitude. For José Arcadio, the pleasure of lovemaking eases his separation anxiety even as it defines the heretofore vague sense of his solitude. Instructed by sex of his isolation, he seeks sex to end it. As he knows, sex paradoxically relieves and reminds him of his sickness of heart; he abandons himself to sex and solitude at the same time. As Paz states: "Solitude is both a sentence and an expiation. It is a punishment but it is also a promise that our exile will [can] end." These paradoxical elements make up that which is the dialectic of solitude. According to Paz, as human beings we strive for solace at the same time we are repelled by it, for solace then functions sharply to betray our solitude. Birth and death are complementary opposites. One initiates us into life, but also initiates us into that primal separation. The other ends the separation, but takes with it the life. Which is true life or true death—creation or destruction? The human being is not sure. Paz states that "although we do not know, our whole being strives to escape the opposites that torment us." Mired in this paradox, the human being has one personal, physical solace: "Creation and destruction become one in the act of love, and during a fraction of a second man has a glimpse of a more perfect state of being." This love is a solace because for its time it defeats solitude; it requires the intimate envelopment of or by another human being; it is a particle of communion, of harmony. For Paz, love becomes "the most human trait of all … something that we have made ourselves and that is not found in nature … a free choosing of our destiny." It is created from the dialectic of solitude. It is fleeting, but it is real.

Just as José Arcadio finds solace in the sexual union with Pilar Ternera and the gypsy girl, other characters strive for and find the same solace. When Aureliano Buendia sees Remedios Moscote and falls in love with her, his feeling becomes an obsession. He seeks her everywhere, but paradoxically finds her image in the condition only she can alleviate and therefore increase: "his private and terrible solitude." He marries her and is happy for a time. After Pietro Crespi's suicide, and after she has rejected Gerineldo Márquez, Amaranta begins an incestuous relationship with Aureliano José, who becomes for her "a palliative for her solitude." When Amaranta terminates this relationship, it is Aureliano José who must seek solace for his solitude. He goes to sleep in the barracks, and on Saturdays he goes to town to the whores for "consolation for his abrupt solitude." It is Petra Cotes who helps Aureliano Segundo, taking him in, loving him, and curing him of his "tendencies toward solitary meditation." The entire town has access to this solace when the gringos of the banana boom bring a whole trainload of whores: "Babylonish women skilled in age-old methods and in possession of all manner of unguents and devices to stimulate the unaroused, to give courage to the timid, to satiate the voracious, to exalt the modest man, to teach a lesson to repeaters, and to correct solitary people." But if there is motion from solitude toward solace in the book, it is a resisted motion.

Paz maintains that it traditionally has been the business of society to complicate individual accessibility to the solace of erotic love. Seeking to conventionalize, society restricts love with monetary, legal, religious, hygienic, and moral constraints. Fertility and communion become the property of religion. The notion that love and sex should occur only in church-sanctioned marriage is society's attempt to achieve harmony. Marriage protects order and with children perpetuates this same order. The effects of the dialectic of solitude are given, then, social and religious antidotes. True erotic communion, growing from the dialectic of solitude, becomes threatening to society because, as Paz states, "whenever it succeeds in realizing itself, it breaks up a marriage and transforms it into what society does not want it to be: a revelation of two solitary beings who create their own world, a world that rejects society's lies, abolishes time and work, and declares itself to be self-sufficient."

The psychological restraints of society are represented again and again in *One Hundred Years of Solitude*: José Arcadio must hide his relationship with Pilar Ternera; Rebeca hides Pietro Crespi's love letters; Fernanda brutally suppresses Meme's love for Mauricio; Fernanda rejects her own husband's love. The perfect example is the Petra Cotes–Aureliano Segundo–Fernanda triangle. Petra Cotes and Aureliano Segundo perfectly express Paz's revelatory natural love: physically and emotionally liberating and even materialistically fecund. Because of social and religious dogma and her own paranoia, Fernanda destroys her husband's love for her.

So the characters in *One Hundred Years of Solitude* are entrenched in solitude, that awareness of the ultimate knowledge of their isolation, their fundamental loss, their disharmony with nature. And according to Paz, everything that a person encounters in the world following this knowledge, "self-awareness, time, reason, customs, habits," serves to heighten this sense of loss, "tends to make us exiles from life." As exiles from life we "are condemned to search for it [communion, harmony] through jungles and deserts or in the underground [psychosexual] mazes of the labyrinth." We seek, like García Márquez's characters, some resolution for the dialectic that tears at us; we seek to sate that primal longing for place and to experience "an instant of that full life in which opposites vanish, in which life and death, time and eternity are united": Macondo.

The founder of Macondo, José Arcadio Buendia, is an exile, running from death, from guilt, from the soul of the man he has killed, who is a nightly reminder of death and solitude: "He [José Arcadio Buendia] was tormented by the immense desolation with which the dead man had looked at him through the rain, his deep nostalgia as he yearned for living people." José Arcadio Buendia leaves Riohacha and undertakes a great search for peace, for a place, and for resolution of his guilt. The direction is simply "opposite to the road to Riohacha," opposite that of civilization and society "so that they would not leave any trace or meet any people they knew." It becomes "an absurd journey," but "after almost two years of crossing, they became the first mortals to see the western slopes of the mountain range," and "from the cloudy summit they saw the immense aquatic expanse of the great swamp": a new land. "After several months of lost wandering through the swamps," they come upon "the banks of a stony river whose waters were like a torrent of frozen glass." Here José Arcadio Buendia has a dream vision of a "city with houses having mirror walls" and decides to build his town.

Metaphorically, this "lost wandering" in search of "place" is the wandering through the labyrinth. It is a psychological journey. Later, when Colonel Aureliano Buendia attempts to find that same route, he realizes that "it was madness." It is the search for the primal place where opposites vanish: a sanctuary from solitude. Rita Guibert writes that the real Macondo in Colombia was a similarly tiny and remote place near the boyhood home of Gabriel García Márquez, a "town in the middle of nowhere, which García Márquez used to explore when he was a child."[2]

His fictional Macondo becomes a new, idyllic, and beautiful place: "a village of twenty adobe houses, built on the bank of a river of clear water that ran along a bed of polished stones, which were white and enormous, like prehistoric eggs. The world was so recent that many things lacked names, and in order to indicate them it was necessary to point." Here José Arcadio Buendia does indeed create Paz's place of the full life:

José Arcadio Buendia, who was the most enterprising man ever to be seen in the village, had set up the placement of the houses in such a way that from all of them one could reach the river and draw water with the same effort, and he had lined up the streets with such good sense that no house got more sun than another during the hot time of day. Within a few years Macondo was a village that was more orderly and hard-working than any known until then by its three hundred inhabitants. It was a truly happy village where no one was over thirty years of age and where no one had died.

Macondo is a place where the magical and real are uniquely intertwined. Yellow flowers fall from the sky; a man is constantly surrounded by a halo of butterflies; people soar about on carpets: to the innocent and childlike people of Macondo these magical things are an accepted part of their reality. Manipulated by gypsies from the world outside Macondo, these same people believe that commonplace objects—magnets, magnifying glasses, ice—are mysterious and magical. Macondo is a place where for a time opposites relax, where there is harmony and a sense of human communion—for a time. Ultimately Macondo cannot resist the outside world, which cannot promise to relieve the citizens of their sense of loss. Instead, they are provided with systems to protect them from it. Paz states that in simple, primitive cultures like Macondo "solitude is a dangerous and terrifying condition." Therefore, society offers "complex and rigid systems of prohibition, rules and rituals," that protect "the individual from solitude." Foremost among these systems is religion.

A visiting priest, appalled by the innocent and effective pagan system of "natural law," decides to stay and build a church. Religion provides its own system of redemption, communion, and fertility that suppresses the positive dialectic of solitude. Paz states that a god is introduced "who is also a son, a descendant of ancient creation-gods—dies and is resurrected at fixed periods." This introduction of a new god is well illustrated in another García Márquez story, "The Handsomest Drowned Man in the World." Here redemption for a town comes in the form of death, the drowned man, and his appearance completely reorders the town, giving it purpose and saving it from its narrow existence and its solitude. The people even bury the body in the sea without an anchor "so that he could come back if he wished and whenever he wished."[3] The drowned man becomes a fertility symbol when in his memory the people of the town completely decorate with flowers a promontory that can be seen from far out to sea. In *One Hundred Years of*

Solitude, however, the introduction of Christ as a god marks the decline and physical death of Melquiades, who brought magic and wisdom to the town and the Buendias. He functioned as a god for them. He also has died—on the beach at Singapore—and is resurrected and appears to various male generations of the Buendias until the end of the novel.

The death of the town's ancient, magical fertility comes symbolically when a "monster" is caught in a trap near the town. It bleeds a "green and greasy liquid" from its wounds. Its description also seems to symbolize the decline and death of all of the magic wrought in the town: "Its human parts were more like those of a sickly angel than of a man, for its hands were tense and agile, its eyes large and gloomy."

The problem posed by the dialectic of solitude is evaded by a religious communion. The problem of fertility is subsumed by the Christian resurrection myth. With the expectance of death, a cemetery is established in Macondo. Paz states that to protect the individual from solitude, "religious ritual, and the constant presence of the dead, create a [the] center of relationships."

The Buendias help establish this religion through their second son, Aureliano, who seeks solace from his solitude in the relationship with Remedios Moscote. Through this relationship, the Moscotes and the government they represent are firmly established in the town. The marriage of Remedios and Aureliano brings the priest, and the ongoing relationship between the Buendias and the Moscotes establishes the rule of law. Apolinar Moscote brings in a school and the government authority that had been resisted to that point. Armed soldiers appear in Macondo to enforce the edicts of the government. Magic is replaced by reason, a further refuge from solitude. Macondo becomes the prophesied "city with houses having mirror walls." Retreating to the protection of reason, the inhabitants of Macondo create a town that is a mirror image of this irresponsible retreat: foreign and loveless. Paz writes that when this retreat is most pronounced, man's "creations, like those of an inept sorcerer, no longer obey him. He is alone among his works, lost—to use the phrase by José Gorostiza—in a 'wilderness of mirrors'."

Paz goes on to write later, concerning the destruction of the bourgeois world, that man is awakened into a new labyrinth: "the mazes of a nightmare in which the torture chambers are endlessly repeated in the mirrors of reason." The reader realizes this at the end of *One Hundred Years of Solitude* when Macondo, gripped in the vise of an apocalyptic wind, is referred to as "the city of mirrors." It is a city that has evaded solitude through reason and religion, but has not escaped or resolved it. Central to this concept of unresolved solitude is the character of Colonel Aureliano Buendia, who has retreated into the self-obsessive grip of solitude. He is the man who cannot love. He is the man who was born with his eyes open. At the end of his book Paz expresses a hope for modern society that cannot help Macondo: "Perhaps we will realize that we have been dreaming with our eyes open, and that the dreams of reason are intolerable."

Macondo has slipped away into the intolerable. A society based on religion and reason is established. Politics replaces the idyllic balance of José Arcadio Buendia's magical natural order. The civil wars come in a futile and bloody attempt to resist the corrupt and corrosive alliance of religion, greed, and politics. The wars further alienate the people from their magical past, for in order to win, the Liberals who want self-rule have to adopt the same brutal methods as the Conservatives; Colonel Aureliano Buendia realizes that he has come to fight for nothing. Imperialist exploitation, repression, and natural and economic ruination come to Macondo, where the people lapse into the self-centered and self-obsessive retreat from solitude, no longer willing to react to solitude in self-awareness, human contact, and action—the "indolence of the people" is "in contrast to the voracity of [the] oblivion" that overtakes them. The Buendia family becomes locked into the hopeless pattern of futile reaction to the self-obsessive solitude of José Arcadio Segundo, to the decadent, repressive, escapist religion of Fernanda, and to the bourgeois, hedonistic revelry of Aureliano Segundo. Because of solitude and the unhealthy reaction to it, the Buendias and Macondo speed to their mutual apocalypse.

It is obvious that the last of the Buendias have nothing for the future. José Arcadio, the last, returns from Rome when his mother finally dies. Instead of studying for the priesthood he has lived a bohemian life in Rome. He proceeds to live a life of perverse, foppish decadence until killed by his young playmates while soaking in one of his scented baths. The last Aureliano has remained true to his name by growing and maturing alone, spending his time in the workroom and nurturing his solitude. When Amaranta Ursula returns with her husband, Gaston, it is obvious that she has developed a carefree and domineering zest for life, but not much else. She, Gaston, and Aureliano exist there in the crumbling mausoleum of a house. Shortly before Gaston leaves for Europe, Amaranta Ursula and Aureliano begin a wild, passionate, and all-consuming incestuous romance that is the perfect balm for young Aureliano's solitude. They become increasingly preoccupied and self-absorbed, rarely venturing out of the house or beyond the confines of their mutual solitude: "secluded by solitude and love and by the solitude of love." The world around them rapidly disintegrates.

Paz states on the last page of his book that the modern myth is that "the sterility of the bourgeois world will end in suicide or a new form of creative participation." It is obvious that Macondo, mired in the backwash of neglect and indolent solitude, has chosen suicide. After Amaranta Ursula bleeds to death in childbirth, Aureliano places the child in a basket and wanders through town consumed by nostalgia, seeking his own friends and solace in the past. But events have caught up with him while he has frolicked hedonistically with Amaranta Ursula, and time has literally run out. He returns to see the baby dragged away by carnivorous ants, and as he translates the last of the parchments, the destruction they foretell takes place around him. No one shall survive, "because races condemned to one hundred years of solitude did not have a second opportunity on earth."

All that is left, then, as an alternative to this solitude is the choice of some form of "creative participation." García Márquez does not give us any obvious indication of what this would be, but certain characters suggest some form of action and rebellion—some form of resolution to the solitude, resolution that is not completely self-centered and self-obsessive like that of most of the Buendias, some manner of dealing with the collective solitude of the community, the collective problem of being.

The novel does not simply end with a statement about the ultimate solitude of man, unredeemable and irrevocable, as stated by Linda Hall. García Márquez confirms this himself in his published interview with Rita Guibert:

> The whole disaster of Macondo—which is a telluric disaster as well—comes from this lack of solidarity—the solitude which results when everyone is acting for himself alone. That's then a political concept, and interests me as such—to give solitude the political connotation I believe it should have.

The reader needs to draw some conclusions that define García Márquez's role for the solitary man in order to appreciate fully the implications of the novel's ending.

Solidarity implies community: a purposeful bonding of people with like needs and intentions. But this solidarity must at first be an individual thing, a personal decision to act or rebel or resist a negative conformity. This decision must be made before people can combine their hearts and minds for purposeful action. It is an individual decision, a constructive attempt to raise oneself from the easier self-obsessive preoccupation with solitude with which García Márquez's characters have so much trouble. The French existential thinker Albert Camus deals with the concept of action in much of his work. A socialist, like García Márquez, he is very much interested in the suitable form of action for the modern absurd man. The absurd man is quite similar to the solitary man. Both suffer from the oppression of the schism between their needs as human beings and the hostile reality that can never meet those needs. In *The Myth of Sisyphus*, Camus creates various personae and then demonstrates the ideal mode of action or reaction to the absurd. The persona that is closest to a revolutionary action in the face of absurdity is the Conqueror:

> There always comes a time when one must choose between contemplation and action.... One must live with time and die with it, or else elude it for a greater life. I know that one can compromise and live in the world believing in the eternal. That is called accepting. But I loathe this term and want all or nothing. If I choose action, don't think that contemplation is like an unknown country to me. But it cannot give me everything, and, deprived of the eternal, I want to ally myself with time. I do not want to put down to my account either nostalgia or bitterness, and I merely want to see clearly.... I establish my lucidity in the midst of what negates it. I exalt man before what crushes him, and my freedom, my revolt, and my passion come together then in that tension, that lucidity, and that vast repetition.

I have chosen this passage because it expresses a well-known principle of French existentialism, the absurd revolt. Indeed, the hopeless necessity of the revolt is very similar to the process of the dialectic of solitude and would find voice in the struggles of García Márquez's characters, had he chosen to give it to them. Notice that the Conqueror first rejects accepting, the submersion of the absurd by the eternal, by religion. He then goes on to reject the sanctuary of nostalgia for the past and the pointless negativity of bitterness in the present. He also realizes that he must establish his lucidity in the very midst of or by the very thing that negates it; just as Paz realizes that the very thing that eases solitude also defines it. What the Conqueror proposes is actually a dialectic process: "together then in that tension." And the necessary feature of this revolt is that it is constant: "that vast repetition." A revolt against solitude must take this same form. It is a revolt against the primal separation, the solitude, a revolt with no hope of real resolution; it is a revolt that finds meaning in its own processes, in the maintenance of the dialectic, and should not be escaped through religion, self-obsessive nostalgia, or pointless bitterness. The decision to revolt must be made by the individual. Then collectively, with solidarity, the community can maintain itself against the corrosive forces—imperialism, religion—that society naturally seems to impose.

This call to action is much different from another accepted stance for the artist and for all men. In American letters we have a traditional perception of the role of the solitary man. Emerson writes the following in his essay titled "The Poet":

> O poet! a new nobility is conferred in groves and pastures, and not in castles or by the sword-blade any longer. The conditions are hard, but equal. Thou shalt leave the world, and know the muse only. Thou shalt not know any longer the times, customs, grades, politics, or opinions of men, but shalt take all from the muse.

This is obviously antithetical to the call that Camus makes. It brings to mind Colonel Aureliano Buendia and his little goldfishes, creating and melting and creating again in the pristine vacuum of his solitude, or any of the singular and self-centered pursuits of the various Buendias. To leave the world is to abandon the dialectic of solitude that is common to all men. To abandon the dialectic of solitude in this manner, in this kind of self-centered artistic solitude, is to abandon solidarity and to invite the same condemnation that is expressed at the end of *One Hundred Years of Solitude*. This for the Latin American and for all men is to forfeit continuing existence, "a second opportunity on earth."

García Márquez's call for solidarity is the same call that Paz makes. Paz states that "each man's fate is that of man himself" and that "world history has become everyone's task, and our own labyrinth is the labyrinth of all mankind."

This positive human response to the dialectic of solitude can be seen in several of the characters in *One Hundred Years of Solitude*, and although only fleeting, this response is in sharp contrast to the remaining characters. Remedios the Beauty's presence is a saintlike symbol of revolt against the day to day relinquishing of individuality to the drab commonality of solitude: "Remedios the Beauty stayed there wandering through the desert of solitude, bearing no cross on her back, maturing in her dreams without nightmares, her interminable baths, her unscheduled meals, her deep and prolonged silences that had no memory." A regretful Ursula realizes late in her life the source of solitude's bitter conformity:

> She felt irrepressible desires to let herself go and scamper about like a foreigner and allow herself at last an instant of rebellion, that instant yearned for so many times and so many times postponed, putting her resignation aside and shitting on everything once and for all and drawing out of her heart the

infinite stacks of bad words that she had been forced to swallow over a century of conformity.

"Shit!" she shouted.

Amaranta, who was starting to put the clothes into the trunk, thought that she had been bitten by a scorpion.

"Where is it?" she asked in alarm.

"What?"

"The bug!" Amaranta said.

Ursula put her finger on her heart.

"Here," she said.

In what seems to be in contradiction to Ursula, Meme refutes the intransigence of solitude by conforming with the world. This is not Ursula's conformity with solitude, however, but conformity as an active and personally productive interaction with the world:

> It was obvious from then on that she had inherited very little of her mother's character. She seemed more of a second version of Amaranta when the latter had not known bitterness and was arousing the house with her dance steps at the age of twelve or fourteen before her secret passion for Pietro Crespi was to twist the direction of her heart in the end. But unlike Amaranta, unlike all of them, Meme still did not reveal the solitary fate of the family and she seemed entirely in conformity with the world.

In fact, Meme shows no sign of solitude until she falls in love. Then, as with the other characters, she experiences the pangs of love that soothe yet define for her the solitude she had heretofore not experienced. Because her love affair is brutally ended by Fernanda, and Meme is sent to a convent, the reader never knows how she might have lived her life in Macondo.

José Arcadio Segundo turns from solitude to action when he helps lead the strike against the banana company: "A short time later the drumbeats, the shrill of the bugle, the shouting and running of the people told him that not only had the game of pool come to an end, but also the silent and solitary game that he had been playing with himself ever since that dawn execution." What he had learned from that execution was the certainty and irrevocability of death, and how wrong it was to take someone's life. This realization played upon his conscience like a painful foreshadowing: a "solitary game." He goes on to lead the strike and witness the massacre of the workers. He returns to solitude only when he is driven to madness by the suffocating ignorance and apathy of his fellow citizens.

The contrast made by these brief reactions of other characters to solitude—the many characters who simply surrender to unproductive nostalgia or correct their solitude with religion or reason—shows that *One Hundred Years of Solitude* does offer an alternative to solitude. It is, however, a pessimistic book. Most characters choose not to rise from the dialectic of solitude with the revolt of the Conqueror, but to be subsumed by it. Once again, this is most obvious at the end of the novel. Instead of working through the labyrinth of options of revolt, instead of making the decision to react to the social, religious, and political repression around himself, instead of even continuing to seek the temporary solace of eroticism outside of his family, Aureliano is ultimately so weak that he enters the protective incestuous relationship with Amaranta Ursula. He is not only unwilling to join in a collective involvement with the people of his community, he is even unwilling to join in a sexual involvement with one member of that community. He is, then, seeking solace in the "labyrinths of blood"; incest becomes the symbol of the farthest extreme of solitude. García Márquez shows that a union such as this can only fulfill the private and tragic mythology of the family, can only result in the perversely deformed mythological off-spring. Joining the destruction of Macondo as a symbol for the result of one hundred years of solitude is the child with a tail of a pig.

So this is not a novel that simply seeks to illustrate the isolation of man. This novel is García Márquez's warning to the artist, to the citizen, to the community of Latin America, and to the world. Paz's *The Labyrinth of Solitude* confirms García Márquez's revolutionary ideas—ideas that are not revolutionary in the sense of violence, but of change. In the following sentence Paz figuratively outlines the solitary man's options: "He shouts or keeps silent, stabs or prays, or falls asleep for a hundred years."

NOTES

1. Octavio Paz, *The Labyrinth of Solitude: Life and Thought in Mexico* (New York: Grove Press, 1961), p. 208.

2. Rita Guibert, *Seven Voices: Seven Latin American Writers Talk to Rita Guibert* (New York: Alfred A. Knopf, 1973), p. 306.

3. Gabriel García Márquez, "The Handsomest Drowned Man in the World," in *Leaf Storm and Other Stories* (New York: Harper & Row, 1972), p. 103.

JONATHAN BALDO

Solitude as an Effect of Language in García Márquez's
Cien años de soledad

Of the many mirrors in that "city of mirrors," Gabriel García Márquez's Macondo, not the least important is the text itself, the mirror into which the reader gazes. Engaged in a solitary occupation, sooner or later the reader will recognize his or her kinship with the Buendías, a family "marcada para siempre y desde el principio del mundo por la viruela de la soledad" (p. 333) ["marked forever and from the beginning of the world with the pox of solitude" (p. 363)].[1] And like every character in *Cien años de soledad*, the reader is destined to develop a "dominant obsession," an obsession with one of several themes that recur with increasing frequency as the tale moves forward and that promise to serve as a key for decoding it. Language is the particular thread in the densely woven fabric of the novel that has become my dominant obsession. It is a more slender and less visible thread than others that wind their way through the narrative, scarcely allowing us to trace a growing complicity between language and solitude.

Language is preeminently social. A shared system of codes is a precondition of any social existence whatsoever. (At the beginning of the novel, before Macondo's entry into a socio-political existence, the system of language is, appropriately, still nascent: "The world was so recent that many things lacked names.") But in sly ways *Cien años de soledad* insinuates that language may have as intimate a liaison with solitude as it does with

From *Criticism* 30, 4 © 1988 by Wayne State University Press.

solidarity. Nostalgia, the novel suggests, is a constant lure or trap for any user of language. An offspring as well as an expression of the compulsion to repeat that is everywhere in evidence in the novel, language may also be the seat of obsessional behavior and hence of solitude.

But what I shall be arguing is an implicit alliance between language and solitude makes the reverse argument plausible as well. Tracing a hidden filiation between language and solitude, the novel puts a decidedly social spin on a familiar theme. Rather than recording the privatization—to use an ugly term from the Reagan era—of what is social, it is more likely that the novel is telling the story of the socialization of the private, of the very domain of solitude.

Cien años de soledad is almost a *reductio ad absurdum* of the theme of solitude, arguably the most prominent theme—to the point of banality—of the literature of our century. Or to use a metaphor close to the novel's concerns, *Cien años de soledad* is solitude's imperial hour. García Márquez's novel shows solitude to have insinuated itself into every nook of experience. No one is immune from solitude: neither those who repeat, in an apparent attempt to unburden themselves of memory, nor those who scrupulously resist the temptation to repeat; neither those who are most susceptible to nostalgia (which may seem an attempt to seek relief from solitude by rescuing our past selves who are restlessly pacing the corridors of the labyrinth of time), nor those who resolutely live only in the present or for the future; neither the vivacious nor the withdrawn or solitary. Carrying the theme to the excesses that the novel does has two effects. It drains it of the pathos that is solitude's constant companion in lesser works of fiction: e.g., the novels of Thomas Wolfe. And it causes us to rethink the whole tradition of solitude in our literature. Although *Cien años de soledad* proffers no easy political solutions to the predicament of solitude (it stops short of a metaphysically grounded concept of community), it does amount to an implicit critique of and alternative to more conventional readings of solitude as the pathos of the isolated subject. The novel, then, is both a *reductio ad absurdum* of the theme of solitude, and a pursuit of solitude to a place—the relation of the subject to discourse—where it is permanently entrenched.

Language and nostalgia

On the first page of the novel words are conceived as a substitute for pointing, for the more immediate relation of the indexical sign to its referent: "El mundo era tan reciente, que muchas cosas carecían de nombre, y para mencionarlas había que señalarlas con el dedo" (p. 9) ["The world was so recent that many things lacked names, and in order to indicate them it was necessary to point" (p. 11)]. C. S. Peirce, one of two founders of modern semiotics, established a tripartite classification of the sign into icons, indices, and symbols. The index Peirce defined as "a sign determined by its Dynamic object by virtue of being in a real relation to it."[2] In other words, the index has a present or immediate relation, often a relation of contiguity, with its referent. Examples are a weathervane, a symptom of illness, and the gesture of pointing. The index is not only contiguous but also contemporaneous with the object it designates. It might appear to be free from the temporal gap, the deferral of presence described by Jacques Derrida in his influential essay "Differance," that characterizes the relation between linguistic signs and their referents.[3] Like the world when it was "so recent" that it had scarcely entered the course of history, the index, too, is without memory.

Near the beginning of the novel, you will remember—or may remember, for the narrative is constructed in such a way as to vex the reader's memory—the recently founded town of Macondo suffers a collective lapse of memory brought on by a plague of insomnia. "La primera manifestación del olvido" (p. 47) ["The first manifestation of a loss of memory" (pp. 52–53)], we are told, is the forgetting of names. During the plague, words are made to function as indices, in a desperate attempt by José Arcadio Buendía to reverse the loss of memory and of language. Armed with brush and ink, he decides to mark everything with its name: the objects in his laboratory, furniture, animals, plants, even the town itself. In this frantic effort to resist the erosion of memory, words are forced into a relation of contiguity with their referents, in apparent violation of one of the essential features of the linguistic sign. "A sign," writes Eco, "… stands in place of something which is absent, which could even not exist, or at least not be present anywhere at the time I use the sign."[4]

In ordinary circumstances words are neither contiguous nor contemporaneous with their referents. Whether one understands the linguistic sign along the lines of Saussurean semiology, which conceives of the sign as referring to an original and lost presence, as a provisional detour to which we must have recourse when the "thing itself" designated by the sign cannot present itself; or whether one holds, with Derrida, that the notion of language as marking the absence of a modified or deferred presence is an error of metaphysics, and that language is the "trace" of a past that was itself a trace rather than an original and lost presence: in either case, language has a memorializing function. Words, the insomnia episode suggests, are a memory system, and in *Cien años de soledad* all acts of recollection lead to nostalgia, which is as prolific as vegetation in the tropical climate of Macondo. The forgetting of names of objects during the insomnia plague therefore has a special status. It is not like the simple forgetting of events, José Arcadio Buendía's forgetting of "hasta los hechos más impresionantes de su niñez" (p. 47) ["even the most impressive happenings of childhood" (p. 53)]. For language itself functions as a kind of "máquina de la memoria" (p. 48), a memory machine. José Arcadio Buendía becomes preoccupied with constructing such a machine, "fundaba en la posibilidad de repasar todas las mañanas, y desde el principio hasta el fin, la totalidad de los conocimientos adquiridos en la vida" (p. 48) ["based on the possibility of reviewing every morning, from beginning to end, the totality of knowledge acquired during one's life" (p. 54)], first "para acordarse de los maravillosos inventos de los gitanos" (p. 48) ["in order to remember the marvelous inventions of the gypsies" (p. 54)], and later, during the insomnia plague, to restore memory to "un pueblo que se hundía sin remedio en el tremedal del olvido" (p. 48) ["a town that was sinking irrevocably into the quicksand of forgetfulness" (p. 54)]. But language is such a machine for storing, if not the totality of one's personal memories, the collective memory of the race. (Later in the novel, the encyclopedia, which Aureliano Babilonia reads "de la primera página a la última, como si fuera una novela" (p. 316) ["from the first page to the last … as if it were a novel" (p. 344)], also functions as such a machine.) Language is always, in a sense, memorial, commemorative, so when the people of Macondo forget how to match things with their names, they have forgotten the faculty of memory itself. The possession of a language, then, may be a sufficient condition for Macondo to become a town "abatido por los recuerdos" (p. 324) ["bowed down by memories" (p. 353)].

Repetition as a language-compulsion

Toward the end of the novel, Aureliano Babilonia leaves the Buendía house after long confinement in his room, in search of the books that will help him decipher the gypsy Melquíades' cryptic parchments. His first and only destination is the bookshop of the wise Catalonian, a former professor of classical literature: "No le interesó nada de lo que vio en el trayecto, acaso porque carecía de recuerdos para comparar" (p. 310) ["Nothing he saw along the way interested him, perhaps because he lacked any memories for comparison" (p. 337)]. The episode suggests a motive for the pervasive compulsion to repeat that is everywhere in evidence in the novel (at the level of narration as well as that of the narrated events): e.g., in the Colonel's two favorite activities, manufacturing little gold fishes that he will later melt down, and fighting revolutions. To repeat is to transform the world into a text. Experiences are able to signify through repetition insofar as they may stand for or refer back to prior events or experiences. The compulsion to repeat is a compulsion to make over one's experiences as a language. If the language that results is a "private language," or as private as a language may be, that too may be an important feature of the desire to repeat: to formulate an alternative language to the public and acquired one, which most of us experience as, in the words of one of Beckett's characters, always "the language of others."

This "language-compulsion" beneath the impulse to repeat also derives from the fact that all cognition is re-cognition, and that all so-called perception is never immediate but always already semiotic and therefore memorial or nostalgic. That Aureliano does not notice his surroundings when after long confinement he emerges from the Buendía household suggests as much. Otherwise his impressions of the outside world would be strongest at this moment, most immediate because not yet mediated by the memory of past experiences. The repetition-compulsion, therefore, would appear to be a necessary feature of all perception and cognition.

Traditionally, characters who are marked by repetitive behavior or ruled by a dominant obsession are "humors" and favored by writers of comic literature, like Ben Jonson or Dickens. Humors are petrified characters, whose mechanical and ritualized behavior, as Northrop Frye observes, ordinarily dehumanizes them and cuts off sympathy.[5] García Márquez's characters seem as if they should be humors. But they do not quite fit that category, I believe, because, as the episode we have been examining indicates, the novel holds repetition to be constitutive of all cognition (or re-cognition). To forego repetition, therefore, would be to exist in a conceptual vacuum.

In addition, obsessions with another person or activity (leading to repetitive behavior) are not merely an encumbrance in this novel. They do not necessarily, as in Frye's formulation, cut a character off from the community of the living by making them appear lifeless and mechanical. García Márquez makes them seem, rather, a desperate attempt to remain with the living by prevailing against time and death ("y entonces aprendieron que las obsesiones dominantes prevalecen contra la muerte," p. 346), and so they are as heroic as they are comic. Yet obsessions inevitably lead to that ubiquitous condition García Márquez calls solitude. Now the novel regards death as the final and most extreme form of many forms of solitude. Melquíades "había estado en la muerte ... pero había regresado porque no pudo soportar la soledad" (p. 49). Solitude is "la otra muerte que existía dentro de la muerte" that so terrifies Prudencio Aguilar (p. 73). Any attempt to circumvent this final form of solitude, death, through the cultivation of a dominant obsession therefore leads by another path to the same destination, solitude. To relinquish repetitive and ritualized behavior, however, is to fare no better. When the lovers Aureliano Babilonia and Amaranta Úrsula forego the rhythmic rituals of everyday life, "el ritmo de los hábitos cotidianos," they lose their sense of reality and time, "el sentido de la realidad" and "la noción del tiempo" (p. 341), another form of solitude. In the worlds of comedy, it is possible to restore humors to the living by applying a corrective, curing them of their repetitive behavior or dominant obsession. But since the reward for relinquishing ritual habit and obsessions seems to be another form of solitude, the notion of cure or correction, so indigenous to comedy, has little or no meaning in *Cien años de soledad*.

Aureliano's second sally into the world beyond the walls of the Buendía house is instigated by José Arcadio, the Seminarist. Following his debauch with the children, he suffers an asthma attack and requires a remedy from a nearby drugstore, but "la segunda visión del pueblo desierto, alumbrado apenas por las amarillentas bombillas de las calles, no despertó en Aureliano más curiosidad que la primera vez" (p. 315) ["the second view of the deserted town, barely illuminated by the yellowish bulbs of the street lights, did not awaken in Aureliano any more curiosity than the first" (p. 343)]. What explains this lack of interest in his surroundings even after a second viewing, and why does he break the pattern of the Buendías by showing no evidence of a compulsion to repeat? Because the world is already textualized, already a book for Aureliano, which in this novel means already memorialized or committed to memory. He has read a six-volume encyclopedia from beginning to end, we are told, as if it were a novel, and committed it to his prodigious memory. And when Gastón and José Arcadio question him about his source of information after it becomes clear that he knows things that are not in the encyclopedia, he responds cryptically, "Todo se sabe" (p. 316), "Everything is known" (p. 344).

Although Aureliano is, like his progenitors, a creature of memory, his is a purely intellectual memory, neither fed by nor feeding nostalgia. Endowed with a "sabiduría enciclopedica, [una] rara facultad de recordar sin conocerlos los pormenores de hechos y lugares remotos" (p. 343) ["encyclopedic knowledge, a rare faculty for remembering the details of remote deeds and places without having been there" (p. 375)], he is the owner of memories that had been "en su memoria desde mucho antes de nacer" (p. 301) ["in his head since long before he was born" (p. 328)]. When he tries to imaginatively reconstruct "el arrasado esplendor de la antigua ciudad de la compañía bananera" (p. 324) ["the annihilated splendor of the old banana-company town" (p. 353)], it is a purely intellectual enterprise, not an exercise in nostalgia. He meanders through the streets of Macondo, examining "con un interés más científico que humano" ["with scientific interest"] the houses of inhabitants "abatidos por los recuerdos" (p. 324) ["bowed down by memories" (p. 353)]. Aureliano Babilonia suffers personal memories and "las lanzas mortales de las nostalgias proprias" (p. 349) ["the fatal lances of his own nostalgia" (p. 381)] for the first time only after his wife-aunt, Amaranta Úrsula, dies in childbirth:

> y en aquel relámpago de lucidez tuvo conciencia de que era incapaz de resistir sobre su alma el peso abrumador de tanto pasado. (p. 349) [and in that flash of lucidity he became aware that he was unable to bear in his soul the crushing weight of so much past (p. 381)].

Until this time Aureliano manages to avoid the private language that is memory, and the desire to generate such a private language through repetition, because he embodies something like a universal memory.

Repetition, a means of generating signs, might seem an antidote to solitude. If indeed all cognition is re-cognition, then repetition may be a means of becoming aware of the world, as Aureliano Babilonia decidedly is not on his first viewing of it, and even of personalizing the world with the stamp of one's memories. But repetition is, besides the mark of obsessions and solitude, a virtual machine for manufacturing nostalgia. Repetition feeds on itself, since it promises an illusory relief from nostalgia, at the same time that it deepens nostalgia and characters' obsessions with their pasts. For the repeated experience is not a present experience but rather a sign pointing backward. No inhabitant of Macondo succeeds in dodging the trap of nostalgia because everyone is faced with an impossible choice: to repeat in order to emerge from a perceptual isolation like Aureliano Babilonia's, a tactic, I have argued, that paradoxically sentences one to the twin fates of nostalgia and solitude; and to scrupulously avoid repetition, like the vivacious Amaranta Úrsula and her husband Gastón, in which case one's experiences are sentenced to remain dumb, mute, and elusive, an ever-disappearing stream of non-repeatable and therefore irrecuperable moments.

As the ending to the enigmatic last sentence of the novel echoes in our minds—"todo lo escrito en ellos era irrepetible desde siempre y para siemre, porque las estirpes condenadas a cien años de soledad no tenían una segunda oportunidad sobre la tierra" (p. 351) ["everything on [Melquíades' parchments] was unrepeatable since time immemorial and forever more, because races condemned to one hundred years of solitude did not have a second opportunity on earth" (p. 383)]—we wonder which is the more troubling dream: to be condemned to repeat, or to be forbidden to repeat, to be denied what is perhaps our primary means of imparting form to experience.

Toward the end of the novel, several characters try to affirm the idea of an existence without recurrence (whether repetition or memory, a form of recurrence or restaging of the past in the theater of the mind), and without nostalgia. Before examining their strategies and measuring their successes, allow me to pose the dilemma once again, at the risk of repeating myself.

Excursus: solitude and temporality

After returning to his native village on the Mediterranean coast, the Catalonian feels a pang of nostalgia for Macondo, where he had previously been nostalgic for the village of his birth. The experience causes the machinery for producing nostalgia to self-destruct and leads to suspicion of the illusionistic faculty of memory and its capacity for generating mirages.

> Aturdido por dos nostalgias enfrentadas como dos espejos, perdió su maravilloso sentido de la irrealidad, hasta que terminó por recomendarles a todos que se fueran de Macondo ... y que en qualquier lugar en que estuvieran recordaran siempre que el pasado era mentira, que la memoria no tenía caminos de regreso, que toda primavera antigua era irrecuperable, y que el amor más desatinado y tenaz era de todos modos una verdad efímera. (p. 339). [Upset by two nostalgias facing each other like two mirrors, he lost his marvelous sense of unreality and he ended up recommending to all of them [his four young friends] that they leave Macondo ... and that wherever they might be they always remember that the past was a lie, that memory has no return, that every spring gone by could not be recovered, and that the wildest and most tenacious love was an ephemeral truth in the end (p. 370).]

He appears not to recognize the contradiction in a precept that enjoins one to forswear memory, since all precepts (and, arguably, all uses of language) are implicitly both an instance of memory and a call to remember. Contradictions aside, what the Catalonian ignores in his repudiation of all forms of retention is the more important motive for memory and nostalgia: not to recapture a definite past that is beyond recovery, but to stabilize experiences that were so fluid as to be unintelligible until fixed through memory, repetition, even nostalgia. To the notion of nostalgia as a means of recuperating the past, then, we might oppose the idea of nostalgia as a cognitive act whose aim is not so much recovery as a "covering" of the past, a movement that simultaneously falsifies the past and makes it intelligible by lending it a stability and clarity it never had when "present."[6] Instead of merely a ticket to solitude, therefore, memory and nostalgia might as judiciously be regarded as lines of resistance to solitude.[7]

In his reading of Husserl's *The Phenomenology of Internal Time-Consciousness* (1929), Derrida shows that Husserl's phenomenological account of how the mind makes sense of time rests on the notion of a "living present," a moment of raw, unmediated—i.e., uninterpreted and unremembered—experience that serves as the stable ground for our memories. Husserl's account rests largely on a distinction between "retention," a memory of immediate traces of sensory experience, and "representation," memory of experiences over a greater span of time. Derrida shows that this distinction, intended to fortify the notion of a pure present free from all mediation or retention of what is already past, ends up undermining the phenomenological notion of an isolated moment of unmediated presence, and indeed the very distinction between perception and representation. Derrida opposes to the phenomenological notion of a "living present" a notion of the present as a moment hollowed out by its relations to the past and future, a moment compounded of anticipations and what Husserl calls retentions and representations. In other words, memory is not an operation performed upon, or added to, perception. Rather, memory already helps constitute what we call perception. By Derrida's account, the present moment can never serve as an origin or ground by reference to which the mind can master temporality.[8]

Given Derrida's analysis, the pervasiveness of memory, nostalgia, and repetition, that trio of disorders responsible for so much of the solitude in *One Hundred Years of Solitude*, becomes easier to account for. First, since it contains within it "retentions" of the past, the present moment is always already memorial. The Catalonian's injunction to forswear memory, if taken seriously, would result in the disintegration of all psychic functions. Second, what Husserl calls "representations" or memories at a greater remove than "retentions" might prove a strategy for forging out of the flux of temporal experience moments isolated, stabilized, clarified by the rhetorical operations of memory. That so many characters have a "memory fixation" is indicative, I think, of the fixative powers of memory.

The Catalonian's advice rests on a false distinction between recollection, which notoriously edits, and present experience, not only because present experience is already informed or constituted by retentions, but also because it is no less subject to editorial processes than is memory. So-called sensory perception is necessarily rhetorical, and in particular synecdochic, a section of Kenneth Burke's *The Philosophy of Literary Form* suggests. Burke argues that synecdoche is the archtrope of all representation—artistic, political, and sensory. As an instance of the last: "A tree ... is an infinity of events—and among these our senses abstract certain recordings which 'represent' the tree."[9] Burke's remarks suggest that all perception—as Derrida argues, already containing a memory apparatus—is synecdochic, so that memories over a span of time are doubly rhetorical, synecdoches of synecdoches.

To forswear memory not only shows a misplaced confidence in the distinction between recollected and present experience but also fails to recognize the constructive rather than reconstructive or recuperative role of memory. The editorial activities of memory are necessary to fix and to clarify our experiences even, paradoxically, as it necessarily falsifies them. (It is not simply that our memories often tailor past events to make them better fit the vain body of our desires.) Hence, Macondo's inhabitants must choose between two unsatisfactory alternatives: to live in a past that never was, a constructed or fictionalized past, as did the Catalonian before his "awakening"; or, like the Catalonian's protégé Álvaro, to live in a "present" so fluid and heterogeneous that the mind cannot master it. Like Orpheus, we cannot resist the backward glance that promises certainty and possession. And too, like Orpheus's, our backward gaze is bound to lose for us the very thing we would possess.

Although memory is an untrustworthy mechanism that generates hallucinations about what never was, lapses of memory, whether personal— "el olvido remediable del corazón" ["the remediable forgetfulness of the heart"] and the even more cruel and irrevocable "olvido de la muerte" (p. 49) ["forgetfulness of death" (p. 54)]—or collective—the "official" version of the massacre of the workers intended to make the town forget the episode, or the amnesia of the insomnia plague—are equally intolerable forms of isolation or solitude.

Perhaps to avoid getting lost in the labyrinthine corridors of time, at least three characters toward the end of the novel seem to free themselves from both nostalgia and a compulsion to repeat: Álvaro, Aureliano Babilonia, and Amaranta Úrsula. An avoidance of recurrence in both forms, memory and repetition, comes naturally to Aureliano Babilonia and Amaranta Úrsula. Though diametrically opposed personalities, both inhabit worlds that are already textualized or formalized. They therefore lack the need to formalize, through memory, nostalgia, and repetition, a world experienced as fluid and heterogeneous.

On her return to Macondo from schooling in Brussels, Amaranta Úrsula seems to have escaped the pox of solitude that marks so many of her line. With the industry and strength of character of Úrsula Iguarán, she refuses to have any truck with the past or with memory. Naturally inclined to "tirar en la basura las cosas y las costumbres revenidas" (pp. 318–19) ["toss all items and customs from the past into the trash" (p. 347)], she appears to exist in only two dimensions of time, the future and the present. She has the Colonel's clairvoyance and Petra Cotes' powers of prognostication, albeit in trivialized form: "estaba dotada de un raro instinto para anticiparse a la moda" (p. 319) ["she was endowed with a rare instinct for anticipating fashion" (p. 348)]. A profoundly temporal being, "estaba suscrita a cuanta revista de modas, información artística y música popular se publicaba en Europa" (p. 319) ["she subscribed to every fashion magazine, art publication, and popular music review published in Europe" (p. 348)]. Fashion constitutes a succession of languages or sign systems so rapid that they do not have the opportunity to become affiliated with memory and nostalgia. Language is primarily memorial in *Cien años de soledad*, but the languages of fashion, languages that are not retrospective but prospective and prognosticative, represent an inversion of the primary function of language. A decision to live purely in the present may be consummated only through an utter loss of language, as during the insomnia plague, or the manipulation of language ("fashion") so that it is no longer an instrument of memory.

Amaranta Úrsula lives and moves comfortably in the element of time, without nostalgia or remorse. Her husband Gastón's inventiveness in matters of love seems to break the Buendías' pattern of obsessively repetitive behavior. Her interest in fashion even suggests that time is her co-conspirator, helping her to continually renew the present by shedding the burden of the past through the endless succession of fashions. We learn that her husband Gastón, however, has already made the diagnosis upon her return to Macondo: "desde el mediodía mortal en que descendió del tren comprendió que la determinación de su mujer había sido provocada por un espejismo de la nostalgia" (p. 320) ["since that fatal noon when he got off the train he realized that his wife's determination to return to the town of her parents had been provoked by a nostalgic mirage" (p. 349)].

The alternative of the bookstore owner's protégé Álvaro to repetition and nostalgia is, if more successful, also more desperate. Following his master's advice,

> Lo vendió todo … y compró un pasaje eterno en un tren que nunca acababa de viajar. En las tarjetas postales que mandaba desde las estaciones intermedias, describía a gritos las imágenes instantáneas que había visto por la ventanilla del vagón, y era como ir haciendo trizas y tirando al olvido el largo poema de la fugacidad: los negros quiméricos en los algodonales de la

Luisiana, los caballos alados en la hierba azul de Kentucky, los amantes griegos en el crepúsculo infernal de Arizona, la muchacha de suéter rojo que pintaba acuarelas en los lagos de Michigan, y que le hizo con los pinceles un adiós que no era de despedida sino de esperanza, porque ignoraba que estaba viendo pasar un tren sin regreso. (p. 339). [He sold everything ... and he bought an eternal ticket on a train that never stopped traveling. In the postcards that he sent from the way stations he would describe with shouts the instantaneous images that he had seen from the window of the coach, and it was as if he were tearing up and throwing into oblivion some long, evanescent poem: the chimerical Negroes in the cotton fields of Louisiana, the winged horses in the bluegrass of Kentucky, the Greek lovers in the infernal sunsets of Arizona, the girl in the red sweater painting watercolors by a lake in Michigan who waved at him with her brushes, not to say farewell but out of hope, because she did not know that she was watching a train with no return passing by (pp. 370–71).]

Álvaro's postcards from the way stations of his eternal train journey, like fashion for Amaranta Úrsula, constitute an inversion of the memorializing function of images and other classes of signs—e.g., the daguerreotype of the family taken by Melquíades—earlier in the novel. The postcards are an attempt to overcome the commemorative character of language or of signs in general. His messages do not memorialize the places through which he passes, or constitute a record of his journey. Rather, they are messages that, through a kind of intensification of language—they are "gritos," shouts—attempt to make language contemporaneous with its referents. In a way, therefore, they echo José Arcadio Buendía's harnessing of names to objects during the insomnia plague. The shouts recorded on the postcards are approximations of descriptions without duration. They are attempts to circumvent both the syntagmatic axis of discourse and the temporalizing movement of the signifying process, the deferral of the signified analyzed by Derrida in his essay "Differance," both of which make language so fertile a ground for retrospection and prospection. Furthermore, the simplified visual signs of postcards are approximations of signs without referents, ungrounded both in the experience of the sender (postcards are messages cut off from their origins to an even greater degree than letters) and in the places they purport to represent, and they are therefore signs that appear to lack a built-in memory. For Álvaro, therefore, they constitute an ideal class of signs, since the only sign without a temporal gap between signifier and signified is not one in which the signified is fully present to the signifier (an impossible condition), but rather one that purportedly has no signified. Not only is this attempt to resist repetition, nostalgia, memory, and the memory system that is language somewhat desperate and likely to fail, but it also seems more diseased, more marked by the pox of solitude, than the condition it was meant to cure.

Letters

The relative scarcity of reported dialogue in the novel is, of course, consistent with the novel's theme of solitude. Writing, not speech, is the most common form of exchange between characters. Letters are a prominent device throughout the novel, but the flurry of letters increases as the novel moves forward, the solitude of its characters deepens, and the Buendía family line and the town of Macondo reach their apocalyptic end.

A generally unreliable means of communication in *Cien años de soledad*, one that often misses its mark, letters are usually either from a mysterious source (the letter regarding Rebeca, or those to Fernanda from the invisible doctors), or dissimulating (the letters from Gastón's partners and those between Gastón and Amaranta Úrsula), or contradictory (Amaranta Úrsula's letter to Gastón), or unread (the final letter from Barcelona and the letters that Amaranta promises to deliver to the dead).

Their behavior at their destinations is as problematic as their origins: Amaranta Úrsula's letter of "contradictory truths" to Gastón regarding her love for him and for Aureliano, for instance serves Gastón as "el pretexto que él deseaba para abandonarla a su suerte" (p. 343) ["the pretext that he had wanted to abandon her to her fate" (p. 374)]. A drawn-out correspondence, like that between Aureliano and the Catalonian, usually degenerates from "real contacts" (p. 374) to contact that is shadowy or uncertain. Like all literature, the Catalonian's literary manuscripts are letters with addressee unknown. Even more than letters, therefore, literature is that mode of communication destined to misfire. When Alfonso loses a roll of pages he has clandestinely taken, their author remarks that "aquel ere el destino natural de la literatura" (p. 337) ["that it was the natural destiny of literature" (p. 368)]. Writing causes Fernanda, in the course of her interminable correspondence with her son and daughter, to lose her sense of time. Presumably writing erodes a sense of time because it is an activity in which the present is strongly elided. The letter is a prospective communication whose consummation is ordinarily deferred. And by virtue of the syntagmatic axis of discourse, all writing, including letters, is prospective—like features of García Márquez's narrative (e.g., the recurring phrase, "muchos años después," "many years later"), or like Fernanda's letters, which are mostly about projected dates for her son's and daughter's returns—if not prophetic, like Melquíades' manuscripts. Writing in the novel is just as frequently retrospective or nostalgic. Simply because it is composed of language, the stuff of memory, writing induces a profound nostalgia in the wise Catalonian both as he scribbles at his desk at the rear of his bookshop and shortly after returns to his native village, whence he sends a deluge of letters to his old friends. Writing from his home in Catalonia, he is soon overtaken by the old enemy nostalgia: "aunque él mismo no parecía advertirlo, aquellas cartas de recuperación y estímulo se iban transformando poco a poco en pastorals de desengaño (pp. 338-39) ["although he himself did not seem to notice it, those letters of recuperation and stimulation were slowly changing into pastoral letters of disenchantment" (p. 370)].

Because of a reciprocity between speaker and hearer (a written text cannot be interrogated by its reader in the same way that a hearer may question a speaker) and because of the presumption that in speech, unlike writing, meaning or thought is transparent to the signs used to reproduce it, speech in the western tradition has been presumed to be a fuller and more immediate mode of communication which writing can only imperfectly emulate. The voice of living speech, Derrida shows, has been a common metaphor for self-presence and for the transparency of signs to the thought in which they were presumed to originate. The more shadowy and impersonal medium of writing, in contrast, introduces a gap between meaning and intent.[10] Even in the work of Saussure, one of the founders of modern semiotics, Derrida exposes the common gesture of privileging speech, which represents the illusory possibility that "the signifier would become perfectly diaphanous due to the absolute proximity to the signified. This proximity is broken when, instead of hearing myself speak, I see myself write or gesture."[11] Because language is fundamentally a network of relays and system of differences whose operations the speaker cannot hope to master, writing, not speech, is the prototype for all communicative acts, as Derrida argues and as *Cien años de soledad* seems to suggest.

The thematics of writing in *Cien años de soledad* indicates that García Màrquez's version of "soledad" is in part another name for the gap between the self and its signs. Might the subject itself, whose identity or definition is ordinarily bolstered by the feeling of solitude, not be the product of such a gap? We are largely constituted, and not merely limited, by the gap between ourselves and the signs we use. Hence, the peculiar lack of pathos associated with the theme of solitude in this novel—a point to which I will be returning shortly. If the subject were merely limited by this gap, then we would have to postulate a subject that is prior to the systems of signs it employs. But the solitude of Cien años is not that of an isolated consciousness anterior to language, and struggling to find the means of self-expression to emerge from its solitude. The solitude of which García Márquez writes is closer to "the essential solitude" that Blanchot connects with the writer.

Admitting that the word "solitude" has been much abused, Blanchot inquires into its "essential" meaning: "Asking this question should not simply lead us into melancholy reflections. Solitude as the world understands it is a hurt which requires no further comment here."[12] Neither does he intend to evoke the pathos of the artist's solitude, "the complacent isolation of individualism," or the individual's "quest for singularity."[13] For Blanchot the more essential solitude has to do with a relation to language, and is revealed most fully in the writer's relation to his or her work (not, by the way, in the writer's relation to the public which consumes or refuses to consume that work). "The writer belongs to the work," writes Blanchot, "but what belongs to him is only a book, a mute collection of sterile words, the most insignificant thing in the world.... And the work, finally, knows him not. It closes in around his absence as the impersonal, anonymous affirmation that it is—and nothing more."[14] If we generalize Blanchot's remarks so that they refer not only to the writer but to any user of language, then I believe we arrive in the proximity of the meaning of solitude in *Cien años de soledad*.

Language, even as it seems to guarantee a well-defined social identity, a solidarity with a class or community of speakers, and even as it helps round the contours of personality, is far from "user-friendly." It is full of ruses: what are commonly taken to be positive entities, words, that only subsequently acquire relations with one another, turn out to be negative terms, relays in a process of endless referral. And it exposes any user to risks: for example, the risk of what Maurice Blanchot calls fascination. To write, according to Blanchot, "is to let fascination rule language."[15] Whereas seeing "presupposes distance, decisiveness which separates, the power to stay out of contact and in contact avoid confusion ... what fascinates us robs us of our power to give sense. It abandons its 'sensory' nature, abandons the world, draws back from the world, and draws us along.... Fascination is solitude's gaze."[16]

García Márquez's version of the theme of solitude is freighted with far less pathos than most twentieth-century variations on the theme. The difference may be accounted for with the help of what I have been arguing is a cryptic theme of the novel: namely, a complicity between language and solitude. Pathos depends upon the belief that a condition might *theoretically* have been prevented, an outcome reversed. To link solitude to language, however, is to deny any such possibility. *Cien años de soledad* takes on what is arguably the predominant theme of literature in the bourgeois era, though in an absolutely eccentric way that disengages it from subjectivity and the pathos of the subject. It is tempting to regard this novel as a critique, rather than merely a further instance, of the theme of solitude. On the other hand, García Márquez shows that solitude, in the non-contingent and therefore non-pathetic form that his novel explores, has no likely social or political cure. In fact, it may be the "soledad" promulgated by language that engenders a false nostalgia for community.[17]

To say that solitude is an effect of language is to say that it is grounded not in the private experience of a subject, but rather, in what has a public or social origin: language. I am not denying, or implying that the novel denies, the socializing function of language. What I am suggesting is that the novel shows a certain non-psychological form of solitude to be fostered by this same socializing agency. Because of their determination by language, both solitude and solidarity cannot be purified of a fictive element. An awareness of the mechanisms of language fictionalizes both solitude and solidarity. A sense of solidarity or community is inconceivable apart from an arbitary, conventional system of signs. And the subject, I have been arguing, might be understood as the product of certain language-effects. Hence the novel's political ambivalence. In spite of its clear sympathies with the political left, the novel seems deeply suspicious of the ideologies of collectivism as well as bourgeois individualism. Each ideology uses the other as a foundation for its own project, a point of origin for its own turning or troping or rebellion. As a consequence, each commits the same error of presuming the other to be something more than an effect of language. More important, that fictive element helps account for the compensatory violence—i.e., a violence to compensate for the fiction's lack of a metaphysical ground—with which each ideology is asserted, not only in the novel, but also in the polarized spheres of twentieth-century politics.

Coda: solitude, the novel, and the reader

The novelist has isolated himself. The birthplace of the novel is the solitary individual, who is no longer able to express himself by giving examples of his most important concerns, is himself uncounseled, and cannot counsel others. To write a novel means to carry the incommensurable to extremes in the representation of human life. In the midst of life's fullness, the novel gives evidence of the profound perplexity of the living. Even the first great book of the genre, Don Quixote, teaches how the spiritual greatness, the boldness, the helpfulness of one of the noblest of men, Don Quixote, are completely devoid of counsel and do not contain the slightest scintilla of wisdom.[18]

My epigraph is taken from one of the most beguiling stories of twentieth-century criticism, Walter Benjamin's essay on Nikolai Leskov, "The Storyteller." Benjamin's essay tells the story of the rise of the novel and decline of the storyteller at the dawn of modern times. What distinguishes the storyteller, according to Benjamin, is "an orientation toward practical interests," an ability to provide counsel, and above all an interest in communicating experience. The rise of the novel is a symptom of the decline of communicable experience, of the value we grant to experience, and of the ability to give counsel from experience. These changes are reflected in a shift in the ways in which stories are consumed: unlike the storyteller and his or her audience, the writer and reader of novels are isolated, no longer in each other's presence.

Might the solitude of *Cien años de soledad* not be, among other things, the novel's way of allegorizing the conditions in which it is produced and consumed, and the hesitancy or inability of this novel (and, as Benjamin argues, the entire novelistic tradition) to provide counsel and to orient itself toward "practical interests"? Macondo's plague of solitude, we might speculate, is the novelist's plague, a reflection of the condition of the storyteller in modern times, a condition also reflected in García Márquez's own remarks on critics and readers of *Cien años de soledad*. Asked if he were curious to learn the secret of his novel's extraordinary success, he replied, "No, no quiero saberlo. Me parece muy peligroso descubrir por qué razones un libro que yo escribí pensando sólo en unos cuantos amigos se vende en todas partes como salchichas calientes."[19] And explaining his dislike for pontificating critics, he suggests that the novel is filled with signs, markers, passwords addressed only to his most intimate friends. Critics,

> con una investidura de pontífices, y sin darse cuenta de que una novela como *Cien años de soledad* carece por completo de seriedad y esta llena de señas a los amigos más íntimos, señas que sólo ellos pueden descubrir, asumen la responsabilidad de descifrar todas las adivinanzas del libro corriendo el riesgo de decir grandes tonterías.[20]

What is striking about these remarks is not the (justifiable) mistrust of critics like myself that they express, but rather the way they radically circumscribe—like the protective circle that Colonel Aureliano Buendía draws around himself—the community to which the story is addressed.

Of course, like much Latin-American fiction, García Márquez's has its roots in the rich soil of a storytelling tradition. It would be tempting to argue that the narrative itself, rooted in orality and community, is itself immune from the infestation of solitude, and indirectly—that is, not through the events of the narrative but through the narration—shows us a way beyond the Buendías' predicament. The book, as Tzvetan Todorov notes, "recrea el ambiente de la realización oral."[21] Does the narrative itself, a quasi-oral performance, make up for the scarcity of oral communication or reported dialogue in the novel? Does the author of *Cien años de soledad* escape the solitude of the writers *within* the novel? Or does the thematics of writing in *Cien años de soledad* anticipate and head off the familiar critical response of granting priority to an oral tradition, an instance of the act, frequently analyzed by Jacques Derrida, of privileging speech over writing? And does that thematics serve to reveal a hidden partnership between language and solitude?

The latter seems to be suggested not only by the proliferation of various forms of writing but also by a related development, the shifts in the narrative's own conceptions of language. Of the many forms of innocence (sexual, political, scientific) that abound at the beginning of the novel, not the least important is the innocent conception of language as an aggregate of signs, a view that informed seventeenth-century philosophy and speculation on language and that was gradually transformed in the development of modern linguistics to that of a system.[22] A naive conception of language as an aggregate of signs is implicit in the narrator's remark on the first page, cited earlier: "El mundo era tan reciente, que muchas cosas carecían de nombre, y para mencionarlas había que señalarlas con el dedo." The notion of language as a collection of names for objects persists through the insomnia plague, when José Arcadio Buendía labels everything in his surroundings in order to resist the erosion of memory. But this episode intimates a shift in the novel's conception of language that will become more pronounced later in the narrative. Language appears to be so strong an aid in transactions with the world that without it things become ghostly, insubstantial. Towards the end of the insomnia, José Arcadio Buendía's hands "parecían dudar de la existencia de las cosas" (p. 48) ["seemed to doubt the existence of things" (p. 54)]. That the loss of language does not yield, together with the collapse of intelligibility, a more vivid and immediate *perception* suggests that the view of language implicit in José Arcadio Buendía's frantic labeling—that of a collection of names for objects—is mistaken. Those hands that doubt the existence of things already suggest a conception of language as a relational system of differences. "Without language," Saussure writes, "thought is a vague, uncharted nebula. There are no preexisting ideas, and nothing is distinct before the appearance of language."[23]

The notion of language as an arbitrary, conventional system of differences "without positive terms" underlies the more problematic attempts at naming that take place later in the novel, when characters experience difficulty giving a name not to objects but to each other's moods and characters. The ability of García Márquez's characters to "read" one another falters in the later chapters of the novel, in which interpretive gestures abound and in which "solitude" would seem to designate the need for characters to interpret one another as well as the freedom and difficulty they experience in doing so. Amaranta's "hardness of heart" suddenly appears to Úrsula to be in truth supreme tenderness. To Fernanda, Amaranta shows "tal dinamismo en las últimas horas que Fernanda creyó que se estaba burlando de todos" (p. 239) ["such vigor in her last hours that Fernanda thought she was making fun of everyone" (p. 261)]. The primary method characters elect to interpret one another late in the novel is to "read" an act, a motive, a trait, or a condition as its binary opposite. After becoming acquainted with Amaranta Úrsula's husband Gastón, Aureliano no longer thought that he was "tan tonto como lo aparentaba, sino al contrario, un hombre de una constancia, una habilidad y una paciencia infinitas, que se había propuesto vencer a la esposa por el cansancio de la eterna complacencia, del nunca decircle que no, del simular una conformidad sin límites" (p. 331) ["as foolish as he appeared, but, quite the contrary, was a man of infinite steadiness, ability, and patience who had set about to conquer his wife with the weariness of eternal agreement, of never saying no, of simulating a limitless conformity" (pp. 361–62)].

These swings (of which there are many more in the last half of the novel) are instances, to be sure, of the novel's hyperbolic or extravagant mode. But more importantly they derive from the differential, relational character of language. The tendency in *Cien años de soledad* of a judgment or interpretation to reverse itself, *and the figure of paradox in general*, are not aberrations, but rather predictable effects of a fundamental law of language, that of reciprocal difference. Each term in a linguistic system is constituted in opposition to others in accordance with Saussure's principle that "in language there are only differences *without positive terms*," that "concepts are purely differential and defined not by their positive content but negatively by their relations with the other terms of the system."[24] If two terms in a binary opposition help constitute each other, then in a very real sense each "refers" to the other and invites the ambitious reader to interpret it as its negation. Solitude itself, which "al mismo tiempo los separaba y los unía" (p. 316) ["separated and united (Aureliano Babilonia and José Arcadio) at the same time" (p. 344)], is a paradoxical condition, an effect of that principle of language, reciprocal difference, that makes such reversals likely or even inevitable methods of interpretation. Since speech (or orality) is as saturated with difference and with traces of non-present meaning as is writing, it is unlikely that it will serve as a simple vaccination against writing's disease of solitude.

Asked about the source of his peculiar blend of realism and myth or fantasy, García Márquez has testified to the influence of an oral storytelling tradition:

> Quizás … la pista me la dieron los relatos de mi abuela. Para ella los mitos, las leyendas, las creencias de la gente, formaban parte, y de manera muy natural, de su vida cotidiana. Pensando en ella, me di cuenta de pronto que no estaba inventando nada, sino simplemente captando y refiriendo un mundo de presagios, de terapias, de premoniciones, de supersticiones, si tú quieres, que era muy nuestro, muy latinoamericano.[25]

But that his grandmother doesn't represent the storytelling tradition for which the European Benjamin expressed nostalgia is clear. Far from possessing an overriding concern for practical interests, she created a magical or supernatural world apart that fascinated the boy by day, but caused him terror by night. It was the grandfather who represented "la seguridad absoluta dentro del mundo incierto de la abuela. Sólo con él desaparecía la zozobra, y me sentía con los pies sobre la tierra y bien establecido en la vida real."[26]

The oral tradition embodied for García Márquez in his grandmother seems at once communal ("muy nuestro, muy latinoamericano") and a schooling in a peculiar form of solitude: the solitude of the work of fiction, the remoteness of the fictional world from "la vida real." The worlds of fictional works are always, like those of his grandmother's stories, "mundos inciertos." To say as much is not to subscribe to a New Critical definition of the literary work as self-sufficient and complete, a world unto itself that provides its own defining criteria. Blanchot offers a different, purely negative, version of the literary work's isolation: "The solitude of the work has as its primary framework the absence of any defining criteria. This absence makes it impossible ever to declare the work finished or unfinished. The work is without any proof.... It can't be verified.... The work is solitary: this does not mean that it remains uncommunicable, that it has no reader. But whoever reads it enters into the affirmation of the work's solitude, just as he who writes it belongs to the risk of this solitude."[27] Somewhat less neutrally than Blanchot, the ending of *Cien años de soledad* conceives of the work on the model of a house from which its characters cannot escape, like the house in Buñuel's *El angel exterminador*. "Before reaching the final line" of Melquíades' saga of the Buendía family, Aureliano Babilonia "had already understood that he would never leave that room" in which he reads (p. 383). Is it possible that the house of fiction hems the reader in no less than its characters? That it is a Buñuelian house that mysteriously entraps its guests? That the solitude of *Cien años de soledad* is most tellingly the reader's own? If I may return to my opening remarks (and thereby fulfill the Buendía fate of circularity) the novel seems to me, in addition to a family chronicle, a saga of the reader's gradual induction into the Buendía clan—and, again, for many reasons stemming from the nature of language and discourse.

Pilar Ternera, we are told, could predict the future

> porque un siglo de naipes y de experiencia le había enseñado que la historia de la familia era un engranaje de repeticiones irreparables, una rueda giratoria que hubiera seguido dando vueltas hasta la eternidad, de no haber sido por el desgaste progresivo e irremediable del eje. (p. 334). [because a century of cards and experience had taught her that the history of the family was a machine with unavoidable repetitions, a turning wheel that would have gone on spilling into eternity were it not for the progressive and irremediable wearing of the axle (p. 364).]

Despite the grinding repetitions of the Buendía family and of the narration itself, the reader cannot escape the madness of repetition, cannot successfully resist becoming part of this "engranaje de repeticiones irreparables." For in addition to the burden of formulating a sequential discourse on the novel, the reader-critic must hunt for repetitive structures, a standard way of reading a novel, as Hillis Miller notes in his recent book on repetition in fiction.[28] Put in a slightly different way, the reader is called upon to develop a "dominant obsession" with one of the various strands or themes of the narrative, somewhat akin to José Arcadio the Seminarist's obsession with excavating the three canvas sacks of gold Úrsula has buried, for the reader of *Cien años* must become an excavator of meanings in order for the novel to cohere. Literature may be defined as a discourse that requires of its readers a dominant obsession. Or as a discourse that poses these alternatives to its readers: to develop a dominant obsession (necessary to generate a reading of the literary text), or to return from one's sojourn in the text empty-handed, without the means to distill a meaning from it.

Nothing resembles the obsessive behavior of García Márquez's characters so much as the behavior of García Márquez's narrative, with its extraordinary recurrences of names, events, personalities, images, phrases, actions, and themes. The verbal tics in *Cien años de soledad* take place not at the level of reported dialogue, as they do, for instance, in Dickens. Dickensian characters are often defined and delineated by a signature expression, one that will survive intact all changes of context. Their speech is often almost entirely repetition. Largely because there is little dialogue in *Cien años de soledad*, most of the repetition takes place at the level of the narration. A past-tense narrative is a particular form of recurrence, namely a recollection, and every reading, including a first reading, is a reconstruction of what is already written. But in addition, every discourse, whether literary or otherwise, entails repetition, if only as a means of ensuring a hegemony of certain terms, key terms that will make reading or interpretation possible. García Márquez's narrative must repeat—and an essay on García Márquez's narrative must repeat—for the same reason that his characters must repeat: otherwise either a life or a discourse will remain formless, an ever-disappearing stream of moments incapable of recalling or echoing one another. It is probable, therefore, that every discourse is a good deal closer to the verbal tics of the Dickensian character or to the compulsively repetitive behavior of the Buendías than we care to imagine.

The reader's very motivation for reading a novel is mirrored in an interesting way by the narrator's remark about Aureliano Babilonia's first expedition into the world: "No le interesó nada de lo que vio en el trayecto, acaso porque carecía de recuerdos para comparar" (p. 310) ["Nothing he saw along the way interested him, perhaps because he lacked any memories for comparison" (p. 337)]. We would like to think that it is only the naive or simple reader—but certainly not the professor of literature—who only notices what s/he is able to connect to his or her own experience, drawing from a fund of memories. But if such a fund of memories is necessary to accrue enough interest to hold the reader of fiction, then perhaps Aureliano Babilonia's predicament is a mirror of our own. As we leave the house in which *we* read for a sojourn in a world we have never before glimpsed, whether what we see along the way interests us will depend on the memories we have for comparison. If so, then the very concept of the "novel" amounts to a paradox, since its consumption depends on its offering substantially not what is novel, but on the contrary what is already a repetition. Or one might say that the novel's apparent "novelty" is a ruse, a disguise that allows the reader to mask his or her own compulsion to repeat (which, I have been arguing, bears an intimate relation to the very possibility of discourse, and need not be interpreted in the quasi-mystical fashion of the later Freud). There is a sense, then, in which the absurd repetitions in *Cien años de soledad*, on both the level of the narration and the level of the narrated events, while seeming to violate the very premises of the genre to which it belongs, instead exposes to view the whirrings and grindings of the mechanism that drives all novels.

In José Arcadio Segundo and Aureliano Babilonia's extraordinary experience of time, the reader will more than likely recognize the accidents that time is prone to in the room in which she or he reads the novel. In the small, isolated room where they attempt to decipher Melquíades' parchments (much like the reader of *Cien años*, also, no doubt, sitting in an isolated chamber, busily deciphering this manuscript of García Márquez's that for many readers might as well have been written in Sanskrit like the parchments), José Arcadio Segundo and Aureliano Babilonia discovered that José Arcadio Buendía, far from being crazy,

> era el único que había dispuesto de bastante lucidez para vislumbrar la verdad de que también el tiempo sufría tropiezos y accidentes, y podía por tanto astillarse y dejar en un cuarto una fracción eternizada. (p. 296) [was the only one who had enough lucidity to sense the truth of the fact that time also stumbled and had accidents and could therefore splinter and leave an eternalized fragment in a room (p. 322)].

That is an apt description also of the experience of a reader of novels, who generally remembers a lengthy narrative by a handful of its most vivid moments, "eternalized fragments in a room."

And because it is already, on the reader's first experience of it, set in the past tense, a narrative is in a good position to infect the reader with the same plague of nostalgia that infests Macondo. In fact, one might say that the reader's burden of memory and nostalgia develop alongside that of the townspeople of Macondo. In the course of the novel Macondo develops from "un pueblo que se hundía sin remedio en el tremedal del olvido" (p. 48) ["a town that was sinking irrevocably into the quicksand of forgetfulness" (p. 54)] to one whose inhabitants are "abatidos por los recuerdos" (p. 324), "bowed down by memories" (p. 353). The condition of Macondo at the beginning of *Cien años de soledad* reflects that of a reader who has just sat down to read a novel, at least a novel set in an imaginary locale like Macondo, whose history the reader cannot possibly know. Toward the beginning of the novel and at the beginning of Macondo's history, it is the lapse of memory, whether personal (e.g., Rebeca's past, which is a blank tablet to her) or collective, that is the salient danger, precisely because the past, and by extension memory or retention of the past, are such precious commodities. And in a sense the world becomes new again—"tan reciente," like the world on the first page of *Cien años de soledad*—for the reader at the beginning of any novel, as he or she temporarily forgets the familiar world while embarking for a sojourn in a new, alternative world. Similarly, the reader's experience will become more and more retrospective as she or he reads toward the end of the fiction, an ending that will in a limited sense destroy him or her—or at least that part of the reader that has invested in a fund of memories of Macondo—as it destroys Aureliano Babilonia. The act of reading, the apocalyptic ending to the novel makes clear, ends in a consuming, not a consummation, leaving the reader with a sense of solitude vis à vis both a world that no longer exists and its inhabitants, with whom s/he is and always was powerless to communicate. Put in a less sentimental way, the novel's apocalyptic ending is designed to frustrate the confident annexation of another territory and culture by the naturally pluralistic and imperialistic reader of novels. For the motives of the reader are mirrored in a sinister way by the imperialism of the banana company, the politics of solitude. The final pages, in their erasure of this newly acquired and distant colony in the empire of the mind, call attention to those motives. They also cause the reader to re-tally the "profits" of his or her enterprise of reading novels. For the reader of novels is habitually anxious about profits, the "return" on or practical benefits of his or her reading.

Not only do the historical senses of the reader and of Macondo's inhabitants develop in tandem, but also the reader is likely to suffer lapses of memory similar to those of the townspeople of Macondo. The narrative's dizzying circularity and the narrator's telescoping of events, his passing over certain events with such rapidity that they are not likely to remain lodged in the reader's memory, induce in the reader something like "la voracidad del olvido, que poco a poco iba carcomiendo sin piedad los recuerdos" (p. 292) ["the voracity of oblivion, which little by little was undermining memories in a pitiless way" (p. 318)] during the biblical deluge visited upon Macondo following the departure of the banana company.

Time for the reader of *Cien años de soledad* holds other hazards as well. In a novel with so many repetitions, the reader is bound to share Fernanda del Carpio's confusion about time as she corresponds with her children in Brussels and Rome:

> Aquella correspondencia interminable le hizo perder el sentido del tiempo.... Se había acostumbrado a llevar la cuenta de los días, los meses y los años, tomando como puntos de referencia las fechas previstas para el retorno de los hijos. Pero cuando éstos modificaron los plazos una y otra vez, las fechas se le confundieron, los términos se le traspapelaron, y las jornadas se parecieron tanto las unas a las otras, que no se sentían transcurrir. (p. 306) [That endless correspondence made her lose her sense of time.... She had been accustomed to keep track of the days, months, and years, using as points of reference the dates set for the return of her children. But when they changed their plans

time and time again, the dates became confused, the periods were mislaid, and one day seemed so much like another that one could not feel them pass (p. 334).]

Often the "points of reference" offered the reader by the narrator—for example, the day that Colonel Aureliano Buendía faced the firing squad—turn out to be misleading, inconsequential events incapable of serving as an origin, endpoint, or point of reference.[29]

And perhaps the power of language to generate the illusion of presence even as we are reading a past-tense narrative is sufficient to duplicate in the reader the confusion of Úrsula in her old age, her inability to distinguish memory from present experience:

> Llegó a revolver de tal modo el pasado con la actualidad, que en las dos o tres ráfagas de lucidez que tuvo antes de morir, nadie supo a ciencia cierta si hablaba de lo que sentía o de lo que recordaba (p. 290). [She finally mixed up the past with the present in such a way that in the two or three waves of lucidity that she had before she died, no one knew for certain whether she was speaking about what she felt or what she remembered (p. 315).]

Those effects of senility are often duplicated in the experience of reading a past-tense narrative. For reading fiction is such a strongly absorptive activity that (with the exception of much modern and postmodern fiction) it usually entails forgetting the differences between three separate systems of temporality: the time of reading, the time of narration, and the time of the narrated events.

Like so many letters in the novel, the novel itself is a problematic letter since, like the literary scribblings of the Catalonian, it is addressed to an unknown recipient. It is another skewed act of communication, and invites comparison with the mysterious letter from an unknown source to José Arcadio Buendía and Úrsula concerning Rebeca. Or with Amaranta Úrsula's "letter of contradictory truths" (p. 374) to Gastón, which elicits an entirely unanticipated response (as this reading might seem entirely unanticipated to the author to whom it responds). Or with Fernanda's delirious letters to her son and daughter speaking of a fabulous inheritance (for in spite of the narrator's cool, even-handed tone, there is a delirium to the contents and shape of the narrative, and the novel does seem to promise its vast and enthusiastic audience a fabulous inheritance, exotic riches of experience, until the ending which seems to suggest that we, like the last of the Buendía line, will instead inherit the wind).

Engaged in the solitary act of reading, the reader's relationship with the inhabitants of Macondo will be neither one of simple intimacy nor one of comfortable distance and superiority. The illusion of intersubjectivity often entailed by fiction is complicated in *Cien años de soledad* by a peculiarity of the narration. As Todorov has observed, it is a novel that is narrated from the point of view of the auditor. Furthermore, both the narrator ("el sujeto enunciante") and the auditor are as unstable as the world of the novel itself, evolving with time like the fictional characters. The auditor's point of view, to which according to Todorov the narrator continually adapts himself, fluctuates throughout the narrative, thereby matching the pluralization of the "sujetos del enunciado," the six generations of Buendías: "el sujeto enunciante no es fijo sino que se amolda al punto de vista cambiante de su auditorio: suscita su interés, completa sus informaciones, prepara la continuación de la historia por medio de indiscreciones; el narrador es por esto tan múltiples y movible como su mismo auditorio."[30] Because of this instability of both narrator and auditor, it becomes difficult to speak of a solidarity among the members of the community formed by audience, narrator, and characters, a solidarity that would be presupposed by the epic, a genre to which *Cien años de soledad* is often compared.[31] The most apt phrase to describe the reader/auditor's relationship with the narrator and with the inhabitants of Macondo may be the "paraíso de la soledad compartida" (p. 288) ["paradise of shared solitude" (p. 313)] of Petra Cotes and Aureliano Segundo. Renouncing the world for the privilege of understanding it for the duration of his or her reading of the novel, the reader shares the destiny of several of Macondo's inhabitants, including Rebeca who is loath to renounce "los privilegios de la soledad" (p. 191) ["the privileges of solitude" (p. 208)], and Rebeca's archenemy Amaranta, who just prior to her death achieves "la comprensión sin medidas de la soledad" (p. 238) ["the measureless understanding of solitude" (p. 260)].

One final mirror that the novel holds up to its readers. On failing to see any evidence of the passage of time following the departure of his wife and daughter, José Arcadio Buendía goes mad, swearing that "the time machine has broken" (p. 81). He is eventually strapped to the trunk of a chestnut tree, that great symbol of permanence, stability, and narrative as well as genealogical unity and coherence. But that his madness is actually extraordinary lucidity is confirmed by the many characters, and the reader as well, who repeat his experience of the breakdown of the "time machine" or concept of linear time. Lucidity and madness converge so frequently in the novel that any reader attempting to decode García Márquez's mysterious manuscript must worry about his or her own condition, whether it is one of lucidity, madness, or, like that of the aged Úrsula, lucidity peeping through madness. And whether a discourse on *Cien años de soledad* can at best aspire to the lucid madness of José Arcadio Buendía. The particular form of madness that the novel serves up to its readers has to do, I have been speculating, with the way language suspends us between solitude and solidarity. This suspension is not of a comfortable kind that allows us to bridge two distinct domains, the public and the private. For the interpretation of "solitude" as a language-effect, rather than marking a privileged interiority apart from the public and social domain of language and utterance, prevents our ever fully "going private." But the novel also suggests that it is doubtful that discourse can under any circumstances be purified of several linguistic and therefore non-psychologically grounded forms of solitude. The solitude of *Cien años de soledad* is the "solitude" of the speaker or writer's suspension between solitude and solidarity that is one of the most maddening features of language.

NOTES

1. *Cien años de soledad* (Buenos Aires: Editorial Sudamericana, 1967); *One Hundred Years of Solitude*, trans. Gregory Rabassa (New York: Avon Books, 1971). All subsequent references are to these editions.

2. C. S. Peirce, *Collected Papers*, ed. C. Hartshorne and P. Weiss (1932; rpt. Cambridge, Mass.: Harvard Univ. Press, 1960), II, 12.

3. J. Derrida, "Differance," in *Speech and Phenomenon and Other Essays on Husserl's Theory of Signs*, trans. David B. Allison (Evanston: Northwestern Univ. Press, 1973), pp. 129–60.

4. Umberto Eco, "Looking for a Logic of Culture," in *The Tell-Tale Sign: A Survey of Semiotics*, ed. Thomas Sebeok (Lisse: The Peter de Ridder Press, 1975), p. 12.

5. See Northrop Frye, "Dickens and the Comedy of Humors," in *The Victorian Novel: Modern Essays in Criticism*, ed. Ian Watt (Oxford: Oxford Univ. Press, 1971), pp. 47–69.

6. For a reading of the novel in the context of Proust's project of recuperating the past, a reading that proceeds from different premises than mine, see John P. McGowan, "A la Recherche du Temps Perdu in *One Hundred Years of Solitude*," *Modern Fiction Studies*, 28 (1982–83), 557–67.

7. This position has been set forth by Octavio Paz in *The Labyrinth of Solitude: Life and Thought in Mexico*, trans. Lysander Kemp (New York: Grove Press, 1961). He writes, "To live is to be separated from what we were in order to approach what we are going to be in the mysterious future. Solitude is the profoundest fact of the human condition." As García Márquez's novel

also suggests, a preeminent form of solitude is our division not from others but from our past and future selves. It is a condition that, according to Paz, is revocable with age. With maturity, time for us "takes on meaning and purpose and thus becomes history, a vivid, significant account with both a past and a future. Our singularity—deriving from the fact that we are situated in time, in a particular time which is made up of our own selves and which devours us while it feeds us—is not actually abolished, but it is attenuated and, in a certain sense, 'redeemed.' Our personal existence takes part in history" (p. 195). We are redeemed from solitude by recognizing a continuity in time that we call history; the isolated moments of our lives become reunited, as well as united with a larger suprapersonal process. But in the novel, this pathway out of solitude is barred by the disruption of the linear sense of time and of the genealogical metaphor on which the concept of linear time is based. See, for instance, Patricia Tobin, *Time and the Novel: The Genealogical Imperative* (Princeton: Princeton Univ. Press, 1978), which contains a chapter on *Cien años de soledad*.

8. Derrida, *Speech and Phenomenon*, p. 61f.

9. Kenneth Burke, *The Philosophy of Literary Form: Studies in Symbolic Action*, 3rd. ed. (Berkeley: Univ. of California Press, 1973), p. 26.

10. This argument informs much of Derrida's work. See, for example, *Of Grammatology*, trans. Gayatri Chakravorty Spivak (Baltimore: The Johns Hopkins Univ. Press, 1976).

11. Derrida, *Speech and Phenomenon*, p. 80.

12. Maurice Blanchot, *The Space of Literature*, trans. Ann Smock (Lincoln: Univ. of Nebraska Press, 1982), p. 21.

13. Blanchot, p. 21.

14. Blanchot, p. 23.

15. Blanchot, p. 33.

16. Blanchot, p. 32.

17. García Márquez's analysis of the relation between the nostalgia for community on the part of a solitary person or culture and political violence bears comparison with Thomas Mann's analysis of this same relationship in *Doktor Faustus*. I suspect that the difference that would emerge from such a comparison is that Mann's novel, unlike García Márquez's, does not expose this desire for a lost sense of community as a false nostalgia for what never was, a mirage generated by "solitude." On the relation of a desire for community to a humanist metaphysics see Jean-Luc Nancy, "La communauté désoeuvrée," *Aléa*, 4 (1983), 11–50.

18. Walter Benjamin, *Illuminations*, ed. Hannah Arendt, trans. Harry Zohn (New York: Schocken Books, 1969), pp. 87–88.

19. García Márquez, *El olor de la guayaba: Conversaciones con Plinio Apuleyo Mendoza* (Barcelona: Editorial Bruguera, 1982), p. 113.

20. García Márquez, *El olor*, p. 104.

21. Tzvetan Todorov, "Macondo en París," *Texto Crítico*, 11 (1978), p. 38.

22. For an account of this shift, see Stephen K. Land, *From Signs to Propositions: The Concept of Form in Eighteenth-Century Semantic Theory* (London: Longman, 1974).

23. Ferdinand de Saussure, *Course in General Linguistics*, ed. Charles Bally and Albert Sechehaye, trans. Wade Baskin (New York: Philosophical Library, 1959), pp. 111–12.

24. Saussure, pp. 117, 120.

25. García Márquez, *El olor*, p. 84.

26. García Márquez, *El olor*, p. 18.

27. Blanchot, p. 22.

28. J. Hillis Miller, *Fiction and Repetition: Seven English Novels* (Cambridge, Mass.: Harvard Univ. Press, 1982).

29. Todorov notes that episodes, rather than being recounted from beginning to end, usually proceed "del centro a la periferia." See "Macondo en París," pp. 39–40.

30. Todorov, p. 41.

31. Several critics have commented on the relation of *Cien años de soledad* to epic, among them Todorov, *op. cit.*, and Susanne Kappeler, "Voices of Patriarchy: Gabriel García Márquez's *One Hundred Years of Solitude*," in *Teaching the Text*, ed. Susanne Kappeler and Norman Bryson (London: Routledge and Kegan Paul, 1983), pp. 148–63.

IDDO LANDAU

Metafiction as a Rhetorical Device in Hegel's History of Absolute Spirit and Gabriel Garcia Marquez' One Hundred Years of Solitude

"Metafiction" has been defined as "fictional writing which self-consciously and systematically draws attention to its status as an artefact in order to pose questions about the relationship between fiction and reality."[1] Of course, many literary works include some element of self-awareness or self-reference. However, the term "metafiction" is usually applied only to those cases in which the self-relation is used to undermine our traditional understanding of the distinction between fiction and reality. Metafiction shows the rhetorical power to do so by relating a fictional work to *itself*, by including discussions *of* a fictional work as *part* of it. Thus, the distinction between the actual fictional work we are reading and holding in our hands as part of reality and the fictional world which the work describes is blurred or collapses. But this also gives metafiction the rhetorical power to create a feeling of absurdity, subverting temporal, logical, and literary distinctions of before and after the work's completion, of historical narrative and fiction, of true and false. Further, by relating the fictional work to itself, metafiction can also create an impression of recursive chains. Indeed, it is for such "anarchistic" uses that metafiction is most frequently employed, and it is on them that research on it concentrates. However, research has neglected to see that the blurring of fiction and reality can be used not only to confound these categories, but (retaining these categories) to convince the reader that

From *Clio* 21 (Summer 1992). © 1992 by Iddo Landau.

the apparent fictional narrative being read is real, that the events described have actually been happening. Further, it frequently has been overlooked that metafiction has been used as a rhetorical persuasive device not only in literature but also in philosophy. In this paper I shall compare and contrast two uses of metafiction as a rhetorical device, one philosophical, the other literary. The first is the metafiction at the end of Hegel's history of Absolute Spirit. The second, which illuminates dimensions of the first by both similarities and differences, is the use of metafiction at the end of Garcia Marquez' history of Macondo in *One Hundred Years of Solitude*.

In his various writings, Hegel shows how the history of Spirit progressively manifests itself in time as political history, history of legal systems, of art, of religion, and of philosophy. Even the non-temporal, logical categories by which Spirit returns to itself in the *Logic* are present as the essential, guiding concepts of the philosophical systems which progressively appeared in the history of philosophy. All events in these fields are moments in the process by which Spirit strives, through its different manifestations, to achieve self-realization.

The various moments and categories are interrelated by means of the dialectical movement which synthesizes them into ever more inclusive categories. Near the close of the system the Absolute Spirit itself is discussed. The system first describes the manifestation of Absolute Spirit in art, then in religion, and finally in philosophy, the development of which, as of other fields, is outlined from the earliest and most primitive forms. Thus the discussion progresses gradually through the generations up to the modern era. After dealing with Kant, the system discusses German Idealism and shows how Absolute Spirit expresses itself yet more fully with each successive philosopher. But at the end we realize that the final stage of the complete development of Absolute Spirit and of philosophy is the very system we have just been reading.[2] The end of the system (story, narration), then, is the system (story, narration) itself (*Phenomenology of Spirit* 3:14). The story is the story of itself. In *it* Absolute Spirit reaches self-consciousness and self-realization. Although we did not realize it at the time, from the very start we were already reading the system from the point of view of final truth.

Thus, the end of all historical (and logical) events discussed in the system is a fuller and richer understanding of the events themselves. In the end of the system there is a return to previous stages and categories understood in a richer, more complete way. The end of the events discussed in the system is the realization of each one's place in the context of all the other events and processes, of the necessity of their development through the dialectical method, and of their being manifestations of Absolute Spirit. In short, it is the recognition of their necessary development in the process which has led to this very recognition.

Hegel uses metafiction at the end of his system to achieve several philosophical purposes. However, I shall first discuss metafiction as a literary device to create in the reader the impression that what is read is true. The metafictional turn imparts this feeling in the following ways:

1. We are in the habit of seeing truth as the congruence between description and described. Thus we see the statement "snow is white" as true if and only if snow is indeed white. Now, at the end of Hegel's system we reach a special situation: what is described in the system is the very systematic description itself. The system includes assertions about something, but this something is these very assertions. Since the description describes the description itself, a discrepancy between them seems impossible. The metafiction creates the illusion that what we read is true. (Note, however, that this perception is not necessarily correct. A description or a sentence can be about itself and still be false as in, "This sentence is in French and has five words.")

2. The presumption of truth is created not merely by reading a narrative which portrays how a certain system describes itself, but also by the fact that the system *about* which we are reading is the very same system *which* we are reading; it is present right before us. Since the system we are reading about is actually held in our hands, we feel that at least part of what is discussed in the system is real. Put differently, when at the end of the system we understand that this end involves our very present understanding of it, we feel that the system is realized. Thus, we are led to feel by association that the rest of the things described are also realized and hence truly described.

3. The system's special relationship with the reader exists from yet another aspect. The different stages and processes described lie along the Absolute Spirit's way toward self-realization. But according to Hegel, Absolute Spirit cannot reach self-realization by itself; it can do so only through human beings. Thus, the full self-realization of Absolute Spirit (through the self-consciousness of human beings who realize the truth of what is said in the system) described in the system is found to be identical with the reader's all too coincidentally similar self-conscious reading, understanding, and accepting of the system. We as readers, then, are led to believe that the system actually describes the act by which we read it and accept it as true. Put differently, metafictional description induces the supposition of an identity of reference between what is described in the system and the reader's experience which contributes to the impression that what is written in the system is true.

4. Because of the metafiction, there is a sense of synoptical

recapitulation at the end of the system. When we discover that the end of the system is the whole coherent system we have been reading, this whole is recalled at once. But the cohering of theses and descriptions is taken as a mark of truth. Thus, again, a feeling that what we read is true is aroused.

5. Thanks to the metafiction, the system says of itself some things that indeed are true. For example, it says of itself that it discovers itself in the end and indeed it does. Similarly, it says that it reconciles all previous categories, and indeed it does. Thus, when it says or implies of itself that it is true, we may come to think by association that this too is the case.

6. The metafictional turn also creates the impression of a circular mutual affirmation between things said all through the system and things said at its end. Throughout the system we read that we are to reach the complete truth at the end. Then, at the end, we read that all we have been reading up to now is the complete truth. Thus, we feel that what we have read earlier is true, and hence that what is said at the end of the system is true.

Note that the mutual affirmation as constructed by Hegel creates a stronger feeling of truth than would have been aroused by a simple assertion such as "all you have been reading here is true." The affirmation as we are given it appears as a natural continuation of what has been happening in the system according to the dialectical method. In a way, it *relies* on the system. A simple assertion that "all you have been reading here is true" would not be a natural continuation of the system up to that point and would be based on nothing.

All these factors impart a feeling that what we have been reading is true. The feeling is enhanced by the fact that when the system relates to itself all these factors appear at once. Had they appeared one by one, at different stages, the effect would have been weaker. Moreover, the feeling of truth is further enhanced by the fact that these factors are not explicit, and we are less likely to examine critically and consciously whether they indeed are evidence for the truthfulness of the system—an inspection which might lead to a diminution of the impression of truthfulness.

Gabriel Garcia Marquez' *One Hundred Years of Solitude*[3] narrates in a semi-realistic and semi-fantastic way the history of the village Macondo and of a leading family in it—the Buendias. With a few exceptions, the events of this history are narrated chronologically. In the final chapter we learn that one of the last members of the family, Aureliano (lover of Amaranta-Ursula), finds and reads the writings of one Melquiades, composed many years earlier, at the time of José Arcadio Buendia, one of the founders of Macondo. While reading he realizes that these texts discuss the whole history of Macondo and the Buendias. He finds in Melquiades everything that has happened to his family, including the fact that he, Aureliano, has found the book and is reading it, and that this very understanding dawns on him.

Many similarities exist, then, between Garcia Marquez' description of the history of Macondo and Hegel's description of the history of Absolute Spirit. Both works narrate a historical process. In both a metafictional turn appears toward the end of the history, referring directly to itself and reflecting all the other events. In both the metafictional turn takes us back to earlier events, adding to them a dimension which up to that point we had not seen; in the final, metafictional stage we have a richer understanding of the earlier stages.

But most importantly, in both cases the metafictional turn imparts a feeling that what we have read is true. We feel that what we have been reading is not merely a description, but also part of reality. Like Hegel, Garcia Marquez achieves this effect in several ways:

1. As in Hegel, so in the world narrated by Garcia Marquez the description and the described are to some extent one. Aureliano finds a book which describes Macondo and his family, including his finding and reading the book at that very moment. Aureliano is used to the distinction between a description of reality and reality itself. But when he sees that the description of reality is about itself—about the very description he is reading—the description belongs for him to both worlds: the one described and the one he himself experiences. Thus, the events discussed in the book seem more persuasively true to him, and to the extent that we identify with him, to us as well.

2. Again analogously to Hegel, apart from the metafiction that exists *inside* the narrative, there is also one between the narrative and our actual world. Since what is written in *One Hundred Years of Solitude* is similar to what is written in the book Aureliano reads, we feel it might be the same book. In other words, we feel that the book we are reading is the book in Aureliano's hands. It is true, our book was written not by Melquiades but by Garcia Marquez, and not in Sanskrit but in Spanish. But there is sufficient similarity between the two to leave us with the feeling that they are nevertheless one and the same book. Hence, we feel that the book we are reading describes itself and thus both belongs to the world of fiction and that of reality. The distinctions between reality and fantasy are to a large extent obliterated.

3. Again, the metafiction at the end of the book creates a recapitulative synoptic feeling. When Aureliano finds and reads a book which narrates all the events we have been reading about (including his very finding and reading of the book), all we have been reading about at once comes together

as a unity. And since we frequently take the coherence and unity of theses and events to be a mark of their truth, the unity we feel at the end of the book has the effect of truthfulness.

4. Again, thanks to metafiction Melquiades' book can say of itself some things which are indeed true. For example, it says that it discusses Macondo's history and indeed it does. It says that it was found by Aureliano and indeed it was; it is being read by Aureliano at that very moment and indeed it is. It even says that it *says* that it is being read by Aureliano and it does. Thus, when the book implies of itself that it is true, Aureliano, and to a certain extent we, come to think that this is so.

Note that since it is not completely certain that the book Aureliano is reading is the same as ours, some of the things the book says of itself are true only for his and not for ours. For example, we cannot be sure that the book's saying of itself that it was found by Aureliano is true of our book as well as of Aureliano's.

5. Again as before, the metafictional turn creates a feeling of mutual affirmation between the things said all through the system and those said at its end. At the end of the story a book is found that implies that everything that has happened in the story is true; but the book itself is also part of the story, and hence it also is again true. (And again, the affirmation can be taken to continue: since it says, or indicates, that the whole story is true, and since it is part of the story, it again seems true, and thus what it says is true.)

Note that here again this mutual affirmation creates a stronger feeling of truth than a simple assertion that "all you have been reading up to now is true" would have done, since the former seems a natural continuation of the story we have been reading, and the latter would have been foreign to it.

6. In Garcia Marquez, the book found by Aureliano toward the end of the narrative was already fully written out a few generations earlier, at the time of Macondo's founder, José Arcadio Buendia. Thus, both Aureliano and we feel that the events that took place after the writing of the book but which are narrated in it and in *One Hundred Years of Solitude*, were necessary. If the book described events which happened after it was written, then it seems that these events *had* to happen as they did. Thus, there seems to be not only a simple congruence between what was written in Melquiades' book and what happened outside it, but also a necessary, magical congruence. And this enhances our feeling that what was described in the book (which is by and large what is described in *One Hundred Years of Solitude*) was true.

All these factors impart a feeling that what we have been reading is true, a feeling enhanced by the fact that when the book refers to itself all the factors appear at once. Had they appeared separately, their effect would have been weaker. Moreover, none of these factors are explicit. Thus, we are less likely to investigate whether they are indeed evidence for the truth of what the book says—an examination which might weaken the impression of truthfulness.

The similarity between Hegel's history of Absolute Spirit and Garcia Marquez' history of Macondo is clear. It lies, for example, in the appearance of metafiction toward the end of the histories and in the use to which it is put, viz., enhancing the feeling that what is written in them is true. Moreover, even the ways in which metafiction is used to enhance the feeling of truth in these two works are almost similar.

But there are also differences between metafiction in Hegel and in Garcia Marquez. In almost every way, Hegel uses metafiction more fully. Whereas Garcia Marquez uses metafiction only for a literary purpose—to create an aesthetic effect—in Hegel it also advances philosophical purposes. For instance, it allows him to avoid unfounded axioms. The starting point of the system is grounded when the end relates back to it, certifying its necessity in the complete system. Likewise, Hegel uses metafiction to avoid infinite regress. The dialectical method does not go on infinitely, continuously pushing the end forward, but, by relating to itself, overcomes the notion of the end altogether. Similarly, through metafiction Hegel keeps the system continuously dynamic. The movement does not stop once self-consciousness of Absolute Spirit has been reached, but, through the self-relation, continues circularly. Hegel also uses metafiction to help synthesize all the notions contained in the system, yet, since he is an anti-reductionist, without endangering their individual uniqueness. Thus, whereas in the previous phases of the dialectic each inclusive category does not represent the unique natures of the categories included in it, the final category in the system—i.e., the system itself—does.

But even rhetorically, i.e., only in imparting a feeling of truth, Hegel employs this self-relation more fully than Garcia Marquez. First, whereas at the end of Hegel's system we feel that its reading is both experienced by us and implied in the system, we do not feel at the end of Garcia Marquez' novel that *our* reading of it is mentioned or implied in any way. The literary "hero" of Hegel's system—the Absolute Spirit—is taken to exist not only in the system but also in the real world and to achieve self-realization through human beings. Hence we feel that there is a congruence between the acceptance of the system by human beings as described or implied in the system, and our actual acceptance of the system in the real world. The literary "hero" of *One Hundred Years of Solitude*—the Buendia family and Aureliano himself—is not taken to exist in the real world, nor to be connected to our reading of the book in any other way. Thus we are not tempted to feel that our reading the book is described or implied in it.

Second, at the end of Hegel's system we feel that the system we are reading about is similar to the system we actually hold in our hands, whereas at the end of *One Hundred Years of Solitude* we are less certain that the book we are reading about is similar to the one we actually hold. Although the book we are reading about is similar in some respects to the one in our hands (both discuss the same events, including Aureliano's finding and reading it), they are different in others (composed by different authors in different languages). Thus, whereas readers of Hegel's system feel that there is a complete similarity between the system they are reading and the system they are reading about, readers of Garcia Marquez feel that there is only a partial similarity between the book they are reading and the book they are reading about. Hence, the feeling of truthfulness in Garcia Marquez' novel, although still aroused, is weaker.

Third, Hegel's system says of itself a greater number of true things than Aureliano's find does of itself. Hence, the propensity to feel that other things said in these works are also true is shakier in Garcia Marquez than in Hegel.

Fourth, although mutual metafictional affirmation exists in both works, it is stronger in Hegel's, where the final, metafictional stage is clearly anticipated. Moreover, this stage is taken to be a logical continuation of the previous ones. In Garcia Marquez, on the other hand, Aureliano's finding and reading the book is not anticipated. Moreover, it is not seen as a logical, necessary conclusion of the previous stages, but as merely one event among many. Thus in Garcia Marquez the end of the book and the events which precede it still mutually affirm each other, but less powerfully than in Hegel.

All in all, then, Hegel uses metafiction more fully and to achieve stronger effects of truthfulness. There is one way, however, in which Garcia Marquez' use of metafiction creates a stronger feeling of truth than Hegel's: the fact that Melquiades' book describes events that happen after it was written creates a feeling that the congruence between it and the events it (as well as *One Hundred Years of Solitude*) describes is a necessary one. In Hegel's system, on the other hand, the historical realization of the system is taken to be completed only at the end of the narration. It is true that at the end of the system we see that in a sense its end is present also in the beginning; but not in its full form, as is Melquiades' book.

How can the differences between Hegel's and Garcia Marquez' uses of metafiction be explained? Why does the latter not follow Hegel's model of the use of metafiction in all respects, but only in some and less emphatically? The differences have to do with the different natures of their works. Hegel aims at presenting a philosophical, scientific account of the history of Absolute Spirit. The reality or truthfulness of his account is very important to him. Garcia Marquez, on the other hand, is consciously presenting a literary work, and thus he does not aim at convincing his readers that what he is writing is true. His book balances on the fine line between reality and fantasy and he wants to avoid "crossing the border" to reality, as Hegel did. In other words, he does not wish to convey a sense of complete reality, but to leave an impression that the border between fantasy and reality is blurred. Hence, unlike Hegel, he does not use metafiction in all the ways he could.

But if Hegel is interested in using metafiction to achieve the strongest possible effect of truthfulness, why does he not also use Garcia Marquez' method and take his system to exist in its full form already at the beginning of his narrative? This is not possible; Hegel's system is directional. It starts with categories which in themselves are wrong insofar as they are partial, but through an ordered process (the dialectical movement) become incorporated into larger and larger contexts which add to their understanding. Completeness and truth are achieved only at the end of the system, when the development of Absolute Spirit reaches its final stage. Hence, for Hegel the final point could not fully exist at the beginning. In *One Hundred Years of Solitude*, on the other hand, there is no feeling for a gradual philosophical progress. The plot does not seem to go in any specific direction, and at the end of the saga there is a marked feeling of decadence. Hence, there is no difficulty in taking Melquiades' book to exist not only at the end of the story, but also at the beginning.

To sum up, Hegel uses metafiction both as a philosophical device, a structure which fulfills genuine philosophical functions, and as a literary device, a rhetorical tool used to impart to the reader a *feeling* that what is read is true. Does the unmasking of Hegel's use of metafiction as a rhetorical device undermine the philosophical cogency of his system? The answer is no. The existence of a literary device in a philosophical system is in itself irrelevant to the philosophical cogency of the system, which should be measured only by philosophical standards (e.g., the consistency of its theses, the tenability of its assumptions, or the soundness of its arguments). However, identifying the rhetorical devices present in a system is helpful in assessing its philosophical cogency; it enables us to distinguish between philosophical elements in the system (including the philosophical use of metafiction) and rhetorical ones, and thus not to be affected by the latter when only the former should be taken into account.

NOTES

1. Patricia Waugh, *Metafiction: The Theory and Practice of Self-Conscious Fiction* (London: Methuen, 1984), 2.

2. *Lectures on the History of Philosophy*, 20: 460 ff.; all references to Hegel's works are from the Suhrkamp edition, ed. Eva Moldenhauer and Karl Markus Michel, 20 vols. (Frankfurt am Main: 1969). See also *Phenomenology of Spirit* 3:80, 582-83, 589, 591; *Science of Logic* 6:549-50, 567-69, 573; *Encyclopedia of the Philosophical Sciences* section 577.

3. Trans. Gregory Rabassa (New York: Harper and Row, 1970).

DEAN J. IRVINE

Fables of the Plague Years: Postcolonialism, Postmodernism, and Magic Realism in Cien años de soledad [One Hundred Years of Solitude]

Akin to the strain of poststructuralist theory Jacques Derrida practices in his essay "The Law of Genre," governed by "a principle of contamination, a law of impurity, a parasitical economy" and initiated as "a sort of participation without belonging—a taking part in without being part of" (59), the diagnostic method of this paper purports to enchain strains of postcolonialism and postmodernism as a model for the theory and practice of magic realism in Gabriel García Márquez's *Cien años de soledad* [*One Hundred Years of Solitude*].[1] The model of magic realism under construction here is a double-helix: postcolonialism as one genetic strand, postmodernism as the other. In this model, magic realism and the magic realist text are collocated in the twists and gaps of this double discourse, that is, the discursive of enchainment of postcolonialism and postmodernism.

In the essays collected by Lois Parkinson Zamora and Wendy B. Faris for the anthology *Magic Realism: Theory, History, Community* (1995), postmodernism and postcolonialism entwine as nonidentical theoretical discourses in the genealogy of magic realism. Like postmodernism and postcolonialism, magic realism is recognized as a historical product of the discourses of modernism and colonialism. It is accepted among commentators on magic realism that in 1925 the German art critic Franz Roh coined the term in reference to post-expressionist visual art.[2] As well,

From *Ariel: A Review of International English Literature* 29, 4 (October 1998) © 1998 by The Board of Governors, The University of Calgary.

critics generally observe an alternative concept of magic realism, though not the term itself, pioneered by the Cuban novelist Alejo Carpentier, who coined the phrase "lo real maravilloso" ["the marvelous real(ity)"] in his preface to *El reino de este mundo* (1949) in order to disengage his literary practice from that of European surrealism (Zamora and Faris 7; Connell 96). Critics often cite Carpentier's term "the marvelous real(ity)" in conjunction with Roh's "magic realism," sometimes conflating the two terms. In parsing each term, Liam Connell underscores the problematic correlation: "that Carpentier uses *maravilloso* rather than *magico*, and that critics who wilfully mistranslate Carpentier's phrase or, by not translating, imply a simple correspondence between 'the marvelous reality' and Magic Realism—not only obscure a genealogy which includes a Surrealist interest in the marvellous (Breton, *What Is Surrealism?*), but also invoke a number of cultural attributes which follow from the magical ... which are not, I think, similarly associated with the marvellous" (96). The "magic realism" versus "the marvelous real(ity)" debate is now so widespread that I cannot detail it beyond its critical origins: in short, because Roh writes from a European, post-expressionist perspective and Carpentier from a Latin American, post-surrealist perspective, the debate inevitably invites antagonism among critics. Angel Flores's landmark essay "Magical Realism in Spanish American Fiction" (1995) recognizes neither Roh nor Carpentier as the starting point for what he names the "new phase of Latin American literature, of magical realism," opting instead for Jorge Luis Borges's 1935 collection *Historia universal de la infamia* (189). Although Flores does not cite Borges's 1932 essay "El arte narrativo y la magia" as an originary moment in the theorization of magic realism, the widely acknowledged influence of Borges on García Márquez suggests that critics should also consider Borges's essay as a prototype. Moreover, to situate Borges in relation to García Márquez not only avoids the Roh versus Carpentier debate, but also diagnoses better the strain of magic realism in *Cien años de soledad*, especially in the context of Latin American postmodernism and postcolonialism.

Theo D'haen presents the history of the term magic realism as one coextensive with the history of the term postmodernism. For D'haen, magic realism is the progeny of the continental European avant-garde (post-expressionism, surrealism) and, as such, constitutes a discourse "ex-centric" to the "privileged centre" of Anglo-American modernism (203). Citing a consortium of international postmodern theorists (Douwe Fokkema, Allen Thiher, Linda Hutcheon, Brian McHale, Ihab Hassan, David Lodge, and Alan Wilde), D'haen locates the origin of the term postmodernism with the Latin American critic Frederico de Onís in the 1930s (192-93).[3] D'haen suggests that the co-emergence of magic realism and postmodernism in the

1930s occurs when "Latin America was perhaps the continent most ex-centric to the 'privileged centres' of power" (200); that the international acceptance of postmodernism would eventually absorb its "ex-centric" discourse into the "privileged centre" discourses of Europe and the United States; and that, at the same time, magic realism would establish itself as the province of "excentric" cultures including, but not limited to, Latin America. At present, D'haen determines, "in international critical parlance a consensus is emerging in which a hierarchical relation is established between postmodernism and magic realism, whereby the latter comes to denote a particular strain of the contemporary movement covered by the former" (194). D'haen's reconciliation of the critical histories of magic realism and postmodernism leads him to conclude that postmodernism enacts "aesthetic consciousness-raising" and magic realism "political consciousness-raising ... within postmodernism" (202), or, to borrow from Fredric Jameson's *The Political Unconscious*, that their narratives perform "a socially symbolic act." D'haen does not propose an excavation of the Latin American roots of postmodernism in the same way he does the continental European origins of magic realism, but rather advocates a recognition of the dissemination of the theory and practice of postmodernism and magic realism in an international context.

To read the genealogies of postmodernism and magic realism D'haen constructs without skepticism, however, would be to contract the strain of historical amnesia experienced by the town of Macondo in *Cien años de soledad*. D'haen's genealogies infect us with postmodern strains of García Márquez's insomnia and banana plagues; they block our memory of the histories of colonialism and repress theories of postcolonialism designed to unblock our memory. The culturally specific location of the term postmodernism with the Latin American critic Onís is part of the history of colonialism; that is, the appropriation of *postmodernismo* by an international critical community clearly constitutes a kind of colonization of the Latin American term. In fact, to some Latin American critics, the current international application of the term postmodernism to Latin American fiction represents a type of discursive recolonization.

As a reaction to international postmodern theorists, the Latin American critic Iris Zavala decries "the uncritical, normative, univocal acceptance of '(post)modernism' ... in order to object, from a Hispanic perspective, to some Anglo-American and French currents of the philosophical and meta-theoretical mainstream and their tendency to apply the term (post) modernism globally and a-historically" (96). Zavala reminds Anglo-American and continental European critics of the historical and cultural specificity of *modernismo* in Hispanic literature.[4] In augmenting Onís, Zavala then posits a modified definition of *postmodernismo*:

> If one wants to conserve the term 'postmodernism' at least a somewhat more reliable point of reference from which to ask the question is needed. Going back to Onís, we must agree that modernism is the literary expression, and the stylistic motivation, of the entry of the Hispanic world into modernity, adding to his definition that it is the product of a severe rupture with past modes of production and of the emergence of industrialized societies.... This argument can be qualified if modernity is understood as an unfinished project in some societies and cultures, a program which constantly rewrites itself.
>
> (105)

Bill Ashcroft offers an important corrective to the ahistorical and global applications of the term postmodernism to which Zavala objects. The discursive colonization and recolonization of *postmodernismo* is but one international incident in the long history of colonialism in Latin America. According to Ashcroft, "the colonization of Latin America obliges us to address the question of postcolonialism at its roots, at the very emergence of modernity" (13). In this view, not only does modernity originate with European imperial expansion and colonization of Latin America, but also "postmodernity is coterminous with modernity and represents a radical phase of its development ... in the same way postcolonialism is coterminous with colonization, and the dynamic of its disruptive engagement is firmly situated in modernity" (15). "My contention," Ashcroft continues, "is that postcolonialism and postmodernism are both discursive elaborations of postmodernity, which is itself not the overcoming of modernity, but modernity coming to understand its own contradictions and uncertainties" (15). Ashcroft's placement of the discursive category postmodernism at the advent of postmodernity in Latin America obviously extends beyond the reach of postmodern theorists who locate the origin of postmodern aesthetics at the moment of Onís's coinage in the 1930s. Moreover, Ashcroft's conjunction of modernity and postmodernity and enchainment of postcolonialism and postmodernism in a Latin American context constitutes a double discourse analogous to the discursive code of magic realism in *Cien años de soledad*. For at the originary juncture of postcolonialism and postmodernism, *Cien años de soledad* narrates the "contradictions and uncertainties" that follow from imperial expansion, colonization, and modernization of Latin America.

Like postmodernism, magic realism is subject to colonial imperatives. For instance, those critics who limit the term magic realism to its first issue from the European avant-garde claim that "Latin American reality is colonized by the term" (Janes 102). Yet even in a Latin American context, Borges's attempt to reconcile the difference between magic and narrative realism promulgates a colonial imperative. The tacit colonialist project of Borges's essay "El arte narrativo y la magia" is made manifest in his explication of narratives of colonization: William Morris's *Life and Death of Jason* (1867), Edgar Allen Poe's *Narrative of Arthur Gordon Pym* (1838), and José Antonio Conde's *Historia de la dominación de los árabes en España* (1854-55). To interpret the law of cause and effect in narrative, Borges enjoins Sir James Frazer's reduction of magic in *The Golden Bough* to "una conveniente ley general, la del la simpatía, que postula un vínculo inevitable entre cosas distantes, ya porque su figura es igual—magia imitativa, homeopática—ya por el hecho de una cercanía anterior—magia contagiosa" ("El arte" 88) ["a convenient general law, the Law of Sympathy, which assumes that 'things act on each other at a distance through a secret sympathy,' either because their form is similar (imitative, or homeopathic, magic) or because of a previous physical contact (contagious, or contact, magic)" ("Narrative" 37)]. Rather than recognize difference, Borges intends "demonstrar que la magia es la coronación o pesadilla de lo causal, no su contradicción" ("El arte" 89) ["to show that magic is not the contradiction of the law of cause and effect but its crown, or nightmare" ("Narrative" 37)]. Borges's sense of the non-contradictory relation between the law of magic and the law of cause and effect betrays a colonialist tendency to assimilate the former (the premodern discourse of the colonized) to the latter (the modern discourse of the colonizer). As a corollary, the colonizer's discourse is contaminated once it comes into contact with the colonized's discourse, and vice versa; this principle of discursive contamination is manifest, as we will see, in the narratives of the insomnia and banana plagues in *Cien años de soledad*. For at the colonial juncture of the premodern and the modern, narrative discourse functions according to "a principle of contamination, a law of impurity" (Derrida, "Law" 59); this strain of narrative discourse inhabits magic realism, which originates not with Borges himself in the 1930s, but with the colonial narratives of the earliest explorers of Latin America.

Adopting this long historical view, Amaryll Chanady identifies the colonial origins of magic realist narratives in Latin America. Chanady represents and contests several different definitions of magic realism: the portrayal of a supernatural indigenous world-view (magic) combined with the description of contemporary political and social problems (realism); the perception of Latin America as exotic; and the representation of an authentic geographical, ideological, and historical expression of Latin America (50). "In fact," Chanady posits, "magic realism is often defined as the juxtaposition of two different rationalities—the Indian and the European in a syncretic fictitious world-view based on the simultaneous existence of several entirely different cultures in Latin America" (55). Like Borges's "El arte narrativo y la magia," Chanady's location of the emergence of magic realism is coterminous with the emergence of colonialism in Latin America, but Chanady's recognition of difference between Latin American cultures counters Borges's notion of the non-contradictory relation between discursive worlds. For Chanady, neither term in the self-contradictory phrase magic realism is therefore reducible or separable: "magic" cannot be reduced to a premodern native world-view, nor "realism" to a modern European world-view. As a discursive formation, magic realism in the Latin American context elaborates those "contradictions and uncertainties" that arise out of the co-existence of multiple cultures and discourses, and that stem from the simultaneity of imperial colonization and modernization.

Chanady cites Spanish exploration narratives in order to illustrate the history of colonialism as a metanarrative subtending Latin American magic realism.[5] Her first text, from Bernal Díaz del Castillo's *Historia verdadera de la conquista de la Nueva España* on the discovery of the Aztec capital of Tenochtitlán, speaks to colonial textual representations of the new world as fabulous: "[Éstas] grandes poblaciones ... parecía a las cosas y encantamento que cuentan en el libro de Amadís ... y aun algunos de nuestros soldados decían que si aquello que veían si era entre sueños. Y no es maravillar que yo aquí lo escriba desta manera, porque hay que ponderar much en ello, que no sé como lo cuente, ver cosas nunca oídas ni vistas y aun soñadas, como vimos" (238) ["These great towns ... seemed like an enchanted vision from the tale of Amadís. Indeed, some of our soldiers asked whether it was not all a dream.... It was all so wonderful that I do not know how to describe this first glimpse of things never heard of, seen or dreamed of before" (*Conquest* 214; qtd. in Chanady 50)]. Her second text, from Hernán Cortés's second *relación* to Emperor Charles V in 1520, presents a colonial encounter with the new world congruous with the experience García Márquez ascribes to the inhabitants of Macondo: "son tantas y de tantas calidades, que por la prolijidad y por no me ocurrir tantas a la memoria, y aun por no saber poner los nobres, no las expreso" (*Cartas* 52) ["there are so many," that is, things in the New Continent, "and of so many kinds, that because of the great number of them and because I do not remember them all, and also because I do not know what to call them, I cannot relate them" (Chanady 51)].[6] García Márquez, in the opening paragraph of *Cien años de soledad*, introduces a fictional world analogous to the "unnamed" continent faced by Spanish explorers: "El mundo era tan reciente, que muchas cosas carecían de nombre, y para mencionarlas había que señalaras con el dedo" (9) ["The world was so recent that many things lacked names, and in order to indicate them it was necessary to point" (11)]. This condition of namelessness in *Cien años de soledad* predicates the meta-narrative of colonial history. The lack of language necessary to name the colonized world points to the formation and awareness of discursive gaps, disruptive postcolonial sites of "contradictions and uncertainties" at the very origins of colonization in Latin America.

Situating the concept of magic realism in a postcolonial context, as Stephen Slemon proposes, "can enable us to recognize continuities within literary cultures that the established genre systems might blind us to": continuities, that is, between contemporary magic realist texts and texts written at earlier stages of a culture's literary and colonial history ("Magic Realism" 409). The magic realist text enters into a dialogue with genres of colonial and pre-colonial history and mythology; this dialogism marks Latin American magic realism as postcolonial discourse. For this reason, Slemon writes, there is "the perception that magic realism, as a socially symbolic contract, carries a residuum of resistance toward the imperial centre and to its totalizing systems of generic classification" ("Magic Realism" 408). Like D'haen's conception of magic realism as a postmodernist discourse, Slemon holds that magic realism as a postcolonial discourse performs "a socially symbolic act." According to Slemon, the agon between narratives and the decentering of dominant metanarratives of generic classification characterize the magic realist text as postcolonial:

> In the language of narration in a magic realist text, a battle between two oppositional systems takes place, each working toward the creation of a different kind of fictional world from the other. Since the ground rules of these two worlds are incompatible, neither one can fully come into being, and each remains suspended, locked in a continuous dialectic with the "other," a situation which creates disjunction within each of the separate discursive systems, rending them with gaps, absences, and silences. ("Magic Realism" 409)

For García Márquez, the absence of language adequate to describe the phenomenal, unnamed world is signified through the "gaps, absences, and silences" in the magic realist text of *Cien años de soledad*. These silences and memory gaps are fore-grounded in the insomnia plague, where precolonial and colonial discursive systems collide, and again in the banana plague, where neocolonial imperialist and judicial discourses delegitimate and erase the local political histories of the banana workers' revolt and of their massacre. But are such contestations between narratives and collisions between discursive worlds limited to magic realism as a postcolonial discourse?

Brian McHale argues in *Postmodernist Fiction* that one of the functions of the postmodern study of ontology as the "theoretical description of a universe" is to ask such questions as:

> What is a world? What kinds of world are there, how are they constituted, and how do they differ? What happens when different kinds of world are placed in confrontation, or when boundaries between worlds are violated; What is the mode of existence of a text, and what is the mode of existence of the world (or worlds) it projects? How is a projected world structured? And so on. (10)

These questions lead McHale to propose the double thesis that "the dominant of postmodernist fiction is *ontological*," whereas "the dominant of modernist fiction is *epistemological*" (9, 10) and functions as if to ask such questions as:

> What is there to be known? Who knows it? How do they know it, and with what degree of certainty? How is knowledge transmitted from one knower to another, and with what degree of reliability? How does the object of knowledge change as it passes from knower to knower? What are the limits of the knowable? And so on. (9)

What I am forwarding here—as a heuristic strategy—is less the modernist or postmodernist status of *Cien años de soledad* than the notion that the novel, to import McHale's thesis, "dramatizes the shift of dominant from problems of *knowing* to problems of *modes of being*—from an epistemological dominant to an ontological one" (10). In my view, the shift from questions of knowledge to questions of being is dramatized in the acts of reading embedded in *Cien años de soledad*.[7] Melquíades's parchments—and the epistemological task of reading, interpreting, and translating them taken up by successive generations of the House of Buendía—are revealed in the final pages by Aureliano Babilonia, the last Buendía, to be the narratives of his own life and his family's history: the parchments, written prior to the events of the novel by Melquíades himself. Suddenly the embedded reader, Aureliano Babilonia, and the implied reader of *Cien años de soledad* are thrown, as Robert Alter puts it, into an "ontological vertigo" (6). For Aureliano Babilonia, the world of the parchments he reads is indistinguishable from his world, the world of Macondo: for him, reading as a mode of interpretation gives way to a mode of being. So too, for the implied reader of the novel, a mode of interpretation is transformed into a mode of being. The text of *Cien años de soledad* therefore looks back upon both the implied and the embedded reader as "un espejo hablado" (350) ["a speaking mirror"] (383).

The ontological status of the implied reader is called into question in what Jon Thiem names a "fable of textualization" (231):

> Not being literally in the text permits the reader to enjoy the exciting and dangerous fictional world without having to suffer the consequences of living in this world.... In a textualization this balance is upset. The world of the text loses its literal impenetrability. The reader loses that minimal detachment that keeps him or her out of the world of the text. The reader, in short, ceases to be reader, ceases to be invulnerable, comfortable in his or her own armchair, and safely detached, and instead becomes an actor, an agent in the fictional world. (239)

But what is the ontological status of this displaced reader? If we consider the relationship between reader and text in terms of the hierarchized binary of "self" and "other," the displacement of the reader from the privileged position of "self" into the position of "other" performs what Linda Hutcheon in *A Poetics of Postmodernism* terms "aesthetic and political consciousness-raising" (73). From a postcolonial perspective, Chanady argues that the exotic representations of Latin America in magic realist texts are "directed towards a reader who has little knowledge of certain aspects of Latin American nature and civilization. That reader need not be European—he can also live in a large Europeanized metropolis like Buenos Aires" (52). Chanady's location of the (euro) centric reader in relation to the postcolonial, ex-centric text recalls Ashcroft, Griffiths, and Tiffin's construction of post-colonial theory and practice in *The Empire Writes Back*; this displacement of the magic realist text from privileged centres of imperial culture represents a postcolonial discourse writing back from a place "other" than "the" or "a" centre. While D'haen may theorize "the notion of the ex-centric, in the sense of speaking from the margin, from a place 'other' than 'the' or 'a' centre ... [as] an essential feature of that strain of postmodernism we call magic realism" (194), it is critically important to theorize writing back from a place "other" than the centre in that strain of postcolonialism we call magic realism.

The discursive enchainment of postmodernism and postcolonialism— the double-helix of magic realism in *Cien años de soledad*—is foregrounded in what I am calling fables of the plague years: the tales of the insomnia plague and the banana plague. The isolation of these fabulous tales in the text is perhaps analogous to the medical practice of quarantine; but it is, in keeping with my metaphor of the double helix, an attempt to isolate elements of a double code of postmodernism and postcolonialism in the generic code of magic realism. I will first isolate the insomnia plague in chapter three of *Cien años de soledad* as a kind of allegorical narrative, a fable in the broad sense of a fabulous tale, of the theoretical concerns of magic realism as a postmodernist and postcolonialist narrative discourse. Proceeding from the theoretical symptomology of the insomnia plague, I will then isolate the conditions of the banana plague beginning in chapter twelve of *Cien años de soledad* as an allegorical narrative of the sociopolitical concerns of magic realism and as a counter-colonialist and imperialist narrative discourse.

Prior to analysis of such theoretical allegories, however, an account of the insomnia plague itself is in order: an orphan—who is somehow related to Úrsula and José Arcadio Buendía but remembered by neither, who is subsequently named Rebeca (after her mother, so named in a letter of introduction), who refuses to speak until she is spoken to in the Guajiro native language by the servant Visitación, who actually speaks fluently in the Guajiro and Spanish languages, and who suffers from the vice of eating earth until she is cured by Úrsula's homeopathic medicine—is revealed to be a carrier of the insomnia plague which infects the House of Buendía with the illness of insomnia. Visitación relates to the Buendías the critical manifestation of the insomnia plague—the loss of memory—which José Arcadio Buendía dismisses as a native superstition. The town of Macondo is then infected with the illness by eating Úrsula's candied animals. In order to remedy the inevitable loss of memory, José Arcadio Buendía first marks every object in the town with its name and later appends a kind of instruction manual for each object, so transforming the town of Macondo into a text. He then embarks on the construction of "la mánquina de la memoria" (48) ["the memory machine" (54)]: an encyclopedic text in imitation of the marvelous inventions of the gypsies, "se fundaba en la posibilidad de repasar todas las mañanas, y desde el principio hasta el fin, la totalidad de los conocimientos adquiridos en la vida" (48) ["based on the possibility of reviewing every morning, from beginning to end, the totality of knowledge acquired during one's life" (54)]. Despite José Arcadio Buendía's attempts to forestall the decimation of the collective memory of Macondo with his strategies to inscribe and transcribe the totality of language-based knowledge, the insomnia plague ultimately effects the complete erasure of linguistic signifiers and signifieds: "Así continuaron viviendo en una realidad escurridiza, momentáneamente capturada por las palabras, pero que había de fugarse sin remedio cuando olvidaran los valores de la letra escrita" (47) ["Thus they went on living in a reality that was slipping away, momentarily captured by words, but which would escape irredeemably when they forgot the values of the written letters" (53)]. As an alternative system to José Arcadio Buendía's memory machine, the fortune teller Pilar Ternera conceives "el artificio de leer el pasado en las barajas como antes había leído el futuro. Mediante ese recurso, los insomnes empezaron a vivir en un mundo construido por las alternatives inciertas de los naipes" (48) ["the trick of reading the past in cards as she had read the future before. By means of that recourse the insomniacs began to live in a world built on the uncertain alternatives of the cards" (53)]. In the end, the panacea for the insomnia plague, restoring meaning to the meaningless yet textualized world of Macondo, is procured by the gypsy Melquíades. He returns as if from the dead, for it is believed that "la tribu de Melquíades, según contraron los trotamundos, había sido borrada de la faz de la tierra por haber sobrepasado los límites del conocimiento humano" (40) ["Melquíades' tribe, according to what the wanderers said, had been wiped off the face of the earth because they had gone beyond the limits of human knowledge"] (45). While José Arcadio Buendía and Pilar Ternera face the problem of meaning in terms of interpretive or epistemological strategies, the problem of the insomnia plague is revealed to be ontological, a theoretical description of a world "beyond the limits of human knowledge," an ontology of the magical real known only to Melquíades.

From the position of postmodernism, I interpret the insomnia plague in terms of what Thiem calls a "fable of textualization," that is, a type of textualization which takes place when "the world of the text literally intrudes into the extratextual or reader's world" (236). Textualizations, Thiem writes, "partake of a dreamlike quality which aligns them with a host of other magic realist devices and motifs.... [T]he oneiric resonance of textualization..., like so many other dream occurrences,... arises out of the literalization of a common metaphor" (237). The literalization of common metaphors, such as plague and illness in *Cien años de soledad*, parallels the argument of Susan Sontag's book *Illness as Metaphor*, which opens with a kind of fable:

> Illness is the night-side of life, a more onerous [and oneiric] citizenship. Everyone who is born holds dual citizenship, in the kingdom of the well and in the kingdom of the sick. Although we prefer to use only the good passport, sooner or later each of us is obliged, at least for a spell, to identify ourselves as citizens of that other place. (3)

Analogous perhaps to the manner in which we speak of "master narratives," Sontag refers to "master illnesses" (71): so in the phrase "illness as metaphor," metaphor functions as a narrative in miniature. But Sontag urges the demystification of illness as a poetic figure. To argue that García Márquez literalizes the metaphor of "plague" or "illness" forces Sontag's point that "illness is *not* a metaphor" (3). In the textualized town of Macondo, the "illness" is literalized as a text inscribed upon a extratextual world. Thus in a "fable of textualization" such as "la peste del insomnio" (44) ["the insomnia plague" (50)], where "the world of the text literally intrudes into the extratextual or reader's world," both *lector in fabula* (embedded reader) and (perhaps more tentatively) *lector ex fabula* (implied reader) literally become contaminated with the illness of insomnia.[8]

For the oneiric citizen of Macondo, the insomnia plague also stages the exhaustive possibilities of postmodernist metafiction:

> Los que querían dormir, no por cansancio sino por nostalgia de los sueños, recurrieron a toda clase de métodos agotadores. Se reunían a conversar sin tregua, a repetirse durante horas y horas los mismos chistes, a complicar hasta los límites de la exasperación el cuento del gallo capón, que era un juego infinito. (46)

> [Those who wanted sleep, not from fatigue but because of the nostalgia for dreams, tried all kinds of methods of exhausting themselves. They would gather together to converse endlessly, to tell over and over for hours on end the same jokes, to complicate to the limits of exasperation the story about the capon, which was an endless game (51)].

The fictions developed by the insomniacs of Macondo recall John Barth's theorization of postmodernist fiction as "'the literature of exhausted possibility'—or, more chicly, 'the literature of exhaustion'" ("Literature of Exhaustion" 64). The metafictional implication, of course, is the theorization of a "literature of replenishment" (Barth, "Literature of Replenishment" 193): the restoration of dream narratives, that is, the metanarratives of the unconscious. But postmodernist metafiction in the insomnia plague does not deliver the panacea; it theorizes the deferral of sleep, the endless game of exhaustion, the automation of insomnia.

Reading the insomnia plague in the context of a magic realist strain of postmodernism, subtended by Lyotard's definition of the postmodern condition as "incredulity toward metanarratives" (xxiv), demonstrates a corrosion of the semiotic chains of signifier and signified, a collapse of metalinguistic systems of referentiality, and a world without access to legitimation of knowledge based on metanarratives about knowledge. Yet meaning is restored to the world by way of Melquíades's panacea, a magical remedy perhaps for the postmodern condition. But the ontology of the panacea is, of course, but a nostalgia for what Derrida calls the *pharmakon* (*Dissemination* 95ff).

Reading the insomnia plague in the context of a magic realist strain of postcolonialism requires attention to the specific history of a marginal character—Visitación. That the insomnia plague is the same one which exiled Visitación and her brother Cataure from "un reino milenario en el cual eran príncipes" (44) ["an age-old kingdom where they had been prince and princess" (49-50)] suggests that one mutation of the insomnia plague is the history of European imperialism and colonialism in which the critical manifestation of amnesia (loss of memory) effects the violent erasure and expulsion of indigenous people and their cultures. For Visitación, "su corazón fatalista le indicaba que la dolencia letal había de perseguirla de todos modos hasta el último rincón de la tierra" (44) ["her fatalistic heart told her that the lethal sickness would follow her, no matter what, to the farthest corner of the earth" (50)]. For José Arcadio Buendía, "se trataba de una de tantas dolencias inventadas por las super-sticíon de los indígenas" (44-45) ["it was just a question of one of the many illnesses invented by the Indian's superstitions" (50)]. Documentation of lethal sickness in colonial history would support Sontag's point that illness is not a metaphor and give evidence to prove that for colonized people illness is neither a metaphor nor a superstition. Yet the fabled representation of "an age-old kingdom" foregrounds the fabulous origins of the illness of insomnia and the fabulous narrative of the insomnia plague itself. The dialogic form of magic realism in a postcolonial context, then, incorporates the genre of the fable from an immemorial time in Visitación's age-old indigenous culture. According to Chanady, the incorporated genre of the fable in magic realism also originates in the fabulous tales of explorer narratives. To reiterate Chanady's point, "magic realism is often defined as the juxtaposition of two different rationalities—the Indian and the European in a syncretic fictitious world-view based on the simultaneous existence of several entirely different cultures in Latin America" (55). The double code of the insomnia plague in a postcolonial context thus enlists magic realism in what Rawdon Wilson calls the "analysis of postcolonial discourse as the mode of a conflicted consciousness, the cognitive map that discloses the antagonism between two views of culture, two views of history ... and two ideologies" (222-23). Wilson's analysis occasions one final speculation on the double cultural, historical, and ideological code of the insomnia plague: that is, while a colonial strain of the insomnia plague effects Visitación's exile from "an age-old kingdom," it could be argued also that a postcolonial strain of the insomnia plague effects the temporary erasure of the colonial imperialist system of naming. If only for a short spell, as it were, the world of Macondo is suspended in a fabled primordial narrative of namelessness.

Given the strain of colonial imperialism evident in the insomnia plague, the magic realist narrative of "la peste del banano" (199) ["the banana plague" (217)] exhibits the exposure of the inhabitants of Macondo to the sociohistorical epidemic of *neo*colonial imperialism. After the construction of the railroad into Macondo by one of Colonel Aureliano Buendía's illegitimate sons, Aureliano Triste, "no sólo para la modernización de su industria, sino para vincular la población con el resto del mundo" (192) ["not only for the modernization of his business but to link the town with the rest of the world" (209)], the town is exposed to what is, in effect, a modern plague of industrialization and neocolonial imperialism. The railroad, as an effective and historically precedented vehicle for neocolonial imperialism, is the catalyst for the banana plague. Moreover, the narrative of the banana plague and the modernization of Macondo by railroad evidences Jameson's definition of magic realism, which "depends on a content which betrays the overlap or the coexistence of precapitalist with nascent capitalist or technological features" (311).

As a conduit to multinational corporations, the railroad first brings about the "invasión" (197) ["invasion" (215)] and recolonization of Macondo by "los gringos" (197) ["the gringos" (214)], which provokes the town-dwellers to speculate on the relation between recolonization and their past experience of the catastrophic effects of civil war:

> No hubo, sin embargo, mucho tiempo para pensarlo, porque los suspicaces habitantes de Macondo apenas empezaban a preguntarse qué cuernos era lo que establa pasando, cuando el pueblo se había transformado en un campamento de casas de madera con techos de zinc, poblado por forasteros que llegaban de medio mundo en el tren.... Dotados de recursos que en otra época estuvieron reservados a la Divina Providencia, modifacaron el régimen de lluvias, apresuration el ciclo de las cosechas, y quitaron el río de donde estuvo siempre y lo pusieron con sus piedras blancas y sus corrientes heladas en el otro extremo de la población, detrás del cementerio.... Tantos cambios ocurrieron en tan poco tiempo, que ocho meses después de la visita de Mr. Herbert [the banana company representative] los antiguos habitantes de Macondo se levantaban temprano a conocer su proprio pueblo. (196, 197, 198)

> [There was not much time to think about it, however, because the suspicious inhabitants of Macondo barely began to wonder what the devil was going on when the town had already become transformed into an encampment of wooden houses with zinc roofs inhabited by foreigners who arrived on the train from

halfway around the world.... Endowed with means that had been
reserved for Divine Providence in former times, they changed the
pattern of the rains, accelerated the cycle of the harvest, and
moved the river from where it had always been and put it with its
white stones and icy currents on the other side of the town,
behind the cemetery.... So many changes took place in such a
short time that eight months after Mr. Herbert's visit the old
inhabitants had a hard time recognizing their own town (214,
215)].

That the droves of foreigners coming to Macondo by the railroad and
occupying the town are described as "una invasión tan tumultuosa e
intempestiva" (197) ["a tumultuous and intemperate invasion" (215)] invokes
a discourse signifying a neocolonialist invasion; this invasion of Macondo,
therefore, is a recolonization of colonial space. When the authors of *The
Empire Writes Back* argue that "the construction or demolition of houses or
buildings in postcolonial locations is a recurring and evocative figure for the
problematic of postcolonial identity" (28), it suggests that the neocolonialist
invaders settle in Macondo and so transform it into a postcolonial location.
For a definition of the postcolonial in such a context, Slemon proposes that
"the concept proves most useful not when it is used synonymously with a
post-independence historical period in once-colonized nations but rather
when it locates a specifically antior *post*-colonial *discursive* purchase in
culture, one which begins in the moment that colonial power inscribes itself
onto the body and space of its Others" ("Modernism's Last Post" 3). Taken
together, the invasion of Macondo, the construction of encampments, the
rerouting of the river, and the magical alteration of meteorological and
seasonal cycles thus signify the inscription of neocolonial imperialism on an
already colonial location. The invasion of Macondo even extends into the
Buendías' home when "la invasión de la plebe" ["the plebeian invasion"] of
foreigners comes to inhabit and transform the house into "un alboroto de
mercado" (199) ["a marketplace" (216)], and thereafter recolonize the home
of the ancestral colonizers of Macondo, the House of Buendía. However, as
a counter-narrative strategy, García Márquez's defamiliarization of the
historical representation of a neocolonial invasion through the narrative
discourse of magic realism serves to destabilize rather than monumentalize
the history of neocolonial imperialism represented by the invasion of
Macondo.

The invasion is only a preliminary symptom of the banana plague, not
the plague itself. Instigated by the Buendías' hospitable offer of bananas to
Mr. Herbert, who arrives in Macondo as a hot-air balloon businessman and

amateur entomologist, the subsequent "plebeian invasion" by rail and later land survey by "un grupo de ingenieros, agrónomos, hidrólogos, topógrafos y agrimensores que durante varias semanas exploration los mismos lugares donde Mr. Herbert cazaba mariposas" (196) ["a group of engineers, agronomists, hydrologists, topographers, and surveyors who for several weeks explored the places where Mr. Herbert had hunted his butterflies" (213)], leads to the banana company's invasion of Macondo. The banana plague lies dormant for a year following the arrival of Mr. Herbert, after which the invasion of Macondo comes to fruition: "Había pasado más de un año desde la visita de Mr. Herbert, y lo único que se sabía era que los gringos pensaban sembrar banano en la región encantada que José Arcadio Buendía y sus hombres habían atravesado buscando la ruta de los grandes inventos" (199) ["More than a year had gone by since Mr. Herbert's visit and the only thing that was known was that the gringos were planning to plant banana trees in the enchanted region that José Arcadio Buendía and his men had crossed in search of the route to the great inventions" (216)]. Just as the great inventions, the products of capitalist industrialization and ideology, arrive by rail, so too do the banana company and the banana plague, the producers and products of neocolonial imperialism and its ideology. They invade Macondo by the same route. The colonization of "the enchanted region," the barrier isolating the town from the industrial world, thus signifies the exposure of Macondo and its inhabitants to a particular ideological strain of neocolonial imperialism, that is, the banana plague.

The invasion and settlement, exploration and mapping, and later martial government of Macondo by the banana company and its plebeian workers work through the ideology and militant practice of colonial imperialism, though in the modern guise of multinational industrial capitalism. Colonel Aureliano Buendía's planned armed resistance to this neocolonial hegemony—"una conflagración mortal que arrasara con todo vestigio de un régimen de corrupción y de escándalo sostenido por el invasor extranjero" (210) ["a mortal conflagration that would wipe out the vestiges of a regime of corruption and scandal backed by the foreign invader" (229)]—gestures toward a postcolonial resistance narrative, but remains unrealized for the reason that his ideological position, as a militant civil revolutionary, is virtually powerless against the multinational and anonymous forces backing the new colonizer, the banana company. Colonel Aureliano Buendía's dream of "la guerra total" (210) ["the total war" (228)] against the unspecified and unspecifiable "foreign invader" is a nostalgic remnant of an outworn ideology. The imperialist ideology of the new world colonizer, symbolized by the House of Buendía, is absorbed and then displaced by the neocolonial imperialist ideology of multinational industrial capitalism, symbolized by the banana company. Hence the naturalization of this neocolonial imperialist ideology in Macondo is signified by its penetration into the quotidian routines of the House of Buendía:

> La fiebre del banano se había apaciguado. Los antiguos habitantes de Macondo se encontraban arrinconados por los advenedizos, trabajosamente asidos a sus precarios recursos de antaño, pero reconfortados en todo caso por la impresión de haber sobrevido a un naufragio. En la casa siguieron recibiendo invitados a almorzar, y en realidad no se restableció la antigua rutina mientras no se fue, años después, la compañía bananera. (217)

> [The banana fever had calmed down. The old inhabitants of Macondo found themselves surrounded by newcomers and working hard to cling to their precarious resources of times gone by, but comforted in any case by the sense that they had survived a shipwreck. In the house they still had guests for lunch and the old routine was never really set up again until the banana company left years later (236)].

Like a latent disease, the "banana fever" settles into remission; its narrative recedes but does not disappear because its carrier is the House of Buendía, whose narrative is *Cien años de soledad*. Diagnosed by his wife Fernanda to be a carrier of "la sarna de los forasteros" (217) ["the rash of the foreigners" (237)], José Arcadio Segundo, who is later employed as a foreman with the banana company, not only infects the House of Buendía with the neocolonial imperialist ideology of banana plague, but also realizes the narrative of resistance against the same ideological strain.

"Illnesses have always been used as metaphors to enliven charges that a society was corrupt or unjust" (72), Sontag writes in the introduction to her analysis of sociopolitical disease metaphors. For instance, Colonel Aureliano Buendía's metaphor of militant resistance that "would wipe out the vestiges of a regime of corruption and scandal backed by the foreign invader" at once deploys the figurative language of a plague, but it simultaneously redeploys the figure in order to attack it, as it were, using the plague metaphor to counteract the sociopolitical conditions of neocolonial imperialism embodied by the banana plague. As a figure of postcolonial discourse, the banana plague carries a politicized narrative of invasion and resistance; it is a socially symbolic narrative of neocolonial imperialist ideology and postcolonial resistance to this ideological strain. However, the enactment of resistance to the sociopolitical corruption and injustice signified by banana plague is, significantly, not carried out by Colonel Aureliano Buendía, but by an actual carrier of the plague, José Arcadio Segundo.

While the former fable of the plague years, the insomnia plague, presents a positive condition of namelessness, a utopian moment of the deinscription of colonial imperialist power, the latter, the banana plague, presents a negative act of erasure, a dystopian moment of the disempowerment and later depopulation of the banana workers. Like the narrative of the insomnia plague, the banana plague narrates a crisis of representation, but in the context of judicial and political discourse, and a loss of referential meaning, in the context of the banana workers' legal demands against the banana company. Reaper-like harbingers of the death of referentiality in the discursive arena of the court, "[l]os decrépitos abogados vestidos de negro que en otro tiempo asediaron al coronel Aurelano Buendía, y que entonces eran apoderados de la compañía bananera, desvirtuaban estos cargos con arbitrios que parecían cosa de magia" (255) ["[t]he decrepit lawyers dressed in black who during other times had besieged Colonel Aureliano Buendía and who now were controlled by the banana company dismissed those demands with decisions that seemed like acts of magic" (279)]. Masters of illusion and the deferral of meaning, the lawyers represent deft poststructuralist practitioners of judicial discourse; their professional capacity, absorbed into the neocolonial imperialist power structure of the banana company, serves to exercise a sociopolitical hegemony over postcolonial subjects, namely, the banana workers. That the lawyers' "acts of magic" can cloak the neocolonial imperialist reality of the banana company speaks to the danger of discursive fabulation as a rhetorical and narrative device; that is, the reappropriation of magic realism into the judicial discourse of neocolonial imperialism strategically erases and ineffectuates the oppositional narrative discourse of postcolonialism. This discursive erasure of persons through the operations of fabulous judicial processes is evident in the concatenation of events prior to the massacre of the banana workers:

> Los luctuosos abogados demostraron en el juzgado que aquel hombre [Mr. Brown, a banana company executive] no tenía nada que nadie pusiera en duda sus argumentos lo hicieron encarcelar por usurpador.... Cansados de aquel delirio hermenéutico, los trabajadores repudiaron a las autoridades de Macondo y subieron con sus quejas a los tribunales supremos. Fus allí donde los illusionistas del derecho demostraron que las reclamaciones carecían de toda validez, simplemente porque la compañía bananera no tenía, ni había tenido nunca ni tendría jamais trabajadores a su servico, sino que los reclutaba ocasionalmente y con carácter temporal.... [Y] se estableció por fallo de tribunal y se proclamó en bandos solemnes la inexistencia de los trabajadores. (255, 256)

[The mournful lawyers showed in court that that man had nothing to do with the company and in order that no one doubt their arguments they had him jailed as an impostor.... Tired of that hermeneutical delirium, the workers turned away from the authorities in Macondo and brought their complaints up to the higher courts. It was there that the sleight-of-hand lawyers proved that the demands lacked all validity for the simple reason that the banana company did not have, never had had, and never would have workers in its service because they were all hired on a temporary and occasional basis.... [A]nd by a decision of the court it was established and set down in solemn decrees that the workers did not exist (279)].

For Slemon, one of the ways in which the postcolonial is distinguished from the postmodern depends upon the different theorization of the referentiality of language. While the postmodern text "necessarily admits a provisionality to its truth-claims" (2), the postcolonial text maintains "a mimetic or referential purchase to textuality," a claim which admits "the positive production of oppositional truth-claims" ("Modernism's Last Post" 5). However, if the textual referents (contracts, degrees, laws) are governed by a judicial and political system which is controlled by a neocolonial power such as the banana company, the postcolonial purchase to textuality is rendered meaningless and powerless. On the one hand, then, the positive production of oppositional truth-claims subtends the banana workers' contestation of the banana company as a postcolonial resistance narrative; on the other hand, the provisionality of truth-claims underlies the sleight-of-hand lawyers' proof of the non-existence of both Mr. Jack Brown and the banana workers. The lawyers' poststructuralist language games, as a postmodernist strain of magic realist narrative discourse, thus overpower the banana workers' resistance narrative, as a postcolonial strain of magic realist discourse. This double-handed discursive logic ultimately effects the "real" massacre and disappearance of three thousand banana workers who "did not exist."

The prognosis for the banana plague is that of terminal illness. As a historiographic realist narrative—that is, a narrative based on textualized versions of history—the massacre of the banana workers might have terminated with the dissemination of "un bando nacional extraordinario, para informar que los obreros habían obedecido la orden de evacuar la estación, y se dirigían a sus casas in caravanas pacíficas" (262) ["an extraordinary proclamation to the nation which said that the workers had left the station and returned home in peaceful groups" (286)]. Such a narrative, an official record of history sanctioned by the neocolonial imperialist agenda of the banana company, would have erased the other narrative of three thousand banana workers, massacred, then stacked and exported "en el orden y el sentido en que se transportaban los racimos de banano" (260) ["in the same way in which they transported bunches of bananas" (284)]. The collision between these two narratives, one of official neocolonialist history and the other of unofficial postcolonialist history, creates a discursive situation in which both of the separate narratives are rent by silences, absences, and gaps in that each is negated by the existence of the other. Magic realist narrative discourse allows for the coexistence of such contradictory narratives of history. In the postmodernist strain of magic realism, Linda Hutcheon would describe this crisis of representation as "historiographic metafiction" (106)—insofar as the banana massacre narrativizes the construction of historical narratives (although this designation would be dependent upon the textual referent of official history, that is, the neocolonial imperialist textualization of history). In the postcolonial strain of magic realism, conversely, I would posit José Arcadio Segundo's unofficial account of the history of the banana company as a postcolonial resistance narrative. José Arcadio Segundo, the only survivor of the massacre, lives to pass on to Aureliano Babilonia, the last Buendía, "una interpretación tan personal de lo que significó para Macondo la compañía bananera, que muchos años después, cuando Aureliano se incorporara al mundo, había de pensarse que contaba una versión alucinada, porque era radicalmente contraria a la falsa que los historiodores habían admitido, y consagrado en los textos escolares" (296) ["such a personal interpretation of what the banana company had meant to Macondo that many years later, when Aureliano became part of the world, one would have thought that he was telling a hallucinated version, because it was radically opposed to the false one that historians had created and consecrated in the schoolbooks (322)]. What the foregoing attests is how the magic realist text stages a crisis of representation in which the double discourse of postmodernist and postcolonialist narratives, official and unofficial histories, acts out its contestations and contradictions.

Turning back to the final pages of *Cien años de soledad*, which I have already interpreted in terms of a postmodernist code of textualization, an alternate thesis presents itself and a reading in terms of a postcolonial decoding of historical, colonial narrative. In these final pages Aureliano Babilonia deciphers Melquíades's parchments to reveal the historical conditions of colonialism, that is, the absurd history of Sir Francis Drake attacking Riohacha and hunting alligators with cannons and stuffing them as trophies for Queen Elizabeth, which predicates the narrative of the House of Buendía: "Sólo etonces descubrió que Amaranta Úrsula no era su hermana, sino su tía, y que Francis Drake había asaltado a Riohacha solamente para que ellos pudieran buscarse por los labernitos más intrincados de la sangre, hasta engendrar el animal mitológico que había de poner término a la estirpe" (350) ["Only then did he discover that Amaranta Úrsula was not his sister but his aunt, and that Sir Francis Drake had attacked Riohacha only so that they could seek each other through the most intricate labyrinths of blood until they would engender the mythological animal that was to bring the line to the end" (382-83)]. In brief, Aureliano Babilonia's decipherment of the parchments decodes both the *arche* (origin) and *telos* (terminus) of the historical narratives of the House of Buendía and of colonialism. Beyond the code of colonialism hovers the postcolonial possibility, beyond the threshold of the magic realist text, as it were, in the unwritten absence, gap, and silence left after the decoding of the colonial code and the eradication of the House of Buendía: "Sin embargo, antes de llegar al verso final ya había compredido que no saldría jamás de ese cuarto, pues estaba previsto que la ciudad de los espejos (o los espejismos) sería arrasada por el viento y desterrada de la memoria de los hombres en el instante en que Aureliano Babilonia acabara de descifrar los pergaminos, y que todo lo escrito, en ellos era irrepetible desde siempre y para siempre, porque las estirpes condenadas a cien años de soledad no tenían una segunda oportunidad sobre la tierra" (351) ["Before reaching the final line, however, he had already understood that he would never leave that room, for it was foreseen that the city of mirrors (or mirages) would be wiped out by the wind and exiled from the memory of men at the precise moment when Aureliano Babilonia would finish deciphering the parchments, and that everything written on them was unrepeatable since time immemorial and forever more, because races condemned to one hundred years of solitude did not have a second opportunity on earth" (383)]. As both *arche* and *telos*, the final paragraph of the novel reflects upon the unnamed world in the opening paragraph: *Cien años de soledad* is indeed a city of mirrors, a *mise en abîme*. As the colonial narrative of the House of Buendía, Melquíades's parchments (and *Cien años de soledad*) mirror the colonial narrative of Melquíades's tribe, for the Buendías ("exiled from the memory of men") are likewise "borrada de la faz de la tierra por haber sobrepassado los limites del conocimiento humano" (40) ["wiped off the face of the earth because they had gone beyond the limits of human knowledge" (45)]. After Aureliano Babilonia's final act of decoding Melquíades's parchments, the "exile" of the House of Buendía and the erasure of colonial history impose closure upon one narrative and open the possibility for postcolonial narrative.

To rearticulate Slemon's theorization of the confrontation between two oppositional discourses—that is, an encounter in which "each remains suspended, locked in a continuous dialectic with the 'other,' a situation which creates disjunction within each of the separate discursive systems, rending them with gaps, absences, and silences" ("Magic Realism" 409)—also reiterates the agon I have tried to mediate between the strains of postcolonialism and postmodernism and the gaps between their separate discursive systems. Because of the very difficulties theorists have with the term magic realism, it has often been considered a "theoretical void" (González Echevarría, "Isla a su vuelo fugitiva" 18).[9] But magic realism read through a double code of postmodernism and postcolonialism facilitates, if not a unilateral agreement between oppositional discourses, then an arbitration of aporias and theoretical voids.

NOTES

1. All subsequent English translations that follow the original Spanish of *Cien años de soledad* refer to Gregory Rabassa's translation of *One Hundred Years of Solitude*.

2. See Franz Roh, *Nach-Expressionismus: Magischer Realismus. Probleme der neuesten europäischen Malerei* (1925).

3. Among the essays collected in *Postmodern Fiction in Europe and the Americas*, co-edited by D'haen, Iris M. Zavala's "On the (Mis-)uses of the Post-Modern: Hispanic Modernism Revisited" locates Onís's coinage of the term postmodernism in his 1934 *Antología de la poesía española e hispanoamericana (1882-1932)* (Zavala 84).

4. For a current survey of critical discussions of *modernismo* see Gerard Aching's *The Politics of Spanish American* Modernismo (163).

5. Flores first delineated the colonial origins of "magical realism": "realism, since the Colonial Period but especially during the 1880s; the magical, writ large from the earliest in the letters of Columbus, in the chroniclers, in the sagas of Cabeza de Vaca" (189). Where Flores separates realism and the magical into two historical periods, Chanady recombines the two in her analysis of colonial narratives.

6. I have maintained Chanady's own translation of *Cartas de relación de Fernando Cortés, Historiadores primitivos de Indias*.

7. For other analyses of the act of reading in *Cien años de soledad*, see the following: Julio Ortega, "Postmodernism in Latin America" and "La risa de la tribu, el intercambio signico en *Cien años de soledad*"; Jon Thiem, "The Textualization of the Reader in Magic Realist Fiction"; Anibal González, "Translation and the Novel: *One Hundred Years of Solitude*"; Roberto González Echevarría, "*Cien años de soledad*: The Novel as Myth and Archive"; Edwin Williamson, "Magical Realism and the Theme of Incest in *One Hundred Years of Solitude*"; Michael Palencia-Roth, "Los perigamos de

Aureliano Buendía"; and E. Rodríguez Monegal, "*One Hundred Years of Solitude*: The Last Three Pages."

8. In his introduction to Hannes Wallrafen's photographic text *The World of Márquez*, García Márquez describes yet another kind of textualization of the extratextual world:

> I have always had great respect for readers who go off in search of the reality hidden behind my books. I have even greater respect for those who find it, because I've never been able to. In Aracataca, the Caribbean village where I was born, this seems to have become an everyday occupation. Over the last twenty years a whole generation of sharp children has grown up there, lying in wait for the myth hunters at the railroad station so they can introduce them to the places, things, and even the characters from my novels.... These children haven't read my novels, of course, so their knowledge of the mythical Macondo can not have been acquired through them. The places, things and characters they show tourists are real only to the degree that the latter are willing to accept them as so. That is to say, behind the Macondo created by literary fiction there is another Macondo, even more imaginary and mythical, created by readers and authenticated by the children of Aracataca with a third visible and palpable Macondo which is, without a doubt, the falsest of them all. Fortunately, Macondo isn't a place, but a state of mind that allows people to see what they want to see as they see fit. (5-6)

9. I have followed Chanady's quotation and translation of González Echevarría's phrase (Chanady 49).

WORKS CITED

Aching, Gerard. *The Politics of Spanish American* Modernismo: *By Exquisite Design*. Cambridge: Cambridge UP, 1997.

Alter, Robert. *Partial Magic: The Novel as a Self-Conscious Genre*. Berkeley: U of California P, 1975.

Ashcroft, Bill. "Modernity's First Born: Latin America and Postcolonial Transformation." *ARIEL* 29.2 (1998): 7-29.

Ashcroft, Bill, Gareth Griffiths, and Helen Tiffin. *The Empire Writes Back: Theory and Practice in Post-Colonial Literature*. New York: Routledge, 1989.

Barth, John. "The Literature of Exhaustion." *The Friday Book: Essays and Other Non-Fiction*. New York: Putnam, 1984. 62-76.

———. "The Literature of Replenishment." *The Friday Book* 193-206.

Bloom, Harold, ed. *Gabriel García Márquez*. New York: Chelsea House, 1989.

Borges, Jorge Luis. "El arte narrativo y la magia." *Discusión*. 1932. Buenos Aires: Emecé Editores, 1969. 81-91.

———. "Narrative Art and Magic." *Borges: A Reader*. Ed. and trans. Emir Rodríguez Monegal and Alastair Reed. New York: Dutton, 1981.

Carpentier, Alejo. Intro. *El reino de este mundo*. Mexico: Compañía General de Ediciones, 1967. 7-17.

Chanady, Amaryll. "The Origins and Development of Magic Realism in Latin American Fiction." *Magic Realism and Canadian Literature: Essays and Stories*. Ed. Peter Hinchcliff and Ed Jewinski. Waterloo, ON: U of Waterloo P, 1986. 49-60.

Connell, Liam. "Discarding Magic Realism: Modernism, Anthropology, and Critical Practice." *ARIEL* 29.2 (1998): 95-110.

Cortés, Hernan. *Cartas de relación de Fernando Cortés, Historiadores primitivos de Indias*. Vol. 1. Madrid: Biblioteca de autores españols, 1946.

Derrida, Jacques. *Dissemination*. Trans. Barbara Johnson. Chicago: Chicago UP, 1981.

———. "The Law of Genre." Trans. Anita Ronell. *Critical Inquiry* 7 (1980): 55-81.

D'haen, Theo. "Magical Realism and Postmodernism: Decentering Privileged Centres." Zamora and Faris 191-207.

———, and Hans Bertens, eds. *Postmodern Fiction in Europe and the Americas*. Amsterdam: Rodopi, 1988.

Díaz del Castillo, Bernal. *The Conquest of New Spain*. Trans. J. M. Cohen. Penguin: Baltimore, 1963.

———. *Historia verdadera de la conquista de la Nueva España*. Madrid: Alianza Editorial, 1989.

Flores, Angel. "Magical Realism in Spanish American Fiction." *Hispania* 38.2 (1955): 187-92.

García Márquez, Gabriel. *Cien años de soledad*. 1967. Buenos Aires: Editorial Sudamæricana, 1970.

———. *One Hundred Years of Solitude*. Trans. Gregory Rabassa. New York: Avon, 1970.

González, Anibal. "Translation and the Novel: *One Hundred Years of Solitude*" Bloom 271-82.

González Echevarría, Roberto. "*Cien años de soledad*: The Novel as Myth and Archive." Bloom 107-23.

———. "Isla a su vuelo fugitiva: Carpentier y el realismo magico." *Revisto Iberoamericana* 40.86 (1974): 9-63.

Hutcheon, Linda. *A Poetics of Postmodernism: History, Theory, Fiction*. New York: Routledge, 1988.

Jameson, Fredric. "On Magic Realism in Film." *Critical Inquiry* 12 (1986): 301-25.

———. *The Political Unconscious: Narrative as a Socially Symbolic Act.* London: Methuen, 1983.

Janes, Regina. *One Hundred Years of Solitude: Modes of Reading.* Twayne's Masterworks Studies 70. Boston: Twayne, 1991.

Lyotard, Jean-François. *The Postmodern Condition: A Report on Knowledge.* Trans. Geoff Bennington and Brian Massumi. Minneapolis: U of Minnesota P, 1984.

McHale, Brian. *Postmodernist Fiction.* New York: Methuen, 1987.

Ortega, Julio. "Postmodernism in Latin America." D'haen and Bertens 193-208.

———. "La risa de la tribu, el intercambio signico en *Cien años de soledad.*" *Nueva Revista de Fililogica Hispánica* 33.2 (1984): 396-430.

Palencia-Roth, Michael. "Los peragamos de Aureliano Buendía." *Revista Iberoamericana* 123-24 (1983): 403-17.

Rodríguez Monegal, Emir. "*One Hundred Years of Solitude*: The Last Three Pages." *Books Abroad* 47 (1973): 485-89.

Roh, Franz. *Nach-Expressionismus: Magischer Realismus. Probleme der neuesten europäischen Malerei.* Leipzig: Klinkhardt and Biermann, 1925.

Slemon, Stephen. "Magic Realism as Postcolonial Discourse." Zamora and Faris 407-20.

———. "Modernism's Last Post." *Past the Last Post: Theorizing Post-Colonialism and Post-Modernism.* Ed. Ian Adam and Helen Tiffin. Calgary: U of Calgary P, 1990. 1-11.

Sontag, Susan. *Illness as Metaphor.* New York: Vintage, 1978.

Thiem, Jon. "The Textualization of the Reader in Magical Realist Fiction." Zamora and Faris 230-47.

Wallrafen, Hannes, and Gabriel García Márquez: *The World of Márquez: A Photographic Exploration of Macondo.* Trans. Gregory Rabassa. London: Ryan, 1992.

Williamson, Edwin. "Magical Realism and the Theme of Incest in *One Hundred Years of Solitude.*" *Gabriel García Márquez: New Readings.* Ed. Bernard McGuirk and Richard Cardwell. Cambridge: Cambridge UP, 1987.

Wilson, Rawdon. "The Metamorphoses of Fictional Space: Magical Realism." Zamora and Faris 209-33.

Zamora, Lois Parkinson, and Wendy B. Faris, eds. *Magical Realism: Theory, History, Community.* Cornell: Duke UP, 1995.

Zavala, Iris M. "On the (Mis-)Uses of the Post-Modern: Hispanic Modernism Revisited." D'haen and Bertens 83-113.

IRVIN D.S. WINSBORO

Latin American Women in Literature and Reality: *García Márquez's* One Hundred Years of Solitude

As derived from the contemporary Latin American novel, our knowledge of the reality of womanhood is fragmented and distorted. At first glance it seems that all levels of such literature have typecast women in either matrifocal or matrilocal roles, i.e., the mother or family support role, or in supernatural or degrading roles, i.e., the witch or prostitute/mistress role. This appears especially true for the leading figures of the recent Latin American renaissance who style themselves the portrayers of the "real" Latin America. Examples of this school include Carlos Fuentes of Mexico, Mario Vargas Llosa of Peru, Julio Cortazar and Jorge Luis Borges of Argentina, Jorge Amado and Marcio Souza of Brazil, Maria Luisa Bombal of Chile, and arguably the best known, Gabriel Garcia Marquez of Colombia. While the artistic appeal of these writers is widespread and much discussed, in actuality few critics have focused on the fact that their female archetypes are presented much too glibly and, perhaps, too frequently as perceived realities based on their culture's patriarchal practices.

The objective of this essay, therefore, is to present a woman-centered appraisal of a well-known and widely read Latin American novel representative of the realist school, Garcia Marquez's Nobel Prize-winning *One Hundred Years of Solitude* (1971). In particular, the methodology undertaken here focuses on the following question: What is the cultural

From the *Midwest Quarterly* 34, 2 (Winter 1993). © 1993 by Irvin D. S. Winsboro.

intersection in the novelist's mind between the assigned roles of his female figures and the realities of life for women in Latin America? This study refers principally to Garcia Marquez's masterpiece, but it suggests that many of the novel's cultural patterns are valid for other Latin American novels, especially those of the realist school, which have similar sociocultural trajections and connotations and are in other ways reflective of a peculiar genre. By undertaking this approach I hope to build on a growing base of general feminist literary criticism that seeks to expose and redress sexist literary practices and to suggest a fresh methodological approach for the formulation and implementation of similar investigations. Surely the ever-growing stream of feminist consciousness in Latin America underscores the imperative for future studies of this nature, as do the ever-expanding priorities and interests of the academic community itself. As Peter Brooks, noted professor of comparative literature at Yale University, has suggested: "Anyone worth his [or her] salt in literary criticism today has to become something of a feminist" (qtd. in Kolodny, A52).

Feminist analysis of female protagonists underwent a major revision in the late 1960s and 1970s as part of the larger woman-centered praxis that swept both the academic and lay communities. Feminist thinkers at that time concluded that of all the life-determining—and life-restructuring—differences between men and women, the most immutable was woman's childbearing function. To old-line feminists, such as Simone de Beauvoir, this biological function relegated women to an inferior existence behind men (540-88). For new "young Turk" feminist analysts like Dorothy Dinnerstein and Adrienne Rich, the issue equated to one of power between men and women. Since women were "almost universally in charge of infant and early child care" (Dinnerstein, 26), the nature of human development resulted in women controlling the hearth and men controlling the world, these new-line feminists postulated. Initially this analysis provided a variant to the often-cited conclusions of influential psychologist Erik Erikson, who had argued that women were biologically and psychologically drawn to "inner space," i.e., domestic challenges inside the home, while men were universally pulled to "outer space," i.e., worldly challenges outside the home (Erikson, 582-606). While contemporary feminists have condemned Erikson's study as biased and misogynistic, it is interesting to note that both his and other woman-centered studies, those of Michelle Rosaldo and Rayna Reiter, for example, seemed to find common ground on the issue of motherhood being a restrictive and stultifying experience—that is to say, restrictive and stultifying compared to the unlimited environmental vistas of men.

While this mode of analysis is flawed in many respects—especially regarding the political connotations derived from it—it is useful in terms of constructing a working paradigm regarding the roles mothers and women play in society and, in our case, in literature. Expanding on this premise we can ask ourselves two revealing woman-centered questions concerning chosen female characters: Are the protagonists' personalities and role structures totally dependent upon mothering functions and stereotyped roles? and Are the protagonists' roles and personalities not solely those of the domestic sphere but rather larger ones of public life, what Erikson called "outer space"? Approached from another perspective, the question becomes: Does Garcia Marquez in *One Hundred Years of Solitude* allow his female characters access to public life, or is that alternative presumptively closed to them in favor of restrictive, home-centered mothering and collateral roles?

In order to arrive at an answer to these questions one must first look critically at Gabriel Garcia Marquez and his *One Hundred Years of Solitude* from a woman-centered perspective. It is relevant here to deal more with a feminist analysis of Garcia Marquez's work than with literary criticism, which has been presented amply elsewhere. Of necessity this study will highlight certain of the author's stylistic and structural devices in *One Hundred Years of Solitude*, but generally these will be background discussions only. Additionally, it is henceforth understood that a woman-centered analysis of literature is more than analyzing and rethinking the position of the female in the written word: it is drawing new assumptions about the cultural context of women based upon the feminist notion, as Kate Millett has so eloquently argued, that the "personal is political," i.e., what applies to the individual applies equally to the group. It is this belief in particular that has led feminists to focus on the problem of literary sexism, and it is this premise that underlies the following discussion. In focusing on such issues, Garcia Marquez's *One Hundred Years of Solitude* will be presented as indicative of feminist concerns regarding an entire range (genre?) of contemporary Latin American literature.

Gabriel Garcia Marquez was born to Gabriel Eligio Marquez and Santiaga Marquez Iguaran in the Colombian banana town of Aracataca. He grew up with his maternal grandparents, falling particularly under the spell of his paternalistic grandfather, a retired military officer. Garcia Marquez drifted through various jobs and journalistic attempts until 1967 when he completed the Spanish edition of *One Hundred Years of Solitude*. The work became an immediate success and eventually propelled him into the ranks of internationally acclaimed writers. Gregory Rabassa translated the story into English in 1970. Since then it has been translated into twenty-four other languages with combined sales of over ten million copies. Although Garcia Marquez subsequently had seven more works translated into English, including his well-known, *No One Writes to the Colonel and Other Short Stories* and *Love in the Time of Cholera*, which immediately catapulted to the top of the best seller lists of France and the United States after its first translation, *One Hundred Years of Solitude* remains his crowning work. The work received unique acclaim in 1982 when Garcia Marquez won the Nobel Prize in Literature for it. In awarding the prize, the Swedish Academy compared Garcia Marquez to such luminaries as Balzac and Faulkner, all of whom, in the Academy's view, were novelists of "overwhelming narrative talent, breadth and epic richness" (qtd. in Vinocur, A1). The critic Malcolm Cowley recognized the Nobel selection of Garcia Marquez as singularly important, because it signified "overt recognition for Latin American writers in general" (qtd. in Kakutani, A10). The well-known poet Pablo Neruda went even further in his acclaim by characterizing *One Hundred Years of Solitude* as the greatest revelation in the Spanish language since *Don Quixote*" (qtd. in Eustellafau, 3).

One Hundred Years of Solitude itself is a literary tour de force that oscillates between super-realism and super-fantasy, or what critics frequently term "magic realism" (Pynchon, VII-49). But in addition to being a captivating novel, it also doubles as a commentary—many would say an allegory—for modern Latin American history. From the founding of the village of Macondo near the Colombian coast by Jose Buendia and Ursula Iguaran, his wife-cousin, to the prophesied destruction of the once-great but long-moribund city 100 (or 150) years later, the plot erratically follows the six ensuing generations of the Buendias, all condemned to fundamental solitude. The timeline begins in a pleasant and pristine world which comes to endure, among other epochs, brutal civil war, railroads and modernization, and Yankee imperialism, all of which turn Macondo into a run-down banana town of wooden homes and zinc roofs strikingly similar to the author's own home town of Aracataca. In the end, the town, like each Buendia, dies from inexplicable yet long-unfolding events. In essence, the story takes on the force of a metaphor for all the cycles of life that have characterized an entire region.

Garcia Marquez weaves mystical tales of the Buendia family that at times make Tolstoy's Rostovs' genealogical chart pale by comparison. In a large sense, Jose and Ursula are the only two character types in the work; as noted earlier, ensuing generations are simply variants of their strengths and weaknesses. The Buendia men are brooding, introverted, licentious, and impulsive, frequently too impulsive for the women of the family. For their part, the Buendia women are continually concerned with keeping the family together in a dynastic sense. They are stern, naive, and sometimes sexually wanton, but generally they are the mothers and custodians of the Buendia male line. It is the women who provide through various intergenerational mothering functions the glue that holds the work together, the substance that keeps it from becoming a disjointed and fragmented chronicle.

Garcia Marquez's portrayal of Ursula, the prototypical female character, is that of an icon who "worked like a galley slave" (64) and "watched over the survival of the line" (197). Through 316 pages of the 383-page work, Ursula is an actor or voice of the Buendia saga; she, or her thematic variations, serve the Buendia family as mother figure, moral, and common sense force, and, finally, after 100 (or 150) years, as the symbol of Buendia decadence and impotence. Frequently other female characters appear, many of whom are not really blood Buendias, but, as researcher Barbara N. Gantt has determined, the primal motherly qualities of Ursula continue to reflect omnipotently over her family, what Garcia Marquez calls her "planetary system" (245).

In many cases the author imbues Ursula with all the traditional attributes of noble Latin American women. These qualities range from maternal instinct and faith to magical predictive and curative powers. They are the qualities of females as ideals—or as researcher Anne Firor Scott would put it, women on pedestals—but they are in no way reflective of, or even hint of, the true range of life-challenges women face, and have faced, in Latin America.

The author's feelings regarding Ursula's mission surface in the house that she built. It was constructed and maintained for the most traditional of purposes—to promote and arrange the marriages of eligible daughters. Ursula's progeny, like herself, aspired to be no more than wife and mother within the author's scheme of things. They were, as Erikson might have determined, destined by the author for lives of domesticity while the Buendia men went off to conquer worldly challenges. Perhaps here Garcia Marquez simply aped his own phenomenological experience. This becomes plausible when one considers that the author's mother and the story's protagonist shared the same original surname—"Iguaran."

Besides Ursula, there appear eight other Buendia women in the novel. They are Remedios, Rebeca, Amaranta, Santa Sofia de la Piedad, Remedios the Beauty, Fernanda del Carpio, Renata Remedios, otherwise known as Meme, and Amaranta Ursula. The common bonding of these characters throughout the novel is their marriage to or parenting of Buendias, or their supportive familial roles in this process. Some are forceful and intriguing figures in their own right, but generally they are creatures of their own female spheres, different and apart from what Garcia Marquez called "men's affairs" (74).

It would not be incorrect to assume that the author intends to conform his female characters to the classical stereotypes prescribed by *marianismo*, that is, the cultural ideal common to Latin America whereby women are to be, as Gross and Bingham have found, "religious and pious, focused on family, secluded at home, and the moral force of their families" (141). The concept equates rather closely with what North American women have been criticizing as the "cult of domesticity" (Welter, 313-33) and the notion of women's "proper place" (Rothman, 3-9). This belief has translated to submissiveness in the outside world and superiority within the inner space of the household for many women, especially those of Latin America. Other female characters besides the Buendia women appear in *One Hundred Years of Solitude*, for example the ageless concubine Pilar Ternera, but generally they function as mistresses and role adjuncts to the Buendia men. In a literary form they, too, have adopted, or have been forced to adopt, the precepts of *marianismo*, which so many women of Latin America have interpreted as the very necessity for their existence.

The themes of *marianismo* and mothering recur in almost all the female characters. The author continually implies for all the women what he states explicitly for the story's terminal female character, Amaranta Ursula: "The only thing that she needed to be completely happy was the birth of her children" (352). This "maternal instinct" (90) so intoxicates the Buendia women that it sometimes results in incestuous offspring, a condition long feared, yet predicted, by Ursula to result in such offspring being born with the "tail of a pig" (217). Perhaps this is the author's way of suggesting punishment for those female characters who stray from the concept of regal motherhood. The reader is never quite certain of the implicit symbolism of the tail-of-a-pig prediction.

The *marianismo* and mothering themes of the novel prove to be didactic in many ways. Certainly, for example, they are suggestive of Garcia Marquez's concept of gender identity. While the men violate the outside world in their would-be conquests of rival political factions, imperialist Yankee corporations and women—always women—the female Buendias are restricted to an inner world of domestic and motherly concerns. Even though there are exceptions to the pattern, the cultural meaning (or perception) of motherhood remains an imperative throughout the work. In the mind of the novelist there is a rigid intersection between womanhood and motherhood: they are both collateral and self-sustaining images. Perhaps this is not so difficult to understand when one considers that the author himself is the product of a society that embraces both *machismo* and *marianismo*. In this case, the works of the new Latin American "realist" school certainly reveal an important sense of verisimilitude clearly based on sociocultural connotations—their realism *does*, in fact, embody both the experiences and ethos of Latin America. As Garcia Marquez himself has stated: "It always amuses me that the highest praise for my work comes for the imagination, while the truth is that there's not a single line in all my work that does not have a basis in reality" (qtd. in Clemons and Levy-Spira, 60).

What emerges from the foregoing is the thesis that *One Hundred Years of Solitude* reflects the traditional Latin American role of women as adjuncts to men and implies neither qualitative awareness nor literary criticism of the restrictive political and economic systems and notions (i.e., *marianismo*) that perpetuate such notions. As a whole, the women of Macondo are pictured as male-defined, biological reproducers or sexually pleasing objects who are treated thematically as accessories to the men who actually shape and control the world. The examples from *One Hundred Years of Solitude* would, thus, seem to indicate that Garcia Marquez has mingled his own phenomenological experience as a Latin American male with the created artistic images of his female protagonists. As one new feminist voice from Garcia Marquez's home country of Colombia has noted: "We have become women within the family unit, where our model has been woman-mother— victimized, dominated, sacrificing her creativity for the sake of her husband and children; where we have not had the right or the time to explore the continual changes in the world" (Sanchez, 164). In this sense, Garcia Marquez truly is indicative of a Latin verisimilitude, as Vivian Antaki has so aptly documented. The author's own words on this subject once again are instructive; upon receiving the Nobel Prize in 1982, Garcia Marquez stated that *One Hundred Years of Solitude* "did not have to be invented—I took most of it from reality" (qtd. in Simons, A10).

This description highlights two major points about Garcia Marquez's work and the "reality" of life for women in Latin America. First, as Garcia Marquez himself acknowledges, his work is both derivative and reflective of the realities of womanhood in his homeland. Obviously, the incipient feminist movement in Latin America is designed to alter these realities, but nevertheless Garcia Marquez offers a snapshot of both perceived and *actual* cultural norms.

The second point rests on an element of more abstract literary criticism. That is, that such works as Garcia Marquez's *One Hundred Years of Solitude*—realistic literature at its best and, therefore, most didactic— pointedly make no effort to portray female values independent of *marianismo*. Thus, such literature in the popular mind becomes indistinguishable from reality, but it is the age-old Latin American reality of paternalism and what contemporary feminist critics are describing as the confining notions of "woman's proper place."

Latin American feminists might find *One Hundred Years of Solitude* a disturbing element in a sea of so-called "realist" literature which places women in a psychological environment that serves to perpetuate a climate of stereotypes and limited expectations. While the present study cannot presume to speak for the rising tide of feminist voices to our south, it is instructive to note that a new feminist-oriented epistemology is rapidly growing in Latin America and increasingly targeting for analysis the role of women in regional literature. Particularly representative of this new social commitment is a reinvigorated women's movement, which is attacking the notion that women's resources, desires, and achievements should be thematically limited to motherhood roles and corollary pursuits or to degrading and objectified roles as prostitutes and mistresses. Traditionally writers and intellectuals in Latin America have participated in political debates over such causes much more strenuously than their counterparts to the north, and it is therefore almost predictable that the romantic or paternalistic caste/class depiction of literary women as powerless and docile in the face of male domination will increasingly come under attack.

The feminist counter to such a pejorative portrayal is to generate a new literature altogether, one focusing on the female experience as important and valued. Indeed, such writers as Isabel Allende of Chile already are producing new works based on feminist sensibilities, even while conforming to derived styles based on the region's literary tradition of fantasy and hyperbole. Other writers, Elena Poniatowska, specifically, are consciously creating women protagonists in their works as not only movers and shakers, but as complete human creatures. Poniatowska's portrayal in *Hasta no verte Jesus mio* (*Until I see you, my Jesus*, 1969) of a peasant woman who is an active participant in the Mexican Revolution sheds meaningful light on this subject. In fact, Poniatowska herself once commented on the political thrust of her works:

> We write in Latin America to reclaim a space to discover ourselves in the presence of others, of human community—so that they may see us, so that they may love us—to form the vision of the world, to acquire some dimension—so they can't erase us so easily. We write so as not to disappear. (qtd. in Chevigny)

Such statements indicate how modern writers are determined to graft feminist concerns onto the roots of traditional Latin American ideological concerns. The result inevitably will be a new political dialogue on how women *are* portrayed in literature and how they *should be* portrayed by this and ensuing generations of Latin American writers.

As the effort by women to win control over their lives progresses and grows, the complexity and scope of this endeavor will become increasingly embedded in the psyche and literature of Latin America. Its advocates will not be placated by a "realist" literature, written by avowedly leftist authors, such as Gabriel Garcia Marquez, that simply projects women's roles based upon patriarchal, male-oriented concepts. Although, in fact, to a large degree this literature *does* reflect the past imperatives of womanhood in a society that has historically embraced *marianismo* as an article of faith. The new generation of feminist writers will stress the importance of demystifying spurious sociocultural categories and underscore by implication their determination to foment a feminist revolution in life and in literature—an upheaval that will result in redefined opportunities for women in all spheres of public and private life (see Miller). These authors will most certainly take their cue from such analysts as Barbara Warren, who concluded in *The Feminine Image in Literature* that "Before woman can know and accept her human identity, apart from being the object of man's fantasies and desires, she must understand the nature of the images that have been projected upon her; she must separate herself from the man-created myths" (1). Inevitably, the result will be a less biased and patriarchal approach to the role and reality of women in Latin American literature. We are talking, then, of nothing less than a social revolution in the art of literature.

BIBLIOGRAPHY

Antaki, Vivian Jane. "Beyond Political Perspectives: The Literary Craft of Carlos Fuentes, Mario Vargas Llosa and Gabriel Garcia Marquez." Dissertation. University of Colorado, 1978.

Beauvoir, Simone de. *The Second Sex*. Trans. H.M. Parshley. New York: Vintage, 1974 [1952].

Chevigny, Bell Gale. "The Transformation of Privilege in the Work of Elena Poniatowska." *Latin American Literary Review* 13 (1985), 49-62.

Clemons, Walter, and Eduardo Levy-Spira. "The Sweet Plague of Love." *Newsweek*, 25 April 1988, 60-61.

Dinnerstein, Dorothy. *The Mermaid and the Minotaur: Sexual Arrangements and Human Malaise*. New York: Harper Colophon, 1977.

Erikson, Erik. "Inner and Outer Space: Reflections on Womanhood." *Daedalus* 93 (1964), 582-606.

Eustellafau, Margaret. *Gabriel Garcia Marquez: An Annotated Bibliography, 1947-1979*. Westport: Greenwood, 1980.

Gantt, Barbara N. "The Women of Macondo: Feminine Archetypes in Garcia Marquez *Cien Anos de Soledad*." Dissertation. Florida State University, 1977.

Garcia Marquez, Gabriel. *One Hundred Years of Solitude*. Trans. Gregory Rabassa. New York: Avon, 1971.

————. *Love in the Time of Cholera.* Trans. Edith Grossman. New York: Knopf, 1988.

————. *No One Writes to the Colonel and Other Short Stories.* Trans. J.S. Bernstein. New York: Harper and Row, 1979.

Gross, Susan Hill, and Marjorie Wall Bingham. *Women in Latin America: The 20th Century.* St. Louis Park, Minnesota: Glenhurst, 1985.

Kakutani, Michiko. "Nobel Laureate's Writing Brings a Wide Variety of Responses." *New York Times,* 22 October 1982, A10.

Kolodny, Annette. "Respectability Is Eroding the Revolutionary Potential of Feminist Criticism." *The Chronicle of Higher Education,* 4 May 1988, A52.

Miller, Beth, ed. *Women in Hispanic Literature: Icons and Fallen Idols.* Berkeley: California University Press, 1983.

Millett, Kate. *Sexual Politics.* New York: Avon, 1971.

Pynchon, Thomas. "The Heart's Eternal Vow: *Love in the Time of Cholera.*" *New York Times,* 10 April 1988, VII 1, 49.

Reiter, Rayna R., ed. *Toward an Anthropology of Women.* New York: Monthly Review Press, 1975.

Rich, Adrienne. *Of Woman Born: Motherhood as Experience and Institution.* New York: Norton, 1976.

Rosaldo, Michelle Z. "Women, Culture, and Society: A Theoretical Overview." *Women, Culture, and Society.* Eds. Michelle Z. Rosaldo and Louise Lamphere. Stanford: Stanford University Press, 1974, 17-40.

Rothman, Sheila M. *Woman's Proper Place: A History of Changing Ideas and Practices, 1870 to the Present.* New York: Basic Books, 1978.

Sanchez, Luz Helena. "Columbia: Fighting for the Right to Fight." *Sisterhood is Global: The International Women's Movement Anthology.* Ed. Robin Morgan. Garden City: Anchor, 1984, 164-168.

Scott, Anne Firor. *The Southern Lady: From Pedestal to Politics, 1830-1930.* Chicago: Chicago University Press, 1970.

Simons, Marlise. "Storyteller With Bent for Revolution." *New York Times,* 22 October 1982, A10.

Vinocur, John. "García Márquez of Colombia Wins Novel Literature Prize." *New York Times,* 22 October 1982, A1.

Warren, Barbara. *The Feminine Image in Literature.* Rochelle Park: Hayden, 1973.

Welter, Barbara. "The Cult of True Womanhood, 1820-1860." *The American Family in Social-Historical Perspective.* Ed. Michael Gordon. New York: St. Martins, 1978, 313-33.

ALEXANDER COLEMAN

Bloomsbury in Aracataca:
The Ghost of Virginia Woolf

Not long ago, Octavio Paz complained with his usual eloquence about the lack of seminal works of literary criticism in the field of contemporary Latin American letters; his comments might help us direct our attention to what we should be doing when we who are "in the field" take up a book and try to place it in a tradition, or when we divine the existence of an individual talent and attempt to locate that talent in relation to all that has gone on before its birth. The most difficult thing is to define a past into which a new talent might be or has been born. You will recall that in the short note contained in his miscellany entitled *Corriente alterna*, in the piece called "Sobre la crítica" (On Criticism), Paz defined the critical act as being, above all, the sketching out of a mental space for various works to move in and about, in constantly changing relationship to one another. This space, drawn out and defined by the literary critic, should be the meeting point at which one work meets another and others, at which one work speaks to many others and they in turn speak back to it, and tell why it is there.[1] For Paz, the critical act is *not* the mere summa of works read or the catalogues of possible predecessors and sources. It is an almost creative act, composed of affinities and oppositions, whose center lies in the perception of the critic, a field into which the new work may happily function without in any way doing damage to the disruptive, iconoclastic, or revolutionary nature of the work in

From *World Literature Today* 59 (Autumn 1985). © 1985 by *World Literature Today*.

question. A good piece of criticism should be like a Calder mobile, to which new wings and other shapes can be added without disturbing the moving yet stable equilibrium.

These injunctions are directed only to myself as I begin my scrutiny of a topic that could easily be construed as an attempt at the baldest kind of source-hunting, trying to figure out what texts of Virginia Woolf have any bearing on the making of the New Novel in Spanish America, when these texts made their impression on a succession of authors, or what thematic or technical devices of Virginia Woolf had any discernible effect upon a novelist, say, such as Gabriel García Márquez. I am going to take the latter course, searching for the novelistic poetics of Virginia Woolf as they bounced off, springboard fashion, into a poetics of a specific author of the new wave. This possible exercise in literary parallelism may be fruitful whether or not the two parallel lines intersect at any point. In the specific case of García Márquez, I hope to point out that his visionary novels show him to have been an intense yet neighborly reader of Virginia Woolf. The distance between Bloomsbury and Aracataca is not that great—through the medium of literature, she spoke to him in ways he never forgot, and of which we have some record. But even now I am going too far afield too soon.

An obvious presumption in the intercommunication between books is the simple idea that all books are part of one book, and that literature is a medium in which we all participate with greater or lesser achievement, all according to our gifts and energies. As for the relationship between a work of literature and the swirling life around that same work, Virginia Woolf and the majority of the New Latin American novelists will and do insist implicitly or explicitly on the real source of creative energies—not life, but literature itself. Harold Bloom has given us the most truculent version of this now sacred belief: "Poems, I am saying, are neither about 'subjects' nor about 'themselves.' They are necessarily about *other poems*; a poem is a response to a poem, as a poet is a response to a poet, or a person to his parent. Trying to write a poem takes the poet back to the origins of what a poem *first was for him*, and so takes the poet back beyond the pleasure principle to the decisive initial encounter and response that began him."[2] Of course, when Bloom mentions "poets" or "poems," he refers to any genre of a work of literature in the making, in response to a prior seminal literature experience in the distant or not too distant past.

The most obvious reference point to this "challenge and response" theory of literature within literature is *Don Quijote de la Mancha*, the novel which not only gives us a macaronic, parodic reworking of all previously existing genres in Spain as read and transfigured by Miguel de Cervantes— pastoral, chivalric, *novela morisca*, picaresque, among others—but also presents us with a fictional elaboration concerning what happens when fictional characters within fiction read fictions, then lose their bearings and even go mad, their brains having dried up from the digestion of so much print. This novel about previous novels and romances makes literature itself both the subject and the unique kinetic force within the book, for after all, the characters are all believers in books, dupes of the illusory nature of literature, fully aware of the written word as elements in a universe of appearances. More than one might think if read from the usual "idealistic" perspective, *Don Quijote de la Mancha* seems to be a never-ending discourse on the subject of the scrutiny of a library, a backward look at books that brought to Spain the avant-garde of its time.[3] In addition, the book must be read in the light not only of Cervantes's voluminous readings in European literature, but also his dark and somber reading in the ultimate meaning of the total book that was Spanish history of his time. In this sense, Cervantes's fictional story/history and imaginative brand of illusory historiography points to the truth, the destiny of a nation.

So too, we can look at Virginia Woolf and Gabriel García Márquez in relation to the literary and historical traditions into which they were born. Both might be said to have inherited variants of nineteenth-century realistic practice, and both found a way out of the realistic impasse by revisionist readings of texts well outside the realistic canon. The literary past weighed heavily on them both, and this should be said with due recognition and adjustments to the monstrous gap between the immediate forebears of García Márquez within the national literature of Colombia and within the continent at large in contrast to the imposing, granitic fathers and grandfathers against whom Virginia Woolf struggled, fought, and finally prevailed in such masterpieces as *Mrs. Dalloway* (1925), *To the Lighthouse* (1927), and *Orlando* (1928), a trio of works written in succession which can be thought of as a good index of her disruptive response to the literature of her father's generation.

There are two intertwined threads in Virginia Woolf's relation to and final rupture with the literature of her immediate past: above all, her criticism of the novels of Arnold Bennett, H. G. Wells, and John Galsworthy; second, her sharp attitude toward the biographical genre as practiced by the Victorians—not only the biography of a great eminence of the past, but the biography of a nation (and its relationship to the art of a great historian) and, by extension, the biography of the cultural-historical experience of a nation through the centuries, yet in parodic and compressed form. Here, of course, I am referring to Virginia Woolf's *Orlando*, the mock biography of English culture, translated by Jorge Luis Borges in the late thirties and first mentioned by Gabriel García Márquez as early as 1950, some seventeen years before the publication of another kind of epic biography, *Cien años de soledad*. But again, I am getting ahead of my modest proposal.

Woolf's commentaries on her three eminent novelistic predecessors can be best summarized by extracting the arguments contained in her essay entitled "Modern Fiction," first reprinted in *The Common Reader*, volume 1. For her, these authors are "materialists … concerned not with the spirit but with the body": "If we fasten, then, one label on all these books, on which is one word, materialists, we mean by it that they write of unimportant things, that they spend immense skill and immense industry making the trivial and the transitory appear the true and the enduring." With all their stupendous energy and display of detail, Woolf insists that still, "life escapes, and perhaps without life nothing else is worth while." For her, the traditional novel is not a novel made of richness of perception or selectivity of experience, but rather one made of tyrannical restraints, the elements variously called plot, comedy, tragedy, love interest, and a general air of probability and verisimilitude. It should be said that she is not protesting against the abundance of fact in the novelistic machines of her predecessors—not at all. Having so often been accused of estheticism and preciosity, Woolf attacks her forebears with the passionate cry of "Life, more life." Life for her is not hidden in meticulous catalogues and characterological tics, but rather is free and unfettered, a confused realm of half-conscious memories whispering to us, the random vitality of the past lurking into the present, the aleatory disorder of any "character" (not a positive thing in Woolf) at any time of its existence within the novel. In a memorable passage, she tells of the chaotic implosion of sensations and things which befall all of us and certainly her characters in any ordinary day, an implosion which the realist is too blind or simply too gross or bluff to be able to perceive.

> Examine for a moment an ordinary mind on an ordinary day. The mind receives a myriad impressions—trivial, fantastic, evanescent, or engraved with the sharpness of steel. From all sides they come, an incessant shower of innumerable atoms, and as they fall, as they shape themselves into the life of Monday or Tuesday, the accent falls differently from of old … so that, if a writer were a free man and not a slave, if he could write what he chose, not what he must … there would be no plot, no comedy, no tragedy, no love interest or catastrophe in the accepted style.… Life is not a series of gig-lamps symmetrically arranged, life is a luminous halo, a semi-transparent envelope surrounding us from the beginning of consciousness to the end. Is it not the task of the novelist to convey this varying, this unknown and uncircumscribed spirit?

Later in the essay, she urges herself and her readers to the task: "Let us record the atoms as they fall upon the mind in the order in which they fall, let us trace the pattern, however disconnected and incoherent in appearance, which each sight or incident scores upon the consciousness."[4] Similar passages can be found coursing through all her essays and diaries; she simply cannot bear the presumptions of empiricism in the making of a novel, nor can she abide the idea that there is such a thing as a novelistic character "to be nailed down," as it were, by dint of leaden observation and manic accumulation of detail. She is above all a novelist in the process of alluding to a possible personality, producing a flow of perceptions and vagaries which are at the heart of human inconstancy, since an infinite succession of impressions constitutes an *unfinished* totality, and that is all to the good.

In another passage from her diary, written during the catharsis represented by *To the Lighthouse*, she returns to that constant theme—the exhaustion of scientific presumptions in literature.

> Waste, deadness, come from the inclusion of things that don't belong to the moment, this appalling narrative business of the realist: getting on from lunch to dinner: it is false, unreal, merely conventional. Why admit anything to literature that is not poetry—by which I mean saturated? Is that not my grudge against novelists—that they select nothing? The poets succeeding by simplifying: practically everything is left out.[5]

So too for the Victorian biographer. On 30 October 1927 Woolf published in the *New York Herald Tribune* a brisk review of her friend Harold Nicolson's then recent book, *Some People*.[6] The opening salvo of the review goes to the heart of the matter, as is the case so often with her pronouncements.

> On the one hand there is truth, on the other there is personality. And if we think of truth as something of granite-like solidity and of personality as something of rainbow-like intangibility and reflect that the aim of biography is to weld these two into one seamless whole, we shall admit that the problem is a stiff one and that we need not wonder if biographers have for the most part failed to solve it.

Truth is hard and empirical, it feeds on indiscriminate detail, it is sure and obdurate, but it is to be found only in the British Museum, not in the rush of crowds surging around Picadilly. Biographers who aim at truth are dull and unreadable, because they cannot envision the re-creation of something other than truth; that "something other" is personality. As she says, "For in order that the light of personality may shine through, facts must be manipulated, some must be brightened, others shaded." She goes on with high praise of the wonderful table talk in Boswell's *Life of Johnson*, but then goes even further to flay the nonart of the Victorian biographer, "dominated by the idea of goodness. Noble, upright, chaste, severe; it is thus that the Victorian worthies are presented to us." We rummage, she says, through Victorian biographies as if carrying out an onerous task, conscious of "a sense of the prodigious waste, of the artistic wrongheadedness of such a method." The new biographer—Nicolson of course and his master Lytton Strachey, and by inference herself—"chooses, he synthesizes; in short, he has ceased to be the chronicler, he has become an artist.... So it would seem as if one of the great advantages of the new school to which Mr. Nicolson belongs is the lack of pose, humbug, solemnity. They approach their bigwigs fearlessly. They have no fixed scheme of the universe, no standard of courage or morality to which they insist that he shall conform."

Virginia Woolf will insist that the new freedom of the novelist must be accorded to the art of the biographer also; both should attain a wanted "freedom from pose, from sentimentality, from illusion." And finally, she posits the impossible marriage with which she began her review, that of granite and rainbow: "Truth of fact and truth of fiction are incompatible; yet he (the new biographer) is now more than ever urged to combine them." The result of these injunctions to herself will be *Orlando*, at once an imaginative biography of Vita Sackville-West, Nicolson's wife, and a tour de force of temporal compressions under the guise of a rainbowish biography of England's cultural phases.

(Let me anticipate my argument a bit before going to *Orlando*, lest by now you suspect that I am off the track of my subject. Simply put: if the redefinition of novelistic time is fundamental to both Woolf and García Márquez, there is another darker matter to be explored as we examine the silent communication between the near spinster of Bloomsbury and the Rabelaisian temperament of the man from Aracataca. I am here speaking of a critique of power in all its guises in both novelists—parental or political power, overbearing and suffocating, power that is ego in action, trampling over the nuances of an individual sensibility, above all that of a child. Power resides in its temporary command over time and in its energetic command of the world outside through the exercise of the will. Power is manifest in any circle. It is related to self-possession, identity of purpose, and always accompanied by the servility of those condemned to surround that power. If you are a child of that power—and who is not, manipulated as you are by a writer-father, let's say, or a president-for-life power—you will be allowed to exist in a minimal sort of way; this silent power [felt in a study, a parlor, or a palace] will surreptitiously and continually indicate to you that you are permitted to exist, yes, but you cannot be *me* the all-powerful, you cannot equal *me*, and above all you must not be able to be better than I am. Power resists the nurture of alternative egos, alternative ambitions; it erases the possibility of an individual sensibility of total *otherness* to the central emanation. A world ordered by masculinity was the world into which Virginia Woolf was born, a world where clock time was the ultimate truth and fact was God. In mounting her assault upon fact and clock time, she was not only opening her art out onto the world of sensibility and heightened perception, but she was also breaking down the imperious values silently imposed upon her by her eminent Victorian father, Sir Leslie Stephen, prolific biographer by trade, dead since 1904, it is true, but very much alive in her mind and still begging for attention as a Learish presence in her memory. Her essay entitled "The New Biography" is one of the many oblique weapons taken up as she organizes her delayed parricide; the spoofy put-on *Orlando* is another step, with the final laying to rest in *To the Lighthouse*. So the texts or interviews by García Márquez that I am interested in are those related to his reading of time and the solitude of power in Virginia Woolf.) End of parenthesis!

Orlando is not easy to describe, because the description of the imagination (the rainbow) working upon fact (the granite) is the art of literary welding into seamless textures of words. The book avoids a single perspective. The androgynous narrative voice makes its way through four centuries of English history, style, mode, and ornament, the narrator describing a "single" person only in the most outlandish definition of singularity, a "self" who "has a great variety of selves to call upon," a composite accumulation of individual, anonymous existences within the most varied unity, a unity which somehow "contrive[s] to synchronize the sixty or seventy different times which beat simultaneously in every normal human system."[7] Orlando begins as a sixteen-year-old stripling in full Elizabethan flower around 1586, becomes an ambassador to Turkey some 100 years later without a wrinkle, witnesses the age of Swift, Pope, and Johnson, changes sex without an operation, notes the dreaded arrival of the musty and damp Victorian age with its perennial chills, the ubiquitous ivied walls, its good number of bearded eminences, its muffled, stodgy parlors, and dies on 11 October 1928, the very day the book was published. Magically but logically, García Márquez was born in the same year as the writing of *Orlando*, 1927.

Orlando first entered into the world of Spanish American literary criticism in the form of a lengthy lecture given in Buenos Aires by the founder of *Sur*, Victoria Ocampo, on 7 July 1937; it was entitled "Virginia Woolf, Orlando y Cía."[8] Ocampo's passionate advocacy of the work was hardly limited to her lecture presentation of the main themes of *Orlando*; she also commissioned Jorge Luis Borges to translate the work for her publishing house, and thus the book began to make its way in Spanish by means of Borges's splendid version. We know that García Márquez had read the book by 1950, but the question remains: what would have attracted him to the work, and why did it exert a pull over this fledgling author some seventeen years before the publication of *One Hundred Years of Solitude* in Spanish? For once, a date can tell us much—1950 is just two years after the dreadful *Bogotazo*, a period of seemingly endless civil war between opposing bands which followed the assassination of the liberal charismatic leader Jorge Eliécer Gaitán in 1948. García Márquez found himself in the midst of *la violencia* between the *godos* and the *rojos* which would end only after hundreds of thousands of lives had been sacrificed. This war was the bloody source for Aureliano Buendía's similarly futile military exploits, all fought bravely and all ignominiously lost. For the protonovelist who was García Márquez in 1950, the problem was the same as it was for Virginia Woolf, *toutes proportions gardées*: how does the imagination face the apocalypse (*la violencia*, World War I)? How can words put together give off the sense of centuries, having passed, of what is changeless and timeless within violence and apparent change? Here is García Márquez's observation of 1950:

> We in Colombia still have not written the novel which might be fortunately influenced by the Joyces, the Faulkners, or the Virginia Woolfs. And I say "fortunately," because I don't think that we Colombians can be, at this moment, an exception to the play of influences. In her prologue to Orlando, Virginia confesses to her influences.... There is something there—above all in the manipulation of time—between Huxley and Virginia Woolf once again.... If we Colombians were to decide to really do it, we would undoubtedly have to fall into that current. What is lamentable is that such a literary event has not yet taken place, nor do we see even the slightest symptoms that it might ever take place at any time.[9]

Orlando and many of García Márquez's later works affirm in hyperbolic terms the parody of History, or what Suzanne Jill Levine has called "fiction's truth over History or of History as an infinite series of contradictory stories."[10] Through the unchanging and immortal Ursula (in *Cien años*) and the endlessly autumnal patriarch, García Márquez satirizes the history of a continent. As Emir Rodríguez Monegal has observed, "*Orlando* opened a door in Latin America to a world of fantastic narrative, the most ancient form of the art of storytelling and the only form until the eighteenth century, when realistic practice began to be systematically cultivated."[11] Above all, we are looking at a new kind of novelistic freedom from clock time, the curse of the tick-tock and dead fact, and this in turn means that "linear time is an illusion, and that perhaps the circular metaphor corresponds to time as it really functions."[12] It is the time of fable and myth, where the idea of progress is finally seen for what it is, the eighteenth and the nineteenth century's worst joke played on the twentieth century.

Let us now turn our attention to the matter of power and its solitude in the two novelists. I am making use of a passage from part 1, chapter 19 of *To the Lighthouse*, a book I am fairly sure that García Márquez has not read—all the better for my purposes, since such moments in Woolf lurk constantly throughout her works and end by being something close to a manic obsession in both authors. In this instance Mr. and Mrs. Ramsey (Mr. Ramsey being the stand-in for her father Leslie Stephen) take up two significantly different kinds of books and begin to read within view of each other in the parlor. Within the mirror world of fiction, we see both characters reading their books, and we overhear her thinking about him as he reads. The reading is not exactly silent, however; through her eyes and ears, we hear him slapping his thighs in audible but nonverbal enjoyment of the book that he has deliberately chosen for that evening's reading in order to prove a point in his campaign for self-defense which is his life. Mr. Ramsey is engulfed in reading Sir Walter Scott's *Antiquary*, whereas Mrs. Ramsey has significantly chosen Shakespeare's sonnets. He is reading in a straightforward way a traditional text much beloved by Victorian England, but she is not doing the same to Shakespeare. On the contrary, she is reading pointillistically single sentences and phrases from the sonnets, darting in and out, treasuring the perceptions of individual lines and paying no attention to the linear form of the sonnet. Here is a moment:

> She read and turned the page, winging herself, zigzagging this way and that, from one line to another as from one branch to another, from one red and white flower to another, until a little sound roused her—her husband slapping his thighs. Their eyes met for a second, but they did not want to speak to each other. They had nothing to say, but something seemed, nevertheless, to go from him to her. It was the life, it was the power of it, it was

the tremendous humor, she knew that it made him slap his thighs.
It filled him. It fortified him.[13]

Charles Tansley had been saying that "people don't read Scott
anymore." Mr. Ramsey associates Scott's lost readership with his own flawed
life and work, plus his shaky claims on immortality. Mr. Ramsey, like Leslie
Stephen, was a minor writer, a blustery and energetic man who wanted to
command the world from *A* to *Z* but who couldn't get past *Q*. It is no surprise
therefore when we note that Virginia Woolf's father, Sir Leslie, had praised
Scott in a famous piece of 1871, where he alleged that "the pleasures of Scott
are those of a healthy open air life, a literature of the tough indomitable
puritans of his native land." Virginia Woolf consciously intended to exorcise
her father from her mind, to annihilate the oppressive power of his
remembered presence. The entry in her diary of 28 November 1928 is a sign
of her intentional patricide.

> Father's birthday. He would have been 96, yes, today; and could
> have been 96, like other people one has known; but mercifully
> was not. His life would have entirely ended mine. What would
> have happened? No writing, no books; inconceivable. I used to
> think of him and mother daily; but writing *The Lighthouse* laid
> them in my mind. And now he comes back sometimes, but
> differently. (I believe this to be true—that I was obsessed by them
> both, unhealthily; and writing of them was a necessary act.) He
> comes back now more as a contemporary. I must read him some
> day.[14]

I have deliberately chosen this text about the ejection of paternal
consciousness as a convenient entryway into the more explicit subject of
familial or political power in Woolf as seen by García Márquez and as we see
it evolve in his reading of Virginia Woolf at its most intense and fruitful.
There is a certain passage from *Mrs. Dalloway*, read when he was twenty
years old, which had such a lasting effect upon him that he was able to say
just recently, "I would be a different author than I am today if I had not read
such-and-such a text from *Mrs. Dalloway*." This novel was a primal reading
experience for the young García Márquez; no other book in his vast readings
has had such a singular effect.

When we speak of *Mrs. Dalloway*, or any other work by Virginia Woolf
for that matter, we are immediately seized with the paradox that the
description of what is going on cannot be done, since the "subjects" glanced
upon by the narrator are hardly the substance of the book. It is all surfaces.
The author is constantly approaching the unnameable, what is in the air,

what cannot be seized by descriptive fact. So when we describe the events in such a book as *Mrs. Dalloway*, we lose everything all at once, and that is just the point, since the only reality in such a novel is to be found in its style and not at all in relation of word to apparent subject. Nonetheless, a few solid if pedestrian things might be brought to bear, if only to refresh our memory of such an evanescent masterpiece. The story has no proper beginning or ending. It opens with Clarissa Dalloway shopping in the brisk air of a fresh London morning, preparing for a momentous social event planned for that evening in her home. It ends with Mrs. Dalloway busily entertaining her guests at the same party. The major event in Mrs. Dalloway's day is the return from India of a suitor long ago rejected by her, Peter Walsh. She and her solid member-of-parliament husband Richard have one daughter, shown in various moments under the temporary thrall of a religious fanatic and hard-pressed lesbian, Miss Kilman. Other characters in the novel have no apparent relation to Mrs. Dalloway as she passes blithely through her day. She knows nothing of the badly shell-shocked Septimus Smith, a human remnant from World War I, who, after receiving barbarous treatment from the psychiatrists Holmes and Bradshaw, finally defenestrates himself toward the end of the book, impaling himself on Mrs. Filmer's spiked fence just as Holmes climbs the stairs to take him away to a rest home. Dr. Bradshaw reports the story of Septimus's death to those at Clarissa's party, an event which is crowned by the presence of the prime minister, Mr. Hugh Whitbread. Not much else happens in *Mrs. Dalloway*. How could such an *ephemeral* book have caused such a stroke of illumination in a twenty-year-old Colombian journalist? It is all contained in a single moment from the book, a long sentence which García Márquez can recite in Spanish at will. The context: Mrs. Dalloway and Septimus (the latter accompanied by his wife) are ambling along Bond or Oxford street, unknown to each other, but both taking in the air, shopping and window-gazing. Suddenly, a grand limousine, with blinds drawn and "an air of inscrutable reserve," proceeds toward Picadilly; it is in view of both Mrs. Dalloway and Septimus. It is not known whether the presence within the limousine is the queen, the prime minister, or the prince, but that is not the point. Behind the drawn dove-gray velvet curtain, power in disengaged solitude is manifesting itself to the people, bringing awe and submission. Here is the passage recited by García Márquez in Spanish in a recent interview (of course, I quote here the original):

> But there could be no doubt that greatness was seated within; greatness was passing, hidden, down Bond Street, removed only by a hand's breadth from ordinary people who might now, for the first and last time, be within speaking distance of the majesty of England,

of the enduring symbol of the state which will be known to curious antiquaries, sifting the ruins of time, when London is a grass-grown path and all those hurrying along the pavement this Wednesday morning are but bones with a few wedding rings mixed up in their dust and the gold stoppings of innumerable decayed teeth.[15]

García Márquez said, "I would be a different author than I am today if I had not read that sentence." Furthermore, he remembers that he read it "while I was swatting mosquitoes in my dumpy hotel room, delirious with the torrid heat, during the time I was selling encyclopedias and quick-cure medical books to Colombian peasants." The interviewer responded, "Why did it have such an effect upon you?" García Márquez answered:

> Because it completely transformed my sense of time. Perhaps it permitted me to glimpse in one instant the whole process of Macondo's decomposition, and its final destiny. I ask myself also if that passage was not the remote origin of *The Autumn of the Patriarch*, which is a book about the human enigma of power, about the solitude and misery of power.[16]

If, as has been said, "the central metaphor of Clarissa's narrative (and of the novel) is twofold: the exhilarated sense of being a part of the forward moving process," the rush of life as she exultantly takes it in through the bustle of London, then the other fold of the twofold rhythm in the book is one constantly threatened by lonely destroyers or agents of power in various guises—the ominous tolling of Big Ben, controlling all appointments, offices, and duties, along with other more "humane" trashers of life such as Peter Walsh (the drone back from India), Bradshaw and Holmes, the appropriately named Miss Kilman, the cretinous prime minister Hugh Whitbread, also of deserved name.[17] In Woolf and García Márquez, time and power not only turn on themselves; they turn into aggressions against the individual sensibility, life itself. The task of the novelist of any continent is of course to sing of life, but also to register, as elegy, scenes of destruction caused by thuggish power wielded by the clock and by men and mannish women in studies, parlors, living rooms, and palaces—spaces managed by patriarchs and matriarchs, all enemies of poetry, sensibility, flux, and ripeness.

NOTES

1. Octavio Paz, "Sobre la crítica," in his *Corriente alterna*, Mexico City, Siglo XXI, 1967, pp. 39–40. This essay by Paz has previously been put to excellent use by Emir Rodríguez Monegal in his study "La narrativa

hispanoamericana: Hacia una nueva 'poética,' " in *Teoría de la novela*, S. Sanz Villanueva and Carlos J. Barbachano, eds., Madrid, Sociedad General Española de Librería, 1976, pp. 171–228.

2. Harold Bloom, *A Map of Misreading*, New York, Oxford University Press, 1975, p. 18.

3. This is a synthesis of the subtle argument proposed by Mia I. Gerhardt in *Don Quijote: La vie et les livres*, Amsterdam, Hollandsche Uita. Mig., 1953.

4. Virginia Woolf, "Modern Fiction," in her *Collected Essays*, vol. 2, New York, Harcourt Brace & World, 1967, pp. 103–10.

5. *The Diary of Virginia Woolf*, vol. 3, Anne Olivier Bell, ed., Harmondsworth, Eng., Penguin, 1982, pp. 209–10.

6. Virginia Woolf, *Collected Essays*, vol. 4, New York, Harcourt Brace & World, 1967, pp. 229–35.

7. Virginia Woolf, *Orlando: A Biography*, London, Hogarth, 1964, pp. 278, 274.

8. Victoria Ocampo, "Virginia Woolf, Orlando y Cía," in *Testimonios*, 2nd series, Buenos Aires, Sur, 1941, pp. 13–86.

9. Gabriel García Márquez, "¿Problemas de la novela?" in his *Obra periodística*, vol. 1, J. Gilard, ed., Barcelona, Bruguera, 1981, p. 269.

10. Suzanne Jill Levine, "A Second Glance at the Spoken Mirror: Gabriel García Márquez and Virginia Woolf," *Inti*, 16–17 (Autumn 1982–Spring 1983). Levine's major article represents a critical if not revisionist rereading of the initial treatment of the "imaginative biography" in Spanish American letters, to be found in her study *El espejo hablado*, Caracas, Monte Avila, 1975. I am grateful to her for furnishing the manuscript of her piece in *Inti*, and also for having pointed out on various occasions the seminal importance of *Orlando* in García Márquez's literary formation. See also Emir Rodríguez Monegal, *El boom de la novela latinoamericana*, Caracas, Tiempo Nuevo, 1972, p. 99.

11. Emir Rodríguez Monegal, "Novedad y anacronismo en *Cien años de soledad*," *Revista Nacional de Cultura* (Caracas), July-September 1968; now conveniently available in *Gabriel García Márquez*, Peter Earle, ed., Madrid, Taurus, 1981, pp. 114–38.

12. Levine, op. cit.

13. Virginia Woolf, *To the Lighthouse*, New York, Harcourt Brace & World, n.d., p. 179.

14. *The Diary of Virginia Woolf*, vol. 3, p. 53.

15. Virginia Woolf, *Mrs. Dalloway*, San Diego, Harcourt Brace Jovanovich, n.d., p. 23.

16. Plinio Apuleyo Mendoza, *El olor de la guayaba*, Barcelona, Bruguera, 1982, pp. 67–68.

17. Reuben Brower, "Something Central Which Permeated: Virginia Woolf and *Mrs. Dalloway*," in his *Fields of Light*, New York, Oxford University Press, 1951, pp. 123–37.

MARY E. DAVIS

The Haunted Voice: Echoes of William Faulkner in García Márquez, Fuentes, and Vargas Llosa

In the opening pages of *Absalom, Absalom!* William Faulkner threads his way through a long conversation between the twenty-year-old Quentin Compson, who is taking his leave of Mississippi for Harvard University, and Miss Coldfield, the frozen child who has spent forty-three years hating Thomas Sutpen. Miss Coldfield delivers a maniacal diatribe, while Quentin meditates on her past, her house, his own family, and his immediate future as he listens. This long citation will serve as an activation of Faulkner among us and as an introduction to the subject of my essay.

> Her voice would not cease, it would just vanish. There would be the dim coffin-smelling gloom sweet and oversweet with the twice-bloomed wistaria against the outer wall by the savage quiet September sun impacted distilled and hyperdistilled, into which came now and then the loud cloudy flutter of the sparrows like a flat limber stick whipped by an idle boy, and the rank smell of female old flesh long embattled in virginity while the wan haggard face watched him above the faint triangle of lace at wrists and throat from the too tall chair in which she resembled a crucified child; and the voice not ceasing but vanishing into and then out of the long intervals like a stream, a trickle running from

From *World Literature Today* 59 (Autumn 1985). © 1985 by *World Literature Today*.

patch to patch of dried sand, and the ghost mused with shadowy docility as if it were the voice which he haunted where a more fortunate one would have had a house.[1]

Thomas Sutpen, the ghost, must haunt the several voices of *Absalom* because his house, like that of Atreus, has been destroyed. Faulkner's house, like that of all artists, exists firmly in the body of his work, and his voice, at once quite eccentric and aware of tradition, haunts the narrative now being produced in Latin America, to the extent that a mention of Faulkner's influence is almost obligatory in the introduction of particular writers. Here I wish to explore Faulkner's legacy, those aspects of his prose that fascinated three major writers from Spanish America, and the reasons that attracted the sensibility of that region to Faulkner's work.

In 1944 the North American critic Malcolm Cowley was considering a collection of work by William Faulkner to be published along the lines of his earlier *Portable Hemingway*. He had read Faulkner as a reviewer for the *New Republic*, and he had seen allusions to Faulkner's style by writers of the stature of Jean-Paul Sartre, Camus, and Malraux in the newspapers of Paris. Cowley was amazed to discover the difference between the European assessment of Faulkner and that in his native country. At forty-six, Faulkner had published eleven novels, plus *The Unvanquished* and *Go Down, Moses*. For Cowley, this "was a sustained work of the imagination such as no other American writer had attempted," yet "apparently no one knew that Faulkner had attempted it. His seventeen books were effectively out of print and seemed likely to remain in that condition, since there was no public demand for them."[2] Only an early book of verse and *The Hamlet* were listed in the immense catalogue of the New York Public Library. Cowley's task of assembling texts for the *Portable Faulkner* was made quite difficult by the fact that every one of Faulkner's novels except *Sanctuary* was out of print (p. 22). Simultaneously, the French had begun to discuss Faulkner as a strong candidate for the Nobel Prize, which, in fact, he was awarded only five years later.

Latin Americans have looked to France for guidance in literary affairs since the eighteenth century, and just as Baudelaire introduced Edgar Allan Poe to the French (and to Latin Americans), the French reception of Faulkner heightened the interest of Latin American readers in his work. There had been in 1933 (two years after the publication of *Sanctuary*) the first Spanish critical appraisal of Faulkner by the Galician-Cuban short-story writer Lino Novás Calvo, who compared Faulkner to Sherwood Anderson and Eugene O'Neill, both read in Buenos Aires as soon as they were in France. *Sanctuary* was translated into French and Spanish in 1943; Spanish Americans read Faulkner primarily in French, however, and by 1940, *As I Lay*

Dying, Light in August, Sartoris, The Sound and the Fury, and *These Thirteen* had a strong circulation, particularly in Buenos Aires. A young Frenchman, Maurice Coindreau, became a professor at Princeton University, and from 1935 to 1938 he sent a constant stream of articles on Faulkner's prose to *La Nación*, the Buenos Aires newspaper.[3] Later he became a member of the group of writers whom Victoria Ocampo collected for her prestigious journal *Sur*, and his more complex articles were published there. Jorge Luis Borges was also a writer for *Sur*, and his 1940 translation of *The Wild Palms* had exhausted four printings by 1956 (*SAR*, 138). "By 1942, Faulkner had been accepted as a major novelist" (*SAR*, 141). The ease with which Latin Americans entered Faulkner's tortuous world can be understood if we consider for a moment Faulkner's formation and the esteem in which other North American writers were held in Latin America both in the nineteenth century and in the early twentieth.

Faulkner was a man educated by reading an amazing range of authors. Although his major themes were his own from the earliest verse onward, the symbols used to convey those themes and the ability to enter the personalities of his characters were modified by constant reading. Faulkner judged his own work by that of writers whom he admired, and in 1956 he discussed his literary heroes in an interview with Jean Stein.

> The books I read are the ones I knew and loved when I was a young man and to which I return as you do to old friends: the Old Testament, Dickens, Conrad, Cervantes and Don Quijote. I read that every year, as some do the Bible. Flaubert, Balzac—he created an intact world of his own, a bloodstream running through twenty books—Dostoevski, Tolstoi, Shakespeare. I read Melville occasionally, and of the poets Marlowe, Campion, Jonson, Herrick, Donne, Keats, and Shelley. I still read Housman. I've read these books so often that I don't aways begin at page one and read to the end. I just read one scene, or about one character, just as you'd meet and talk to a friend for a few minutes.[4]

Faulkner felt that "the two great men of my time were Joyce and Mann" (*FC*, 135). Joyce, particularly, served as a workshop of technique for the early stages of Faulkner's long prose. Hugh Kenner, Joyce's most perceptive critic, has written a brilliant essay on the uses to which Faulkner put his reading of Joyce.

> In its social and sociological preoccupations *Ulysses* is more like a

Faulkner novel than anyone could have guessed until recently: anyone, that is, but possibly Faulkner.

For Faulkner had, we may guess, the sense of style which turning Joyce's pages could discern, beneath a superficial look of chaos, the control, the brilliant exactness; could intuit too the use of Dublin devices for Mississippi novels equally exact in their genealogies, chronologies, viewpoints, time schemes. The clocks that tick for Quentin Compson, the calendar leaves that turn, measure off phases of a nightmare like that from which Stephen Dedalus says he is trying to escape: that which cannot be undone, and which cannot be forgotten: Faulkner's weightiest theme, and one that needs no symbols to help it out.[5]

Whether it was Joyce's obvious fondness for the world of classical Greece or Faulkner's own reading that activated the Greek patterns in his prose is hard determine. However, the emphasis on fate, on the hubris which dooms not only a major character but whole families, and the symbolic house whose state reflects that of the family—all are as active in Faulkner's universe as they are in Dublin. At the University of Virginia, Faulkner was asked if his characters enjoyed free will. He replied:

Yes. But I think that man's free will functions against a Greek background of fate, that he has the free will to choose and the courage, the fortitude to die for his choice, [that] is my conception of man, is why I believe that man will endure.[6]

Faulkner wanted to be a poet, a desire explained to his students at the University of Virginia.

I think that any writer is better off if he looks on himself as a poet—he's a failed poet. That he has found man's history in its mutations, in the instances in which it becomes apparent, his anguish, his triumph, his failures, the whole passion of breathing, is so strong and so urgent that it must be recorded. (FU, 145)

Faulkner defined poetry as "some moving, passionate moment of the human condition distilled to its absolute essence" (FU, 202). Poetry was a necessary approach to his vision of tragedy, one which haunted his life as well as his work: "The tragedy is the man who didn't find his hour, didn't find his chance to be what he could have been" (FU, 205).

The "brooding lyrical intensity"[7] of Faulkner's prose, the absolute delight which he found in hyperbole, and the startling images that he adapted to his world frequently remind his reader of those great novelists of the nineteenth century whom he listed as his favorite writers. Although he did not mention Edgar Allan Poe or Mark Twain or Walt Whitman in his interview with Jean Stein, their presence animates some of his finest pages. He adapted the deliberate strangeness of Poe's short stories to the more extensive medium of the novel, and the results are equally unsettling for his reader. The Latin Americans often approach Faulkner through the short stories. For them the transition from the uncanny world of Poe to the similarly eerie one of Faulkner is a natural one. The fall of the house of Sutpen or Sartoris or Hightower repeats the catastrophe of the house of Usher.

The Latin Americans were avid readers of the poetry resulting from the disasters of World War I. They were not at all discomforted by Faulkner's images, in which he blends T. S. Eliot's waste land with more epic images from Whitman, a process at work at the same time in the poetry of the Chilean Pablo Neruda. The French and English decadents had prepared the Latin Americans for the intense eroticism of life in Yoknapatawpha tawpha, and no admirer of Aubrey Beardsley or Oscar Wilde could be shocked by the androgynous nature of Faulkner's early heroines or by the seething passion of his later family sagas.

If one reads *Sur* or other periodicals in Latin America in the 1920s, 1930s, and 1940s, one is immediately struck by the frequency of allusions to Baudelaire, whose name becomes an icon, a symbol in itself, of the life devoted to the exploration, both personal and esthetic, of all the possible realities of human life. For a reader who had memorized *Les fleurs du mal*, it was essentially painless to become a traveler in Faulkner's delirious boat in the "Old Man" sections of *The Wild Palms*. Just as the French served as a bridge to Faulkner in Latin America, Faulkner's work, both short stories and novels, would serve as a bridge to Joyce and to the complex stylistic triumphs of modernism. Faulkner himself was not allowed to see the results of his labors, and he believed all his life in the fundamental simplicity of art. He wrote to Malcolm Cowley:

> All the moving things are eternal in man's history and have been written before, and if a man writes hard enough, sincerely enough, humbly enough, and with the unalterable determination never never never to be quite satisfied with it, he will repeat them, because art, like poverty, takes care of its own, shares its bread. (FC, 16)

For as long as we have written or oral forms of their expression, Latin Americans have always loved poetry. That Faulkner, learning his craft from Joyce and Flaubert, perfected a prose organized around techniques common to poetry did not startle Latin Americans in the century dominated by the sensibility of César Vallejo, Pablo Neruda, and Octavio Paz, and they were eager to explore, on their own, regions as bizarre as the master Mississippian's. The Latin Americans would be equally demanding of their readers, but those who had been educated reading the classics and every possible text from France were prepared for what critics clumsily termed the New Novel.

Within languages themselves frequently given to rhetorical flourish and baroque arabesque, these Latin American students of Faulkner were even ready to explore the literary value of silence. Both Joyce in *Dubliners* and Faulkner often in his novels reveal the intensity of silence, an aspect of reality more commonly captured in prose than in the poetry they so longed to write. Faulkner, the creator of characters who talk incessantly, revealed to Jean Stein: "I prefer silence to sound, and the image produced by words occurs in silence. That is, the thunder and music of the prose take place in silence" (*WW*, 136).

Because Faulkner created such a complex imaginary world, writers have taken from him what suited their own genius best. The three novelists I will examine have been attracted by different aspects of his work, and they should be taken as heraldic figures for many other writers in Latin America who cannot be mentioned.

Long before he won the Nobel Prize in 1982, Gabriel García Márquez had been denying his familiarity with Faulkner, much as Faulkner used to deny knowing Joyce. In 1968 he and Mario Vargas Llosa conducted a dialogue on the novel in Latin America, and in the course of it García Márquez stated that "the new Latin American novelists owe the greatest debt to Faulkner." As he elaborated on this opinion, he attributed Faulkner's influence to his style.

> The "Faulknerian" method is very efficient for narrating Latin American reality. This is what we unconsciously discovered in Faulkner. We saw a reality that we wished to narrate, and we knew that neither the European nor the traditional Spanish method would be adequate. Suddenly we found the Faulknerian method quite adequate to narrate our reality. This is not so strange, because Yoknapatawpha County borders the Caribbean, so that in a manner of speaking, Faulkner is a Caribbean writer, in a sense, he is a Latin American writer.[8]

García Márquez became famous among English readers after the publication in 1970 of Gregory Rabassa's translation of *Cien años de soledad*

(*One Hundred Years of Solitude*), the family saga of the Buendías. The novel so fascinated Vargas Llosa that he wrote a long critical study entitled *Historia de un deicidio*, wherein he compares García Márquez's style, his characters, and the impact of his work to those of Faulkner and attributes the similarity to the native regions of the two novelists. García Márquez grew up in a little town named Aracataca lost in the coastal region of Colombia. Vargas Llosa visited Aracataca and was amazed at its closeness to Faulkner's county: "Lacking anything better, Aracataca lived on myths, ghosts, solitude, and nostalgia." After García Márquez left for Europe, "Aracataca became a wound that time irritated rather than healed, a nostalgia that grew with the passing days, a subjective presence by which he felt obliged to measure the new world that surrounded him."[9]

García Márquez had intended to entitle this tortuous novel *La casa* (The House), but as he worked on it, the Buendías' fate demanded a more thematic title. *One Hundred Years of Solitude* follows the structure of Sophoclean tragedy: there is a prognostication concerning the family, there are mythic characters, there is a matriarch of incredible vitality, a futile war, hubris, a moment of anagnorisis, and a catastrophic end. The novel constantly reminds the reader of *Sartoris*, of *The Unvanquished*, and of *Go Down, Moses*. Whereas Faulkner built narrators into his novels, García Márquez prefers the third person, and with such splendid characters the outside view is generally effective. He uses repetitive images—the house, the river, the plague, the storm of yellow butterflies, the whirlwind—to guide his reader, and he winds clusters of themes around images in the manner of Faulkner. Although the Buendías' history is tragic (they perish because they cannot break out of a radical solitude), García Márquez includes the humorous aspects of daily life, as Faulkner did in exploring the history of the Snopeses. The world of Macondo, García Márquez's Yoknapatawpha, appears in short stories, in other novels which he wrote in the course of exorcising *One Hundred Years of Solitude*, and in movie scripts. Earlier works are just as Faulknerian. *La hojarasca* (*Leaf Storm*) is a simplified *As I Lay Dying* with the number of narrators reduced to three and the object of all the attention (a doctor who has committed suicide) appearing only in the consciousness of the narrators, in the same manner that Thomas Sutpen materializes in *Absalom*. The shorter novel *La mala hora* (*In Evil Hour*) uses pasquinades that mysteriously appear all over town, much as Faulkner used minor characters to function as the voice of the people. The surface of *El otoño del patriarca* (*The Autumn of the Patriarch*), with its endless sentences, enormous paragraphs, and entrapment in a bifurcated first-person narration (the Patriarch narrates his own history, and he has a double, to confuse things further), is more reminiscent of *Light in August* and Faulkner's later novels.

Crónica de una muerte anunciada (*Chronicle of a Death Foretold*), García Márquez's most recent novel, is, as was *Sanctuary*, an imaginative expansion of a real event reported in the newspapers. In it the novelist reverts to the almost Greek simplicity of *Sartoris* and *The Unvanquished*.

The Mexican novelist Carlos Fuentes wrote the best single study of García Márquez only two years after the publication of *One Hundred Years of Solitude*. In "García Márquez: La segunda lectura" (García Márquez: The Second Reading) Fuentes states:

> One of the extraordinary aspects of the novel by García Márquez is that its structure corresponds to that of the deep history of Spanish America: the tension between Utopia, Epic, and Myth. The New World was conceived as Utopia. On losing its geocentric illusion (destroyed by Copernicus), Europe needed to create a new space that would confirm the extension of the known world.
>
> America is, above all else, the renewed possibility of Arcadia.[10]

Fuentes emphasizes the creation of a complete world in García Márquez's prose, one in which certain characters "are continuously reborn, in order to assure the permanency of the cosmos with strange, ritual acts. Such mythification is not gratuitous: the characters defend themselves with their imagination against the chaos that surrounds them. Nature contains demons. The characters contain demons. They, the clan of the Buendía, are all possessed, founders and usurpers, creators and destroyers, Snopes and Sartoris in one single family" (*NNH*, 63). Fuentes's own novels and short stories reiterate the concern for history and the mythic foundation of a habitable world that he analyzed in García Márquez. Fuentes called *One Hundred Years of Solitude* the *Quijote* of the New World, because the last Buendía is allowed to read the text the reader is also reading just before the final destruction of Macondo, and in the same manner as Don Quijote heard about his own exploits in part 2 of *Don Quijote*, Aureliano Babilonia possesses an identity confirmed only by a written text.

Fuentes's diplomatic career and that of his father have given him a facility with languages and the intimate knowledge of cultures that are reflected in his novels. He is the Joyce of the New World, and in 1975 he published Mexico's *Ulysses*, a gigantic novel entitled *Terra Nostra*. During a lecture given at the 1983 Puterbaugh Conference in Norman, Fuentes explained that in *Terra Nostra* he had worked to create a complete Freudian (or symbolic) space, a place of encounter for styles, for history, and for characters from Spain (Celestina, Don Juan, Phillip II), as well as from the Europe that conquered the New World. In counterpoint to the European world he interweaves the mythology, the characters, and the modern reality of the region that several pre-Columbian civilizations referred to as the land closest to the gods.

The many allusions to Poe in this work help the reader follow the constant doubling and reappearance of characters, one of whom writes: "One lifetime is not sufficient. Many existences are needed to fulfill one personality."[11] The process of *Terra Nostra* is startlingly like that which Faulkner attempted, with marginal success, in *A Fable*.

Fuentes is as confident as were Joyce and Faulkner that the alchemy of words does conjure up new realities. The words that he prefers are as freighted with the past as were Faulkner's: "There is no word that is not laden with forgetfulness and memories, colored with illusions and failures; nevertheless, there is no word that is not the bearer of imminent renovation; each word we say simultaneously announces a word we do not know because we desire it" (*TN*, 538). Desire itself finds incarnation in female figures who are at once goddesses and women of distinctly human personalities. They recall, often directly, Caddy Compson and Dilsey, the matriarch who survives the demise of the Compsons, Granny and the fearless Drusilla of *The Unvanquished*. The power of Fuentes's females is as vital as it was for Faulkner, as he creates structure based on images rather than plot.

Perhaps ultimately more important than *Terra Nostra* is Fuentes's earlier novel *La muerte de Artemio Cruz* (*The Death of Artemio Cruz*), another version of *As I Lay Dying*. Artemio reconstructs his whole life as he dies, and his stubbornness, his solitude, and the courage with which he crosses the last river seduce the reader in spite of the fact that Artemio had failed as a revolutionary, failed as a lover, failed as a father. Through the magic of Fuentes's text, he did not fail as a man. This is still the work that makes the most rigorous demands upon the reader. Fuentes's desire is exactly that described by R. W. B. Lewis: "The aim of Faulkner's deliberate deformations is not finally aesthetic; he wants the reader to participate not in a creative act but in a moral act. He wants to define a moral experience of mythological proportions and of ambiguous reality, an aim which of necessity makes heavy demands on the reader."[12]

Fuentes and García Márquez generally reflect the Sartoris rank of Faulknerian characters. Vargas Llosa, on the other hand, prefers ordinary people, and he presents them (or they present themselves) in highly idiosyncratic speech and in gestures eccentric enough to have derived from Dickens. As Faulkner moved into the later stages of his prose, the Snopeses, those triumphs of vulgarity, absorbed the power once held by the Sartoris clan. No matter how ordinary they might be, these characters have a startling ability to express themselves. In the words of Irving Howe: "There remains available to each character the gesture, striking or subdued, by which he defines himself. For Faulkner's characters, the gesture becomes the outer shape of their integrity."[13]

Vargas Llosa's early texts concentrated violence in gestures and epithets as did the works of Hemingway, but as he read Flaubert and Faulkner, he deepened both his presentation of characters and his view of reality. In 1965 he published *La casa verde* (*The Green House*), and in its complex pages he had become the complete Faulknerian. The method of *Absalom, Absalom!* is adapted to the Peruvian jungle, and Vargas Llosa uses five styles to narrate five strands of the plot. Just as Thomas Sutpen materialized in the mind of Quentin Compson, so the character of the deaf-mute Antonia materializes only in the mind of her lover Anselmo, the creator of the Green House. Recognizing the secret Mark Twain that dwells in Faulkner's work, Vargas Llosa devotes one segment of this novel to the voyage of two old friends traveling down the river to death. Twain would have enjoyed their long conversation immensely.

Conversación en La Catedral (*Conversation in The Cathedral*) gives Vargas Llosa the opportunity to present Lima as the Jefferson of Peru, and he concentrates on the seamy underside of Peru's political life, a sordid reality whose structure owes much to *Sanctuary*. Vargas Llosa's characters are presented as dramatically as were Faulkner's, as if they were seen on a stage only momentarily lit, and their revelation is always a combination of eccentric gestures and absolutely appropriate words.

After his critical exploration of García Márquez, Vargas Llosa began to lighten the tone of his prose with the hyperbolic extension common throughout Faulkner and García Márquez. He made fun of his own amorous life in *La tía Julia y el escribidor* (*Aunt Julia and the Scriptwriter*), and in *Pantaleón y las visitadoras* (*Captain Pantoja and the Special Service*) he recounted with enjoyment the minor tragedy of the failure of the grandiose scheme of a military man in a text whose narrative pace closely resembles Faulkner's "Spotted Horses."

Vargas Llosa creates a universe like Yoknapatawpha, one in which tragedy does not produce catharsis but rather repeats itself through generations of characters. His humor is as acidic as Faulkner's was, but the singular poetry in his world is that produced by silence, that sudden pause in the dialogue, that fleeting moment when friends bid each other good-bye forever, that power of memory to re-create the past or to form another version of the past.

Why did Faulkner surpass his more famous contemporaries as the literary model for Latin America? The lyricism of his texts struck a lasting resonance in a continent dedicated to poetry. His exploration of how an entire society is organized and acts itself out is a continuing challenge to writers from societies in the midst of severe ferment. Faulkner's consciousness of other texts, the presence in his work of his favorite authors, is quite stimulating for a continent wherein the baroque style is a natural fact of life. Faulkner's celebration of the individual moral act that redeems history becomes irresistible for countries whose history has yet to be redeemed. Finally, Faulkner's stubborn, relentless determination to work out his genius in words serves as a paradigm in Latin America, the region where words are in terrible danger and where survival itself may only be brought about by equally stubborn imagination.

NOTES

1. William Faulkner, *Absalom, Absalom!*, New York, Random House, 1936, p. 8.

2. Malcolm Cowley, *The Faulkner-Cowley File*, New York, Penguin, 1978, pp. 5, 6. Subsequent references use the abbreviation *FC*.

3. Arnold Chapman, *The Spanish American Reception of U.S. Fiction*, Berkeley, University of California Press, 1966, p. 135. Subsequent references use the abbreviation *SAR*.

4. *Writers at Work: The* Paris Review *Interviews*, Malcolm Cowley, ed., New York, Viking, 1958, p. 136. Subsequent references use the abreviation *WW*.

5. Hugh Kenner, "Faulkner and Joyce," in *Faulkner, Modernism, and Film: Faulkner and Yoknapatawpha*, Evans Harrington and Ann J. Abadie, eds., Jackson, University Press of Mississippi, 1979, p. 33.

6. *Faulkner at the University*, Frederick Gwynn and Joseph Blotner, eds., Charlottesville, University of Virginia Press, 1959, p. 38. Subsequent references use the abbreviation *FU*.

7. The term is Hyatt Waggoner's in *William Faulkner: From Jefferson to the World*, Lexington, University Press of Kentucky, 1959, p. 220.

8. Gabriel García Márquez, Mario Vargas Llosa, *La novela en América Latina: Diálogo*, Lima, Milla Batres, 1968, pp. 52-53. The translations are my own.

9. Mario Vargas Llosa, *Historia de un deicidio*, Barcelona, Monte Avila, 1971, pp. 20, 30. The translations are my own.

10. Carlos Fuentes, *La nueva novela hispanoamericana*, Mexico City, Mortiz, 1969, pp. 59-60. Subsequent references use the abbreviation *NNH*. The translations are my own.

11. Carlos Fuentes, *Terra Nostra*, Margaret Sayers Peden, tr., New York, Farrar, Straus & Giroux, 1976, p. 532.

12. R. W. B. Lewis, "William Faulkner: The Hero in the New World," in *Faulkner*, Robert Penn Warren, ed., Englewood Cliffs, N.J., Prentice-Hall, 1966, p. 211.

13. Irving Howe, *William Faulkner: A Critical Study*, Chicago, University of Chicago Press, 1975, p. 152.

Chronology

1928	Gabriel José García Márquez born on March 6 in Aracataca, Colombia. It is also the year of the banana company massacre, an event Márquez would dwell on at length, and which would appear in *One Hundred Years of Solitude*. His parents are not a presence in his early life. García Márquez is reared in the home of his maternal grandfather, Colonel Nicolás Ricardo Márquez Mejía. (Gabriel García, García Márquez's father, was considered by the Colonel to be a philanderer, part of the rabble drawn to the banana industry, and of a political bent exactly the opposite of the Colonel. Nonetheless, his persistence eventually resulted in marriage to Luisa Santiaga Márquez Iguarán, and the story of their courtship is the inspiration for *Love in the Time of Cholera*.) Living in the house, García Márquez is surrounded by his aunts. As he tells Plinio Apuleyo Mendoza, the aunts storytelling and love of the fantastic and of superstition are a shaping force in García Márquez's writing.
1936	Grandfather dies. His Grandmother is going blind, so García Márquez goes to live with his parents in Sucre. His father had, by then, found work as a pharmacist. Given that the family now had financial footing, they sent young Gabito to Barranquilla for primary school.
1940	García Márquez awarded a scholarship to attend secondary school in Zipaquirá.

1946	Graduates secondary school. His first story, "The Third Resignation," published in *El Spectador*.
1947–1949	Studies law at the National University in Bogotá and at the University of Cartagena, both in Colombia. Begins journalism career as a reporter for *El Espectador* in Bogotá. Also during this time, reads Kafka's "Metamorphosis," translated by Jorge Luis Borges, and is "liberated" at the idea that writing need not follow linear narrative and familiar plots.
1947	Meets Mercedes Barcha Pardo and declares her "the most interesting person" he had ever met. They swear fealty to one another, but will not be married for years.
1950	Leaves law school to pursue journalism full time. Works as a freelancer for several different newspapers and some magazines. Lives in a brothel, begins a number of literary friendships.
1953	Restless and not confident in his writing, García Márquez sells encyclopedias for a short time.
1955	Writes serial installments about a Colombian sailor who survives ten days at sea, the source for what García Márquez would later publish as *Story of a Shipwrecked Sailor*.
1955	Sent to Eastern Europe on assignment. Associates of García Márquez send his first book to a publisher. The novella *Leaf Storm* is released, and it is set in Macondo.
1956	Military shuts down the main paper that employs García Márquez, *El Espectador*. He is trapped in Europe, where he stays for a year. During that time, he writes *No One Writes to the Colonel*. He also tours socialist countries in Europe, intrigued by the possibilities socialism offers for political troubles in Colombia. He sends articles back to newspapers and magazines in Colombia, and also writes *90 Days Behind the Iron Curtain*.
1957	Military regime steps down in Colombia and García Márquez returns home. He settles in Caracas and writes for *Momento*.
1958	Marries Mercedes Barcha in Barranquilla. He will dedicate the majority of his work to her.
1959	The couple welcome their first son, Rodrigo.
1959–1961	García Márquez works in Cuba and, briefly, New York covering the political turmoil in Havana. When he moves his family to Mexico City, after resigning his post at *Prensa Latina*, he would be denied entrance back into the United States until 1971.

1961	Friends arrange for publication of *No One Writes to the Colonel.*
1962	Friends arrange for publication of *Big Mama's Funeral.* Second son, Gonzalo, born. *In Evil Hour* also published, but in heavily bowdlerized edition which Marquez rejects. The corrected version will not be published for years.
1965	Begins work on *One Hundred Years of Solitude.*
1967	*One Hundred Years of Solitude* is published to instant international acclaim, numerous awards, and three years of selling out print runs.
1967	Moves to Barcelona during the last years of the Franco dictatorship.
1972	*Innocent Eréndira* published.
1974	Founds *Alternativa*, a leftist newspaper in Bogotá.
1975	Publishes *Autumn of the Patriarch.*
1975–present	Maintains residences in both Mexico City and Bogotá and is active in political causes while founding several civic and political organizations.
1977	Publishes *Operación Carlota.*
1981	Publishes *Chronicle of a Death Foretold.* Wins the French Legion of Honor.
1982	Wins the Nobel Prize for Literature. Publishes *The Fragrance of Guava*, interviews with Plinio Apuleyo Mendoza.
1985	Publishes *Love in the Time of Cholera.*
1989	Publishes *The General in His Labyrinth.*
1992	Publishes *Strange Pilgrims.*
1994	Publishes *Love and Other Demons.*
1996	Publishes *New of a Kidnapping.*
2000	Declares himself "retired."

Contributors

HAROLD BLOOM is Sterling Professor of the Humanities at Yale University and Henry W. and Albert A. Berg Professor of English at the New York University Graduate School. He is the author of over 20 books, including *Shelley's Mythmaking* (1959), *The Visionary Company* (1961), *Blake's Apocalypse* (1963), *Yeats* (1970), *A Map of Misreading* (1975), *Kabbalah and Criticism* (1975), *Agon: Toward a Theory of Revisionism* (1982), *The American Religion* (1992), *The Western Canon* (1994), and *Omens of Millennium: The Gnosis of Angels, Dreams, and Resurrection* (1996). *The Anxiety of Influence* (1973) sets forth Professor Bloom's provocative theory of the literary relationships between the great writers and their predecessors. His most recent books include *Shakespeare: The Invention of the Human*, a 1998 National Book Award finalist, and *How to Read and Why*, which was published in 2000. In 1999, Professor Bloom received the prestigious American Academy of Arts and Letters Gold Medal for Criticism.

DAVID T. HABERLY is a Professor of Portuguese at the University of Virginia. He is the author of *Three Sad Races: Racial Identity and National Consciousness in Brazilian Literature*. In addition to writing on García Márquez, he has written extensively on Luso-Brazilian literature, nineteenth-century North American and Argentine literature, Borges, and Catalan literature.

KEITH HARRISON, at the time the article was written, was a lecturer at Dawson College in Quebec.

ROBERTO GONZÁLEZ-ECHEVARRÍA is the Sterling Professor of Spanish at Yale. He is the author of *Myth and Archive: A Theory of Latin American Narrative*, *The Voice of the Masters: Writing and Authority in Modern Latin American Literature*, *Celestina's Brood: Continuities of the Baroque in Spanish and Latin American Literatures* and several other books.

JOHN J. DEVENY is Professor of Foreign Languages at Oklahoma State University.

JUAN MANUEL MARCOS is the author of *Roa Bastos, precursor del postboom* (Roa Bastos forerunner of the Postboom 1983) and *De García Márquez al postboom* (From García Márquez to the Postboom 1986), and the publisher of the journal, *Discurso*.

ELIZABETH A. SPILLER is Assistant Professor of English at the University of North Texas.

PAUL M. HEDEEN is Associate Professor of English at Wartburg College. His critical and creative writings have appeared in numerous magazines and journals including *The North American Review, Confrontation, Rosebud, Philosophy and Literature, The Maine Scholar, Modern Fiction Studies, Language and Style, The Great Lakes Review, Southwest Review, The Mid-America Poetry Review*, and *Voices International*.

JONATHAN BALDO is Associate Professor of English and Chair of the Humanities Department at the University of Rochester's Eastman School of Music. He is the author of *The Unmasking of Drama: Contested Representation in Shakespearean Tragedy* and *Acts of Oblivion: Stages of Forgetfulness and the Sense of Nationhead in Shakespeare*.

IDDO LANDAU is Senior Lecturer in the Department of Philosophy at the University of Haifa. His critical work has appeared in *CLIO, Cardozo Law Review, The Monist, Philosophy, The Philosophical Quarterly, Philosophy Today*, and Australasian *Journal of Philosophy*.

DEAN J. IRVINE'S reviews of Canadian poetry, fiction, anthologies, and literary criticism have appeared in *Canadian Literature, Essays on Canadian Writing*, and *Filling Station*. He is editor of *Archive for Our Times: Previously Uncollected and Unpublished Poems of Dorothy Livesay*.

IRVIN D.S. WINSBORO is Associate Professor of History at Florida Gulf Coast University. He is the author of *Feminism and Black Activism in Contemporary America: An Ideological Assessment* and *Thomas Edison: The Fort Myers Collection*, and has authored numerous scholarly articles.

ALEXANDER COLEMAN is Professor Emeritus of Spanish and Comparative Literature at New York University and the author of *Other Voices: A Study of the Late Poetry of Luis Cernuda* and *Eça de Queirós and European Realism*, as well as numerous articles and reviews.

MARY E. DAVIS is Associate Professor of Spanish and Women's Studies at the University of Oklahoma.

Bibliography

Alonso, Carlos J. "The Mourning After: García Márquez, Fuentes and the Meaning of Postmodernity in Spanish America." *MLN* 109 (March 1994): 252-67.

Antoni, Robert. "Parody or Piracy: The Relationship of *The House of the Spirits* to *One Hundred Years of Solitude.*" *Latin American Literary Review* 16 (July/December 1988): 16-28.

Barciauskas, Jonas. "Leaves of Light: The Textual Journeys of Dante and García Márquez." *Cross Currents* 43 (Summer 1993): 212-29.

Bell-Villada, Gene. *García Márquez: The Man and his Work.* Chapel Hill: University of North Carolina Press, 1990.

Bloom, Harold ed. *Modern Critical Views: Gabriel García Márquez.* New York: Chelsea House, 1989.

Bost, David. "Historiography and the Contemporary Narrative: Dialogue and Methodology." *Latin American Literary Review* 16 (January/June 1988): 34-44.

Castano, Patricia and Holly Aylett. "Of Love and Levitation: Interview with G. García Márquez" *The Times Literary Supplement* no. 4516 (October 20-26, 1989): p. 1152.

Clark, Gloria Jeanne Bodtorf. *A Synergy of Styles: Art and Artifact in Gabriel García Márquez.* Lanham: University Press of America, 1999.

Cohn, Deborah. "'The Paralysis of the Instant': the Stagnation of History and the Stylistic Suspension of Time in Gabriel García Márquez's *La Hojarasca.*" *College Literature* 26 no. 2 (Spring 1999): p. 59-78.

Columbus, Claudette Kemper. "The Heir Must Die: One Hundred Years of Solitude as a Gothic Novel." *Modern Fiction Studies* 32 (Autumn 1986): 397-416.

Conniff, Brian. "The Dark Side of Magical Realism: Science, Oppression, and Apocalypse in *One Hundred Years of Solitude.*" *Modern Fiction Studies* 36 (Summer 1990): 167-79.

de Valdés, María Elena, ed. *Approaches to teaching García Márquez's* One Hundred Years of Solitude. New York: Modern Language Association of America, 1990.

Dolan, Sean. *Gabriel García Márquez*. New York: Chelsea House, 1994.

Fiddian, Robin ed. *García Márquez*. New York: Longman, 1995.

Fuentes, Carlos. *Gabriel García Márquez and the Invention of America*. Liverpool: Liverpool University Press, 1987.

Halka, Chester S. *"One Hundred Years of Solitude*: two additional translation corrections." *Journal of Modern Literature* 24, no. 1 (Fall 2000): 173-5

————. *Melquíades, Alchemy and Narrative Theory: The Quest for Gold in* Cien años de soledad. Lathrup Village: International Book Publishers, 1981.

Hahn, Hannelore. *The Influence of Franz Kafka on Three Novels by Gabriel García Márquez*. New York: P. Lang, 1993.

Hamill, Pete. "Love and Solitude." *Vanity Fair*, March 1988: 124-31, 191-2.

Harss, Luis and Barbara Dohmann. *Into the Mainstream: Conversations with Latin-American Writers*. New York: Harper & Row, 1967.

Hoeg, Jerry. "The Social Imaginary/Symbolic: Technology and Latin American Literature." *Mosaic* 30 (December 1997): 95-108.

Janes, Regina. *Gabriel García Márquez: Revolutions in Wonderland*. Columbia: University of Missouri Press, 1981.

Jones, Anny Brooksbank. "Utopia and Other Commonplaces in García Márquez's *El amor en los tiempos del colera.*" *The Modern Language Review* 89 (July 1994): 635-44.

Krapp, John. "Apathy and the Politics of Identity: García Márquez's *One Hundred Years of Solitude* and Contemporary Cultural Criticism." *Literature Interpretation Theory* 11, no. 4 (2001): 403-27.

Mendoza, Plinio Apuleyo. *The Fragrance of Guava*. London: Faber and Faber, 1982.

McGuirk, Bernard and Richard Cardwell, ed. *Gabriel García Márquez: New Readings*. New York: Cambridge University Press, 1987.

McMurray, George R., ed. *Critical essays on Gabriel García Márquez*. Boston: G.K. Hall, 1987.

McNerney, Kathleen. *Understanding Gabriel García Márquez*. Columbia: University of South Carolina Press, 1989.

Mills, Moylan C. and Enrique Gronlund. "Magic Realism and García Márquez's *Erendira.*" *Literature/Film Quarterly* 17, no. 2 (1989): 113-22.

Minta, Stephen. *Gabriel García Márquez: Writer of Colombia.* London: J. Cape, 1987.

Munoz, Elias Miguel. "Into the Writer's Labyrinth: Storytelling Days with Gabo." *Michigan Quarterly Review* 34 (Spring 1995): 172-93

Oberhelman, Harley D. *García Márquez and Cuba: A Study of Its Presence in His Fiction, Journalism, and Cinema.* Fredericton: York Press, 1995.

Oberhelman, Harley D., ed. *Gabriel García Márquez: A Study of the Short Fiction.* Boston: Twayne Publishers, 1991.

Ortega, Julio and Claudia Elliott, ed. *Gabriel García Márquez and the Powers of Fiction.* Austin: University of Texas Press, 1988.

Palencia-Roth, Michael. "Gabriel García Márquez: Labyrinths of Love and History." *World Literature Today* 65 (Winter 1991): 54-8

————. "The Art of Memory in García Márquez and Vargas Llosa." *MLN* 105 (March 1990): 351-66.

Paternostro, Silvana. "Three Days with Gabo." *The Paris Review* 38 (Winter 1996): 220-47.

Pedoto, Constance A. *Painting Literature: Dostoevsky, Kafka, Pirandello, and García Márquez in Living Color.* Lanham: University Press of America, 1993.

Pelayo, Rubén. *Gabriel García Márquez: A Critical Companion.* Greenwood Press, 2001.

Penuel, Arnold M. *Intertextuality in García Márquez.* York: Spanish Literature Publications Co., 1994.

Pérez, Janet and Wendell Aycock, ed. *Climate and Literature: Reflections of Environment.* Lubbock: Texas Tech University Press, 1995.

Rincon, Carlos. "The Peripheral Center of Postmodernism: On Borges, García Márquez, and Alterity." *Boundary 2* 20 (Fall 1993): 162-79.

Rogachevsky, Jorge R. and Ivan Jaksic. *Politics and the Novel in Latin America: García Márquez and Asturias.* Amherst: Council on International Studies, State University of New York at Buffalo, 1980.

Shaw, Bradley A. and Nora Vera-Godwin, ed. *Critical perspectives on Gabriel García Márquez.* Lincoln: Society of Spanish and Spanish-American Studies, 1986.

Simas, Rosa. *Circularity and Visions of the New World in William Faulkner, Gabriel García Márquez, and Osman Lins.* Lewiston: E. Mellen Press, 1993.

Sims, Robert Lewis. *The First García Márquez: A Study of His Journalistic Writing from 1948 to 1955.* Lanham: University Press of America, c1992.

————. *The Evolution of Myth in García Márquez from* La hojarasca *to* Cien años de soledad. Miami: Ediciones Universal, 1981.

Williams, Raymond L. *Gabriel García Márquez*. Boston: Twayne Publishers, 1984.

Wood, Michael. *Gabriel García Márquez*: One Hundred Years of Solitude. New York: Cambridge University Press, 1990.

Acknowledgments

Haberly, David T. "Bags of Bones: A source for Cien Años de Soledad." *Modern Language Notes* 105 (1990), 392-394. © The Johns Hopkins University Press. Reprinted by permission of The Johns Hopkins University Press.

" 'The Only Mystery' in *One Hundred Years of Solitude*" by Keith Harrison. From *Literature and Psychology* 32, no. 2 (1986): 47-52. © 1986 by Keith Harrison. Reprinted by permission.

Echevarría, Roberto González. "Cien Años de Soledad: The Novel as Myth and Archive." *Modern Language Notes* 99:2 (1994), 358-380. © The Johns Hopkins University Press. Reprinted by permission of The John Hopkins University Press.

"Women and Society in *One Hundred Years of Solitude*" by John J. Deveny, Jr. and Juan Manuel Marcos. From *Journal of Popular Culture* 22 (Summer 1988): 83-90. © 1988 by Popular Press. Reprinted by permission.

"Searching for the route of inventions: Retracing the Renaissance Discovery Narrative in Gabriel Garcia Marquez." From *Clio* v. 28 (Summer 1999): 375-98. © 1999 by *Clio*. Reprinted by permission.

"Gabriel García Márquez's Dialectic of Solitude" by Paul Hedeen. From *Southwest Review* 68 (Autumn 1983): 350-64. © 1983 by Paul Hedeen. Reprinted by permission.

Reprinted of material of Jonathan Baldo, "Solitude as an Effect of Language in García Márquez's Cien Años de Soledad" in *Criticism* Vol. 30:4 with the permission of Wayne State University Press.

"Metafiction as a Rhetorical Device in Hagel's History of Absolute Spirit and Gabriel García Márquez's *One Hundred Years of Solitude*" by Iddo Landau. From *Clio* 21 (Summer 1992): 401-410. © 1992 by Iddo Landau. Reprinted by permission.

"Fables of the Plague Years: Postcolonialism, Postmodernism, and Magic Realism in *Cien Años de Soledad*" by Dean J. Irvine. From *ARIEL: A Review of International English Literature* 29, 4 (October 1998): 53-80. © 1998 by *ARIEL*. Reprinted by permission of The Board of Governors, The University of Calgary.

"Latin American Women in Literature and Reality: García Márquez's *One Hundred Years of* Solitude" by Irvin D. S. Winsboro. From *the Midwest Quarterly* 34, 2 (Winter 1993): 192-205. © 1993 by Irvin D.S. Winsboro. Reprinted by permission.

"Bloomsbury in Aracataca: The Ghost of Virginia Woolf" by Alexander Coleman. From *World Literature Today* 59 (Autumn 1985): 543-49. © 1985 by *World Literature Today*. Reprinted by permission.

"The Haunted Voice: Echoes of William Faulkner in García Márquez, Fuentes, and Vargas Llosa" by Mary E. Davis. From *World Literature Today* 59 (Autumn 1985): 531-35. © 1985 by *World Literature Today*. Reprinted by permission.

Index

NOTE: Page numbers followed by an "*n*" indicate endnotes. All characters in the novel are listed under *Cien años de soledad* characters.